OMENS AND SUPERSTITIONS OF SOUTHERN INDIA

OMENS AND SUPERSTITIONS OF SOUTHERN INDIA

By

EDGAR THURSTON, C.I.E.

GYAN

Published by

Gyan Publishing House
5, Ansari Road
Daryaganj, New Delhi-110002
Phone: 011-47034999, 9811692060
E-mail: books@gyanbooks.com

Distribution Network
gyanbooks.com
India, USA, Canada, UK, Australia, France

ISBN : 978-81-212-6420-4 (PB)
First Published, 1912

2nd Impression 2022

Printed at: Gyan Press, Delhi.

OMENS AND SUPERSTITIONS OF SOUTHERN INDIA
Author: EDGAR THURSTON

MALAYAN EXORCIST, WITH FOWL IN HIS MOUTH.
(See p. 246.)

Frontispiece.

OMENS AND SUPERSTITIONS OF SOUTHERN INDIA

BY

EDGAR THURSTON, C.I.E.

1912

PREFACE

THIS book deals mainly with some aspects of what may be termed the psychical life of the inhabitants of the Madras Presidency, and the Native States of Travancore and Cochin. In my "Ethnographic Notes in Southern India" (1906), I stated that the confused chapter devoted to omens, animal superstitions, evil eye, charms, sorcery, etc., was a mere outline sketch of a group of subjects, which, if worked up, would furnish material for a volume. This chapter has now been remodelled, and supplemented by notes collected since its publication, and information which lies buried in the seven bulky volumes of my encyclopædic "Castes and Tribes of Southern India" (1909). The area dealt with (roughly, 182,000 square miles, with a population of 47,800,000) is so vast that I have had perforce to supplement the personal knowledge acquired in the course of wandering expeditions in various parts of Southern India, and in other ways, by recourse to the considerable mass of information, which is hidden away in official reports, gazetteers, journals of societies, books, etc.

To the many friends and correspondents, European

and Indian, who have helped me in the accumulation of facts, and those whose writings I have made liberal use of, I would once more express collectively, and with all sincerity, my great sense of indebtedness. My thanks are due to Mr L. K. Anantha Krishna Iyer for supplying me with the illustrations of Malabar yantrams.

CONTENTS

		PAGE
I.	OMENS	13
II.	ANIMAL SUPERSTITIONS	73
III.	THE EVIL EYE	109
IV.	SNAKE WORSHIP	121
V.	VOWS, VOTIVE AND OTHER OFFERINGS	137
VI.	CHARMS	180
VII.	HUMAN SACRIFICE	199
VIII.	MAGIC AND HUMAN LIFE	224
IX.	MAGIC AND MAGICIANS	237
X.	DIVINATION AND FORTUNE-TELLING	273
XI.	SOME AGRICULTURAL CEREMONIES	289
XII.	RAIN-MAKING CEREMONIES	305
	INDEX	312

LIST OF ILLUSTRATIONS

MALAYAN EXORCIST WITH FOWL IN MOUTH (*see* p. 246) *Frontispiece*

PAGE

SACRED VULTURES, TIRUKAZHUKUNRAM 86

EVIL EYE FIGURES, MALABAR 112

EVIL EYE FIGURES SET UP IN FIELDS 114

IMPRESSIONS OF HAND ON WALL OF HOUSE 119

PRAYING FOR OFFSPRING BEFORE LINGAM, SNAKE-STONES, AND FIGURE OF GANĒSA 124

PULLUVAN WITH POT-DRUM 129

VETTUVANS WEARING LEAFY GARMENTS 152

SILVER VOTIVE OFFERINGS 160

CLAY AND METAL OFFERINGS, SOUTH CANARA 162

SUBRAMANIYA YANTRAM 185

HANUMĀN YANTRAM 186

MERIAH SACRIFICE POST 202

JUMADI BHUTHA, SOUTH CANARA 237

FIGURE WASHED ASHORE AT CALICUT 249

KORAVA WOMAN TELLING FORTUNE 283

OMENS AND SUPERSTITIONS OF SOUTHERN INDIA

I

OMENS

In seeking for omens, Natives consult the so-called science of omens or science of the five birds, and are guided by them. Selected omens are always included in native calendars or panchāngams.

To the quivering and throbbing of various parts of the body as omens, repeated reference is made in the Hindu classics. Thus, in Kalidāsa's Sakuntala, King Dushyanta says: "This hermitage is tranquil, and yet my arm throbs. Whence can there be any result from this in such a place? But yet the gates of destiny are everywhere." Again, Sakuntala says: "Alas! why does my right eye throb?" to which Gautami replies: "Child, the evil be averted. May the tutelary deities of your husband's family confer happy prospects!" In the Raghuvamsa, the statement occurs that "the son of Paulastya, being greatly incensed, drove an arrow deep into his right arm, which was throbbing, and which, therefore, prognosticated his union with Sīta." A quivering sensation in the right arm is supposed to indicate marriage with a beautiful woman; in the right eye some good luck.

During a marriage among the Telugu Tottiyans, who have settled in the Tamil country, a red ram without blemish is sacrificed. It is first sprinkled with water, and, if it shivers, this is considered a good omen. It is recorded,* in connection with the legends of the Badagas of the Nīlgiris, that "in the heart of the Banagudi shola (grove), not far from the Doddūru group of cromlechs, is an odd little shrine to Karairāya, within which are a tiny cromlech, some sacred water-worn stones, and sundry little pottery images representing a tiger, a mounted man, and some dogs. These keep in memory, it is said, a Badaga who was slain in combat with a tiger; and annually a festival is held, at which new images are placed there, and vows are paid. A Kurumba (jungle tribe) makes fire by friction, and burns incense, throws sanctified water over the numerous goats brought to be sacrificed, to see if they will shiver in the manner always held necessary in sacrificed victims, and then slays, one after the other, those which have shown themselves duly qualified."

In many villages, during the festival to the village deity, water is poured over a sheep's back, and it is accepted as a good sign if it shivers. "When the people are economical, they keep on pouring water till it does shiver, to avoid the expense of providing a second victim for sacrifice. But, where they are more scrupulous, if it does not shiver, it is taken as a sign that the goddess will not accept it, and it is taken away."†

Before the thieving Koravas set out on a predatory expedition, a goat is decorated, and taken to a shrine. It is then placed before the idol, which is asked whether the expedition will be successful. If the body of the

* "Gazetteer of the Nilgiris," 1908, i. 338.

† Bishop Whitehead, *Madras Museum Bull.*, 1907, No. 3, v. 134.

animal quivers, it is regarded as an answer in the affirmative; if it does not, the expedition is abandoned.

If, in addition to quivering, the animal urinates, no better sign could be looked for. Thieves though they are, the Koravas make it a point of honour to pay for the goat used in the ceremony. It is said that, in seeking omens from the quivering of an animal, a very liberal interpretation is put on the slightest movement. It is recorded by Bishop Whitehead * that, when an animal has been sacrificed to the goddess Nukalamma at Coconada, its head is put before the shrine, and water poured on it. If the mouth opens, it is accepted as a sign that the sacrifice is accepted.

At the death ceremonies of the Idaiyans of Coimbatore, a cock is tied to a sacrificial post, to which rice is offered. One end of a thread is tied to the post, and the other end to a new cloth. The thread is watched till it shakes, and then broken. The cock is then killed.

Of omens, both good and bad, in Malabar, the following comprehensive list is given by Mr Logan †:—

"Good.—Crows, pigeons, etc., and beasts as deer, etc., moving from left to right, and dogs and jackals moving inversely, and other beasts found similarly and singly; wild crow, ruddy goose, mungoose, goat, and peacock seen singly or in couples either at the right or left. A rainbow seen on the right and left, or behind, prognosticates good, but the reverse if seen in front. Buttermilk, raw rice, puttalpira (*Trichosanthes anguina*, snake-gourd), priyangu flower, honey, ghī (clarified butter); red cotton juice, antimony sulphurate, metal mug, bell ringing, lamp, lotus, karuka grass, raw fish, flesh, flour, ripe fruits, sweetmeats, gems, sandalwood, elephants, pots filled with water, a virgin, a couple of Brāhmans, Rājas,

* *Madras Museum Bull.*, 1907, No. 3, v. 139-40.

† Malabar, 1887, i. 177-8.

respectable men, white flower, white yak tail,* white cloth, and white horse. Chank shell (*Turbinella rapa*), flagstaff, turban, triumphal arch, fruitful soil, burning fire, elegant eatables or drinkables, carts with men in, cows with their young, mares, bulls or cows with ropes tied to their necks, palanquin, swans, peacock and crane warbling sweetly. Bracelets, looking-glass, mustard, bezoar, any substance of white colour, the bellowing of oxen, auspicious words, harmonious human voice, such sounds made by birds or beasts, the uplifting of umbrellas, hailing exclamations, sound of harp, flute, timbrel, tabor, and other instruments of music, sounds of hymns of consecration and Vēdic recitations, gentle breeze all round at the time of a journey.

"Bad.—Men deprived of their limbs, lame or blind, a corpse or wearer of a cloth put on a corpse, coir (cocoanut fibre), broken vessels, hearing of words expressive of breaking, burning, destroying, etc.; the alarming cry of alas! alas! loud screams, cursing, trembling, sneezing, the sight of a man in sorrow, one with a stick, a barber, a widow, pepper, and other pungent substances. A snake, cat, iguana (*Varanus*), blood-sucker (lizard), or monkey passing across the road, vociferous beasts such as jackals, dogs, and kites, loud crying from the east, buffalo, donkey, or temple bull, black grains, salt, liquor, hide, grass, dirt, faggots, iron, flowers used for funeral ceremonies, a eunuch, ruffian, outcaste, vomit, excrement, stench, any horrible figure, bamboo, cotton, lead, cot, stool or other vehicle carried with legs upward, dishes, cups, etc., with mouth downwards, vessels filled with live coals, which are broken and not burning, broomstick, ashes, winnow, hatchet."

In the category of good omens among the Nāyars of Travancore, are placed the elephant, a pot full of water, sweetmeats, fruit, fish, and flesh, images of gods, kings, a cow with its calf, married women, tied bullocks, gold

* Used as a fly-flapper (chamara).

lamps, ghī, and milk. In the list of bad omens come a donkey, broom, buffalo, untied bullock, barber, widow, patient, cat, washerman. The worst of all omens is to allow a cat to cross one's path. An odd number of Nāyars, and an even number of Brāhmans, are good omens, the reverse being particularly bad. On the Vinayakachaturthi day in the month of Avani, no man is allowed to look at the rising moon, on penalty of incurring unmerited obloquy.

By the Pulayas of Travancore, it is considered lucky to see another Pulaya, a Native Christian, an Izhuva with a vessel in the hand, a cow behind, or a boat containing sacks of rice. On the other hand, it is regarded as a very bad omen to be crossed by a cat, to see a fight between animals, a person with a bundle of clothes, or to meet people carrying steel instruments.

It is a good omen for the day if, when he gets up in the morning, a man sees any of the following:—his wife's face, the lines on the palm of his right hand, his face in a mirror, the face of a rich man, the tail of a black cow, the face of a black monkey, or his rice fields. There is a legend that Sīta used to rise early, and present herself, bathed and well dressed, before her lord Rāma, so that he might gaze on her face, and be lucky during the day. This custom is carried out by all good housewives in Hindu families. A fair skinned Paraiyan, or a dark skinned Brāhman, should not, in accordance with a proverb, be seen the first thing in the morning.

Hindus are very particular about catching sight of some auspicious object on the morning of New Year's Day, as the effects of omens seen on that occasion are believed to last throughout the year. Of the Vishu festival, held in celebration of the New Year in Malabar, the following account is given by Mr Gopal Panikkar.*

* "Malabar and its Folk," Madras, 2nd edition, 99-100.

"Being the commencement of a new year, native superstition surrounds it with a peculiarly solemn importance. It is believed that a man's whole prosperity in life depends upon the nature, auspicious or otherwise, of the first things that he happens to fix his eyes upon on this particular morning. According to Nair, and even general Hindu mythology, there are certain objects which possess an inherent inauspicious character. For instance, ashes, firewood, oil, and a lot of similar objects, are inauspicious ones, which will render him who chances to notice them first fare badly in life for the whole year, and their obnoxious effects will be removed only on his seeing holy things, such as reigning princes, oxen, cows, gold, and such like, on the morning of the next new year. The effects of the sight of these various materials are said to apply even to the attainment of objects by a man starting on a special errand, who happens for the first time to look at them after starting. However, with this view, almost every family religiously takes care to prepare the most sightworthy objects on the new year morning. Therefore, on the previous night, they prepare what is known as a kani. A small circular bell-metal vessel is taken, and some holy objects are arranged inside it. A grandha or old book made of palmyra leaves, a gold ornament, a new-washed cloth, some 'unprofitably gay' flowers of the konna tree (*Cassia Fistula*), a measure of rice, a so-called looking-glass made of bell-metal, and a few other things, are all tastefully arranged in the vessel, and placed in a prominent room inside the house. On either side of this vessel, two brass or bell-metal lamps, filled with cocoanut oil clear as diamond sparks, are kept burning, and a small plank of wood, or some other seat, is placed in front of it. At about five o'clock in the morning of the day, some one who has got up first wakes the inmates, both male and female, of the house, and takes them blindfolded, so that they may not gaze at anything else, to the seat near the kani. The members are seated, one after another, in the seat, and are then, and not till then, asked to open their eyes, and carefully look at the kani. Then each is made to look at some venerable member of the house, or sometimes a stranger even. This over, the little playful urchins of the house fire small crackers which they have bought for the occasion. The kani is then taken round the place from house to house, for the benefit of the poor families, which cannot afford to prepare such a costly adornment."

I gather further, in connection with the Vishu festival, that it is the duty of every devout Hindu to see the village deity the first of all things in the morning. For this purpose, many sleep within the temple precincts, and those who sleep in their own houses are escorted thither by those who have been the first to make their obeisance. Many go to see the image with their eyes shut, and sometimes bound with a cloth.*

If a person places the head towards the east when sleeping, he will obtain wealth and health; if towards the south, a lengthening of life; if towards the west, fame; if towards the north, sickness. The last position, therefore, should be avoided.† In the Telugu country, when a child is roused from sleep by a thunderclap, the mother, pressing it to her breast, murmurs, "Arjuna Sahādēva." The invocation implies the idea that thunder is caused by the Mahābhārata heroes, Arjuna and Sahādēva.‡ To dream of a temple car in motion, foretells the death of a near relative. Night, but not day dreams, are considered as omens for good or evil. Among those which are auspicious, may be mentioned riding on a cow, bull, or elephant, entering a temple or palace, a golden horse, climbing a mountain or tree, drinking liquor, eating flesh, curds and rice,

* N. Sunkuni Wariar, "Ind. Ant.," 1892, xxi. 96.

† K. Srikantaliar, "Ind. Ant.," 1892, xxi. 193.

‡ M. N. Venkataswami, "Ind. Ant.," 1905, xxxiv. 176.

wearing white cloths, or jewelry set with precious stones, being dressed in white cloths, and embracing a woman, whose body is smeared with sandal paste. A person will be cured of sickness if he dreams of Brāhmans, kings, flowers, jewels, women, or a looking-glass. Wealth is ensured by a dream that one is bitten in the shade by a snake, or stung by a scorpion. One who dreams that he has been bitten by a snake is considered to be proof against snake-bite; and if he dreams of a cobra, his wife or some near relative is believed to have conceived. Hindu wives believe that to tell their husband's name, or pronounce it even in a dream, would bring him to an untimely end. If a person has an auspicious dream, he should get up and not go to sleep again. But, if the dream is of evil omen, he should pray that he may be spared from its ill effects, and may go to sleep again.

The arrival of a guest is foreshadowed by the hissing noise of the oven, the slipping of a winnow during winnowing, or of a measure when measuring rice. If one dines with a friend or relation on Monday, Wednesday, Friday, or Saturday, it is well; if on a Tuesday, ill-feeling will ensue; if on a Thursday, endless enmity; if on a Sunday, hatred. While eating, one should face east, west, south, or north, according as one wishes for long life, fame, to become vainglorious, or for justice or truth. Evil is foreshadowed if a light goes out during meals, or while some auspicious thing, such, for example, as a marriage, is being discussed. A feast given to the jungle Paliyans by some missionaries was marred at the outset by the unfortunate circumstance that betel and tobacco were placed by the side of the food, these articles being of evil omen as they are placed in the grave with the dead. Chewing a single areca nut, along with betel leaf secures vigour, two nuts are inauspicious, three are excellent, and more bring indifferent luck. The basal portion of the betel leaf must be rejected, as it produces disease; the apical part, as it induces sin; and the midrib and veins, as they destroy the intellect. A leaf on which chunam (lime) has been kept, should be avoided, as it may shorten life.

Before the Koyis shift their quarters, they consult the omens, to see whether the change will be auspicious or not. Sometimes the hatching of a clutch of eggs provides the answer, or four grains of four kinds of seed, representing the prosperity of men, cattle, sheep, and land, are put on a heap of ashes under a man's bed. Any movement among them during the night is a bad omen.*

When a Kondh starts on a shooting expedition, if he first meets an adult female, married or unmarried, he will return home, and ask a child to tell the females to keep out of the way. He will then make a fresh start, and, if he meets a female, will wave his hand to her as a sign that she must keep clear of him. The Kondh believes that, if he sees a female, he will not come across animals in the jungle to shoot. If a woman is in her menses, her husband, brothers, and sons living under the same roof, will not go out shooting for the same reason.

It is noted by Mr F. Fawcett† that it is considered unlucky by the Koravas, when starting on a dacoity or housebreaking, "to see widows, pots of milk, dogs urinating, a man leading a bull, or a bull bellowing. On the other hand, it is downright lucky when a bull bellows at the scene of the criminal operation. To see a man goading a bull is a good omen when starting, and a bad one at the scene. The eighteenth day of the Tamil month,

* "Gazetteer of the Godāvari District," 1907, i. 66.

† "Note on the Koravas," 1908.

Avani, is the luckiest day of all for committing crimes. A successful criminal exploit on this day ensures good luck throughout the year. Sundays, which are auspicious for weddings, are inauspicious for crimes. Mondays, Wednesdays, and Saturdays are unlucky until noon for starting out from home. So, too, is the day after new moon." Fridays are unsuitable for breaking into the houses of Brāhmans or Kōmatis, as they may be engaged in worshipping Ankalamma, to whom the day is sacred.

Some Bōyas in the Bellary district enjoy inām (rent free) lands, in return for propitiating the village goddesses by a rite called bhūta bali, which is intended to secure the prosperity of the village. The Bōya priest gets himself shaved at about midnight, sacrifices a sheep or buffalo, mixes its blood with rice, and distributes the rice thus prepared in small balls throughout the village. When he starts on this business, all the villagers bolt their doors, as it is not considered auspicious to see him then.

When a student starts for the examination hall, he will, if he sees a widow or a Brāhman, retrace his steps, and start again after the lapse of a few minutes. Meeting two Brāhmans would indicate good luck, and he would proceed on his way full of hope.

If, when a person is leaving his house, the head or feet strike accidentally against the threshold, he should not go out, as it forebodes some impending mischief. Sometimes, when a person returns home from a distance, especially at night, he is kept standing at the door, and, after he has washed his hands and feet, an elderly female or servant of the house brings a shallow plate full of water mixed with lime juice and chunam (lime), with some chillies and pieces of charcoal floating on it. The plate is carried three times round the person, and the contents are then thrown into the street without being seen by the man. He then enters the house. If a person knocks at the door of a house in the night once, twice, or thrice, it will not be opened. If the knock is repeated a fourth time, the door will be opened without fear, for the evil spirit is said to knock only thrice.

A tickling sensation in the sole of the right foot foretells that the person has to go on a journey. The omens are favourable if any of the following are met with by one who is starting on a journey, or special errand :—

Married woman.
Virgin.
Prostitute.
Two Brāhmans.
Playing of music.
One carrying musical instruments.
Money.
Fruit or flowers.
A light, or clear blazing fire.
Umbrella.
Cooked food.
Milk or curds.
Cow.
Deer.
Corpse.
Two fishes.
Recital of Vēdas.
Sound of drum or horn.
Spirituous liquor.
Bullock.
Mutton.
Precious stones.
One bearing a silver armlet.
Sandalwood.
Rice.
Elephant.
Horse.
Pot full of water.
Married woman carrying a water-pot from a tank.
Pot of toddy.
Black monkey.
Dog.
Royal eagle.
Parrot.
Honey.
Hearing kind words.
A Gāzula Balija with his pile of bangles on his back.

If, on similar occasions, a person comes across any of the following, the omens are unfavourable :—

Widow.
Lightning.
Fuel.
Smoky fire.
Hare.
Crow flying from right to left.
Snake.
New pot.
Blind man.
Lame man.
Sick man.
Salt.
Tiger.
Pot of oil.
Leather.
Dog barking on a housetop.
Bundle of sticks.
Buttermilk.
Empty vessel.
A quarrel.
Man with dishevelled hair.
Oilman.
Leper.
Mendicant.

Sometimes people leave their house, and sleep elsewhere on the night preceding an inauspicious day, on which a journey is to be made. Unlucky days for starting on a journey are vāra-sūlai, or days on which Siva's trident (sūla) is kept on the ground. The direction in which it lies, varies according to the day of the week. For example, Sunday before noon is a bad time to start towards the west, as the trident is turned that way. It is said to be unlucky to go westward on Friday or Sunday, eastward on Monday or Saturday, north on Tuesday or Wednesday, south on Thursday. A journey begun on Tuesday is liable to result in loss by thieves or fire at home. Loss, too, is likely to follow a journey begun on Saturday, and sickness a start on Sunday. Wednesday and Friday are both propitious days, and a journey begun on either with a view to business will be lucrative. The worst days for travelling are Tuesday, Saturday, and Sunday.* On more than one occasion, a subordinate in my office overstayed his leave on the ground that his guru (spiritual preceptor) told him that the day on which he should have returned was an unlucky one for a journey.

If a traveller sees a hare on his way, he may be sure that he will not succeed in the object of his journey. If, however, the hare touches him, and he does not at once turn back and go home, he is certain to meet with a great misfortune. There is an authority for this superstition in the Rāmayana. After Rāma had recovered Sīta and returned to Ayodha, he was informed that, whilst a washerman and his wife were quarrelling, the former had exclaimed that he was not such a fool as the king had been to take back his wife after she had been carried away by a stranger. Rāma thought this over, and resolved to

* M. J. Walhouse, "Ind. Ant.," 1881, x. 366.

send his wife into the forest. His brother, Lutchmana, was to drive her there, and then to leave her alone. On their way they met a hare, and Sīta, who was ignorant of the purpose of the journey, begged Lutchmana to return, as the omen was a bad one.*

If a dog scratches its body, a traveller will fall ill; if it lies down and wags its tail, some disaster will follow. To one proceeding on a journey, a dog crossing the path from right to left is auspicious. But, if it gets on his person or his feet, shaking its ears, the journey will be unlucky.

A person should postpone an errand on which he is starting, if he sees a cobra or rat-snake. In a recent judicial case, a witness gave evidence to the effect that he was starting on a journey, and when he had proceeded a short way, a snake crossed the road. This being an evil omen, he went back and put off his journey till the following day. On his way he passed through a village in which some men had been arrested for murder, and found that one of two men, whom he had promised to accompany and had gone on without him, had been murdered.

Sneezing once is a good sign; twice, a bad sign. When a child sneezes, those near it usually say "dirgāyus" (long life), or "sathāyus" (a hundred years). The rishi or sage Markandēya, who was remarkable for his austerities and great age, is also known as Dirgāyus. Adults who sneeze pronounce the name of some god, the common expression being "Srimadrangam." When a Badaga baby is born, it is a good omen if the father sneezes before the umbilical cord has been cut, and an evil one if he sneezes after its severance. In the Teluga country it is believed that a child who sneezes on a

* "Manual of the Cuddapah District," 1875, 293.

winnowing fan, or on the door-frame, will meet with misfortune unless balls of boiled rice are thrown over it; and a man who sneezes during his meal, especially at night, will also be unlucky unless water is sprinkled over his face, and he is made to pronounce his own name, and that of his birthplace and his patron deity.*

Gaping is an indication that evil spirits have effected an entrance into the body. Hence many Brāhmans, when they gape, snap their fingers as a preventive.† When a great man yawns, his sleep is promoted by all the company with him snapping their fingers with great vehemence, and making a singular noise. It was noted by Alberuni ‡ that Hindus "spit out and blow their noses without any respect for the elder ones present, and crack their lice before them. They consider the *crepitus ventris* as a good omen, sneezing as a bad omen." In Travancore, a courtier must cover the mouth with the right hand, lest his breath should pollute the king or other superior. Also, at the temples, a low-caste man must wear a bandage over his nose and mouth, so that his breath may not pollute the idols.§ A Kudumi woman in Travancore, at the menstrual period, should stand at a distance of seven feet, closing her mouth and nostrils with the palm of her hand, as her breath would have a contaminating effect. Her shadow, too, should not fall on any one.

A Kumbāra potter, when engaged in the manufacture of the pot or household deity for the Kurubas, should cover his mouth with a bandage, so that his breath may not defile it. The Koragas of South Canara are said to be regarded with such intense loathing that, up to quite

* "Gazetteer of the Godāvari District," 1907, i. 47.
† M. J. Walhouse, "Ind. Ant.," 1876, v. 21.
‡ India, Trübner, Oriental Series, 1888, i. 182.
§ Rev. S. Mateer, "Native Life in Travancore," 1883, 330-52.

recent times, one section of them called Ande or pot Kurubas, continually wore a pot suspended from their necks, into which they were compelled to spit, being so utterly unclean as to be prohibited from even spitting on the highway.* In a note on the Paraiyans (Pariahs), Sonnerat, writing in the eighteenth century,† says that, when drinking, they put the cup to their lips, and their fingers to their mouths, in such a way that they are defiled with the spittle. A Brāhman may take snuff, but he should not smoke a cheroot or cigar. When once the cheroot has touched his lips, it is defiled by the saliva, and, therefore, cannot be returned to his mouth.‡

At the festivals of the village deities in the Telugu country, an unmarried Mādiga (Telugu Pariah) woman, called Mātangi § (the name of a favourite goddess) spits upon the people assembled, and touches them with her stick. Her touch and saliva are believed to purge all uncleanliness of body and soul, and are said to be invited by men who would ordinarily scorn to approach her. At a festival called Kathiru in honour of a village goddess in the Cochin State, the Pulayans (agrestic slaves) go in procession to the temple, and scatter packets of palm-leaves containing handfuls of paddy (unhusked rice) rolled up in straw among the crowds of spectators along the route. "The spectators, both young and old, scramble to obtain as many of the packets as possible, and carry them home. They are then hung in front of the houses, for it is believed that their presence will help to promote the prosperity of the family, until the festival comes round

* M. J. Walhouse, *Journ. Anthrop. Inst.*, 1874, iv. 373.

† Voyage to the East Indies, 1777 and 1781.

‡ Rev. J. A. Sharrock, "South Indian Missions," 1910, 9.

§ *See* Emma Rosenbusch (Mrs Clough), "While sewing Sandals, or Tales of a Telugu Pariah Tribe."

again next year. The greater the number of trophies obtained for a family by its members, the greater, it is believed, will be the prosperity of the family." *

In a note on the Kulwādis or Chalavādis of the Hassan district in Mysore, Captain J. S. F. Mackenzie writes † as follows:—

"Every village has its Holigiri—as the quarters inhabited by the Holiars (formerly agrestic serfs) is called—outside the village boundary hedge. This, I thought, was because they are considered an impure race, whose touch carries defilement with it. Such is the reason generally given by the Brāhman, who refuses to receive anything directly from the hands of a Holiar, and yet the Brāhmans consider great luck will wait upon them if they can manage to pass through the Holigiri without being molested. To this the Holiars have a strong objection, and, should a Brāhman attempt to enter their quarters, they turn out in a body and slipper him, in former times it is said to death. Members of the other castes may come as far as the door, but they must not enter the house, for that would bring the Holiar bad luck. If, by chance, a person happens to get in, the owner takes care to tear the intruder's cloth, tie up some salt in one corner of it, and turn him out. This is supposed to neutralise all the good luck which might have accrued to the trespasser, and avert any evil which might have befallen the owner of the house."

The Telugu Tottiyans, who have settled in the Tamil country, are said by Mr F. R. Hemingway not to recognise the superiority of Brāhmans. They are supposed to possess unholy powers, especially the Nalla (black) Gollas, and are much dreaded by their neighbours. They do

* L. K. Anantha Krishna Iyer, "The Cochin Tribes and Castes," 1909, i. 114.

† "Ind. Ant.," 1873, ii. 65.

not allow any stranger to enter their villages with shoes on, or on horseback, or holding up an umbrella, lest their god should be offended. It is believed that, if any one breaks this rule, he will be visited with illness or some other punishment.

I am informed by Mr S. P. Rice that, when smallpox breaks out in a Hindu house, it is a popular belief that to allow strangers or unclean persons to go into the house, to observe festivals, and even to permit persons who have combed their hair, bathed in oil, or had a shave, to see the patient, would arouse the anger of the goddess, and bring certain death to the sick person. Strangers, and young married women are not admitted to, and may not approach the house, as they may have had sexual intercourse on the previous day.

It is believed that the sight or breath of Muhammadans, just after they have said their prayers at a mosque, will do good to children suffering from various disorders. For this purpose, women carry or take their children, and post themselves at the entrance to a mosque at the time when worshippers leave it. Most of them are Hindus, but sometimes poor Eurasians may be seen there. I once received a pathetic appeal from a Eurasian woman in Malabar, imploring me to lay my hands on the head of her sick child, so that its life might be spared.

In teaching the Grāndha alphabet to children, they are made to repeat the letter "ca" twice quickly without pausing, as the word "ca" means "die." In Malabar, the instruction of a Tiyan child in the alphabet is said by Mr F. Fawcett to begin on the last day of the Dasara festival in the fifth year of its life. A teacher, who has been selected with care, or a lucky person, holds the child's right hand, and makes it trace the letters of the

Malayālam alphabet in rice spread on a plate. The forefinger, which is the one used in offering water to the souls of the dead, and in other parts of the death ceremonies, must not be used for tracing the letters, but is placed above the middle finger, merely to steady it. For the same reason, a doctor, when making a pill, will not use the forefinger. To mention the number seven in Telugu is unlucky, because the word (yēdu) is the same as that for weeping. Even a treasury officer, who is an enlightened university graduate, in counting money, will say six and one. The number seven is, for the same reason, considered unlucky by the Koravas, and a house-breaking expedition should not consist of seven men. Should this, however, be unavoidable, a fiction is indulged in of making the house-breaking implement the eighth member of the gang.* In Tamil the word ten is considered inauspicious, because, on the tenth day after the death of her husband, a widow removes the emblems of married life. Probably for this reason, the offspring of Kallan polyandrous marriages style themselves the children of eight and two, not ten fathers. Lābha is a Sanskrit word meaning profit or gain, and has its equivalent in all the vernacular languages. Hindus, when counting, commence with this word instead of the word signifying one. In like manner, Muhammadans use the word Bismillah or Burketh, apparently as an invocation like the medicinal ℞ (Oh ! Jupiter, aid us). When the number a hundred has been counted, they again begin with the substitute for one, and this serves as a one for the person who is keeping the tally. Oriya merchants say labho (gain) instead of eko (one), when counting out the seers of rice for the elephants' rations. The people of the Oriya Zemindaris often use, not the year of the

* F. Fawcett, "Note on the Koravas," 1908.

Hindu cycle or Muhammadan era, but the year of the reigning Rāja of Puri. The first year of the reign is called, not one, but labho. The counting then proceeds in the ordinary course, but, with the exception of the number ten, all numbers ending with seven or nothing are omitted. This is called the onko. Thus, if a Rāja has reigned two and a half years, he would be said to be in the twenty-fifth onko, seven, seventeen and twenty being omitted.* For chewing betel, two other ingredients are necessary, viz., areca nuts and chunam (lime). For some reason, Tamil Vaishnavas object to mentioning the last by name, and call it moonavadu, or the third.

At a Brāhman funeral, the sons and nephews of the deceased go round the corpse, and untie their kudumi (hair knot), leaving part thereof loose, tie up the rest into a small bunch, and slap their thighs. Consequently, when children at play have their kudumi partially tied, and slap their thighs, they are invariably scolded owing to the association with funerals. Among all Hindu classes it is considered as an insult to the god to bathe or wash the feet on returning home from worship at a temple, and, by so doing, the punyam (good) would be lost. Moreover, washing the feet at the entrance to a home is connected with funerals, inasmuch as, on the return from the burning-ground, a mourner may not enter the house until he has washed his feet. The Badagas of the Nīlgiris hold an agricultural festival called devvē, which should on no account be pronounced duvvē, which means burning-ground.

A bazaar shop-keeper who deals in colours will not sell white paint after the lamps have been lighted. In like manner, a cloth-dealer refuses to sell black cloth,

* S. P. Rice, "Occasional Essays on Native South Indian Life," 1901, 95-6.

and the dealer in hardware to sell nails, needles, etc., lest poverty should ensue. Digging operations with a spade should be stopped before the lamps are lighted. A betel-vine cultivator objects to entering his garden or plucking a leaf after the lighting of the lamps; but, if some leaves are urgently required, he will, before plucking them, pour water from a pot at the foot of the tree on which the vine is growing.

Arrack (liquor) vendors consider it unlucky to set their measures upside down. Some time ago, the Excise Commissioner informs me, the Madras Excise Department had some aluminium measures made for measuring arrack in liquor shops. It was found that the arrack corroded the aluminium, and the measures soon leaked. The shop-keepers were told to turn their measures upside down, in order that they might drain. This they refused to do, as it would bring bad luck to their shops. New measures with round bottoms, which would not stand up, were evolved. But the shop-keepers began to use rings of indiarubber from soda-water bottles, to make them stand. An endeavour was then made to induce them to keep their measures inverted by hanging them on pegs, so that they would drain without being turned upside down. The case illustrates how important a knowledge of the superstitions of the people is in the administration of their affairs. Even so trifling an innovation as the introduction of a new arrangement for maintaining tension in the warp during the process of weaving gave rise a few years ago to a strike among the hand-loom weavers at the Madras School of Arts.

When a Paidi (agriculturists and weavers in Ganjam) is seriously ill, a male or female sorcerer (bejjo or bejjano) is consulted. A square divided into sixteen compartments is drawn on the floor with rice flour. In each compartment are placed a leaf-cup of *Butea frondosa*, a quarter-anna piece, and some food. Seven small bows and arrows are set up in front thereof in two lines. On one side of the square, a big cup filled with food is placed. A fowl is sacrificed, and its blood poured thrice round this cup. Then, placing water in a vessel near the cup, the sorcerer or sorceress throws into it a grain of rice, giving out at the same time the name of some god or goddess. If the rice sinks, it is believed that the illness is caused by the anger of the deity, whose name has been mentioned. If the rice floats, the names of various deities are called out, until a grain sinks. When selecting a site for a new dwelling hut, the Māliah Savaras place on the proposed site as many grains of rice in pairs as there are married members in the family, and cover them over with a cocoanut shell. They are examined on the following day, and, if they are all there, the site is considered auspicious. Among the Kāpu Savaras, the grains of rice are folded up in leaflets of the bael tree (*Ægle Marmelos*), and placed in a split bamboo.

It is recorded by Gloyer* that "when a Dōmb (Vizagapatam hill tribe) house has to be built, the first thing is to select a favourable spot, to which few evil spirits (dūmas) resort. At this spot they put, in several places, three grains of rice arranged in such a way that the two lower grains support the upper one. To protect the grains, they pile up stones round them, and the whole is lightly covered with earth. When, after some time, they find on inspection that the upper grain has fallen off, the spot is regarded as unlucky, and must not be used. If the position of the grains remains unchanged, the omen is regarded as auspicious. They drive in the first post, which must have a certain length, say of

* Jeypore, Breklum, 1901.

five, seven, or nine ells, the ell being measured from the tip of the middle finger to the elbow. The post is covered on the top with rice straw, leaves, and shrubs, so that birds may not foul it, which would be an evil omen."

In Madras, a story is current with reference to the statue of Sir Thomas Munro, that he seized upon all the rice depôts, and starved the people by selling rice in egg-shells, at one shell for a rupee. To punish him, the Government erected the statue in an open place without a canopy, so that the birds of the air might insult him by polluting his face. In the Bellary district, the names Munrol and Munrolappa are common, and are given in hope that the boy may attain the same celebrity as the former Governor of Madras. (I once came across a Telugu cultivator, who rejoiced in the name of Curzon). One of Sir Thomas Munro's good qualities was that, like Rāma and Rob Roy, his arms reached to his knees, or, in other words, he possessed the quality of an Ajanubahu, which is the heritage of kings, or those who have blue blood in them.

In a case of dispute between two Koravas,* "the decision is sometimes arrived at by means of an ordeal. An equal quantity of rice is placed in two pots of equal weight, having the same quantity of water, and there is an equal quantity of fire-wood. The judges satisfy themselves most carefully as to quantity, weights, and so on. The water is boiled, and the man whose rice boils first is declared to be the winner of the dispute. The loser has to recoup the winner all his expenses. It sometimes happens that both pots boil at the same time; then a coin is to be picked out of a pot containing boiling oil."

At one of the religious ceremonies of the Koravas, offerings of boiled rice (pongal) are made to the deity,

* F. Fawcett, "Note on the Koravas," 1908.

Polēramma, by fasting women. The manner in which the boiling food bubbles over from the cooking-pot is eagerly watched, and accepted as an omen for good or evil. A festival called Pongal is observed by Hindus on the first day of the Tamil month Tai, and derives its name from the fact that rice boiled in milk is offered to propitiate the Sun God.

Before the ceremony of walking through fire * (burning embers) at Nidugala on the Nīlgiris, the omens are taken by boiling two pots of milk, side by side, on two hearths. If the milk overflows uniformly on all sides, the crops will be abundant for all the villages. But, if it flows over on one side only, there will be plentiful crops for villages on that side only. For boiling the milk, a light obtained by friction must be used. After the milk-boiling ceremonial, the pūjāri (priest), tying bells on his legs, approaches the fire-pit, carrying milk freshly drawn from a cow, which has calved for the first time, and flowers of *Rhododendron*, *Leucas*, or jasmine. After doing pūja (worship), he throws the flowers on the embers, and they should remain unscorched for a few seconds. He then pours some of the milk over the embers, and no hissing sound should be produced. The omens being propitious, he walks over the glowing embers, followed by a Udaya † and the crowd of celebrants, who, before going through the ordeal, count the hairs on their feet. If any are singed, it is a sign of approaching ill-fortune, or even death.

It is recorded by the Rev. J. Cain ‡ that, when the

* Fire-walking, *see* Thurston, "Ethnographic Notes in Southern India," 1907, 471-86.

† Udaya is one of the divisions of the Badagas, which ranks as superior to the other divisions.

‡ Koyis, *see* Cain, *Madras Christian College Magazine* (old series), v. 352-9, and vi. 274-80; also "Ind. Ant.," v., 1876, and viii., 1879.

Koyis of the Godâvari district determine to appease the goddess of smallpox or cholera, they erect a pandal (booth) outside their village under a nīm tree (*Melia Azadirachta*). They make the image of a woman with earth from a white-ant hill, tie a cloth or two round it, hang a few peacock's feathers round its neck, and place it under the pandal on a three-legged stool made from the wood of the silk-cotton tree (*Cochlospermum Gossypium*). They then bring forward a chicken, and try to persuade it to eat some of the grains which they have thrown before the image, requesting the goddess to inform them whether she will leave their village or not. If the chicken picks up some of the grains, they regard it as a most favourable omen; but, if not, their hearts are filled with dread of the continued anger of the goddess. At the Bhūdēvi Panduga, or festival of the earth goddess, according to Mr F. R. Hemingway, the Koyis set up a stone beneath a *Terminalia tomentosa* tree, which is thus dedicated to the goddess Kodalamma. Each worshipper brings a cock to the priest, who holds it over grains of rice, which have been sprinkled before the goddess. If the bird pecks at the rice, good luck is ensured for the coming year, whilst, if perchance the bird pecks three times, the offerer of that particular bird can scarcely contain himself for joy. If the bird declines to touch the grains, ill-luck is sure to visit the owner's house during the ensuing year.

Concerning a boundary oath in the Mulkangiri tāluk of Vizagapatam, Mr C. A. Henderson writes to me as follows:—

"The pūjāri (priest) levelled a piece of ground about a foot square, and smeared it with cow-dung. The boundary was marked with rice-flour and turmeric, and a small heap of rice and cow-dung was left in the middle. A sword was laid across the heap. The pūjāri touched the rice-flour line with the tips of his fingers, and then pressed his knuckles on the same place, thus leaving an exit on the south side. He then held a chicken over the central heap, and muttered some mantrams. The chicken pecked at the rice, and an egg was placed on the heap. The chicken then pecked at the rice again. The ceremony then waited for another party, who performed a similar ceremony. There was some amusement because their chickens would not eat. The chickens were decapitated, and their heads placed in the square. The eggs were then broken. It was raining, and there was a resulting puddle of cow-dung, chicken's blood, egg, and rice, of which the representatives of each party took a portion, and eat it, or pretended to do so, stating to whom the land belonged. There is said to be a belief that, if a man swears falsely, he will die."

Though not bearing on the subject of omens, some further boundary ceremonies may be placed under reference. At Sāttamangalam, in the South Arcot district, the festival of the goddess Māriamma is said to be crowned by the sacrifice at midnight of a goat, the entrails of which are hung round the neck of the Toti (scavenger), who then goes, stark naked, save for this one adornment, round all the village boundaries.*

It is recorded by Bishop Whitehead † that, in some parts of the Tamil country, *e.g.*, in the Trichinopoly district, at the ceremony for the propitiation of the village boundary goddess, a priest carries a pot containing boiled rice and the blood of a lamb which has been sacrificed to the boundary stone, round which he runs three times. The third time he throws the pot over his shoulder on to another smaller stone, which stands at the foot of the boundary stone. The pot is dashed to pieces, and

* "Gazetteer of the South Arcot District," 1906, i. 98.
† *Madras Museum Bull.*, 1907, No. 3, v. 166.

the rice and blood scatter over the two stones and all round them. The priest then goes away without looking back, followed by the crowd of villagers in dead silence. In the Cuddapah district, when there is a boundary dispute in a village, an image of the goddess Gangamma is placed in the street, and left there for two days. The head of a buffalo and several sheep are offered to her, and the blood is allowed to run into the gutter. The goddess is then worshipped, and she is implored to point out the correct boundary.* In Mysore, if there is a dispute as to the village boundaries, the Holeya † Kuluvādi is believed to be the only person competent to take the oath as to how the boundary ought to run. The old custom for settling such disputes is thus described by Captain J. S. F. Mackenzie : ‡

"The Kuluvādi, carrying on his head a ball made of the village earth, in the centre of which is placed some earth, passes along the boundary. If he has kept the proper line, everything goes well, but, should he, by accident even, go beyond his own proper boundary, then the ball of earth, of its own accord, goes to pieces. The Kuluvādi is said to die within fifteen days, and his house becomes a ruin. Such is the popular belief."

Some years ago Mr H. D. Taylor was called on to settle a boundary dispute between two villages in Jeypore under the following circumstances. As the result of a panchāyat (council meeting), the men of one village had agreed to accept the boundary claimed by the other party if the head of their village walked round the boundary and eat earth at intervals, provided that no harm came to him within six months. The man accordingly perambulated

* "Manual of the Cuddapah District," 1875, 291.

† The Holeyas were formerly agrestic serfs.

‡ "Ind. Ant.," 1873, ii. 66.

the boundary eating earth, and a conditional order of possession was given. Shortly afterwards the man's cattle died, one of his children died of smallpox, and finally he himself died within three months. The other party then claimed the land on the ground that the earth-goddess had proved him to have perjured himself. It was urged in defence that the man had been made to eat earth at such frequent intervals that he contracted dysentery, and died from the effects of earth-eating.*

When the time for the annual festival of the tribal goddess of the Kuruvikkārans (Marāthi-speaking beggars) draws nigh, the headman or an elder piles up *Vigna Catiang* seeds in five small heaps. He then decides in his mind whether there is an odd or even number of seeds in the majority of heaps. If, when the seeds are counted, the result agrees with his forecast, it is taken as a sign of the approval of the goddess, and arrangements for the festival are made. Otherwise it is abandoned for the year.

At the annual festival of Chaudēswari, the tribal goddess of Dēvānga weavers, the priest tries to balance a long sword on its point on the edge of the mouth of a pot. A lime fruit is placed in the region of the navel of the idol, who should throw it down spontaneously. A bundle of betel leaves is cut across with a knife, and the cut ends should unite. If the omens are favourable, a lamp made of rice-flour is lighted, and pongal (boiled rice) offered to it.

It is recorded by Canter Visscher † that, in the building of a house in Malabar, the carpenters open three or four cocoanuts, spilling the juice as little as possible, and put some tips of betel leaves into them. From the way these float on the liquid they foretell whether the house will

* Earth-eating (geophagy), *see* my "Ethnographic Notes in Southern India," 1907, 552-4.

† Letters from Malabar, Translation, Madras, 1862.

be lucky or unlucky, whether it will stand for a long or short period, and whether another will ever be erected on its site.

Korava women, if their husbands are absent on a criminal expedition long enough to arouse apprehension of danger, pull a long piece out of a broom, and tie to one end of it several small pieces dipped in oil. If the stick floats in water, all is well; but, should it sink, two of the women start at once to find the men.*

In the village of Chakibunda in the Cuddapah district, there is a pool of water at the foot of a hill. Those who are desirous of getting children, wealth, etc., go there and pour oil into the water. The oil is said not to float as is usual in greasy bubbles, but to sink and never rise. They also offer betel leaves, on which turmeric and kunkumam have been placed. If these leaves sink, and after some time reappear without the turmeric and kunkumam, but with the marks of nails upon them, the person offering them will gain his wishes. The contents of the leaves, and the oil, are supposed to be consumed by some divine being at the bottom of the pool.† At Madicheruvu, in the Cuddapah district, there is a small waterfall in the midst of a jungle, which is visited annually by a large number of pilgrims. Those who are anxious to know if their sins are forgiven stand under the fall. If they are acceptable the water falls on their heads, but, if they have some great guilt weighing on them, the water swerves on one side, and refuses to be polluted by contact with the sinner.‡

Among the Vādas (Telugu fishermen) the Mannāru is an important individual who not only performs worship, but is consulted on many points. If a man does not

* F. Fawcett, "Note on the Koravas," 1908.
† "Manual of the Cuddapah District," 1875, 288.
‡ *Ibid.*, 285.

secure good catches of fish, he goes to the Mannāru to ascertain the cause of his bad luck. The Mannāru holds in his hand a string on which a stone is tied, and invokes various gods and goddesses by name. Every time a name is mentioned, the stone either swings to and fro like a pendulum, or performs a circular movement. If the former occurs, it is a sign that the deity whose name has been pronounced is the cause of the misfortune, and must be propitiated in a suitable manner.

The Nomad Bauris or Bāwariyas, who commit robberies and manufacture counterfeit coin, keep with them a small quantity of wheat and sandal seeds in a tin or brass case, which they call dēvakadana or god's grain, and a tuft of peacock's feathers. They are very superstitious, and do not embark on any enterprise without first ascertaining by omens whether it will be attended with success or not. This they do by taking at random a small quantity of grains out of the dēvakadana, and counting the number thereof, the omen being considered good or bad according as the number is odd or even.* A gang of Donga Dāsaris, before starting on a thieving expedition, proceed to the jungle near their village in the early part of the night, worship their favourite goddesses, Huligavva and Ellamma, and sacrifice a sheep or fowl before them. They place one of their turbans on the head of the animal as soon as its head falls on the ground. If the turban turns to the right it is considered a good sign, the goddess having permitted them to proceed on the expedition; if to the left they return home. Hanumān (the monkey god) is also consulted as to such expeditions. They go to a Hanumān temple, and, after worshipping him, garland him with a wreath of flowers. The garland hangs

* M. Paupa Rao Naidu, "The Criminal Tribes of India," Madras, 1907, No. 3.

on both sides of the neck. If any of the flowers on the right side drop down first, it is regarded as a permission granted by the god to start on a plundering expedition; and, conversely, an expedition is never undertaken if any flower happens to drop from the left side first.* The Kallans are said by Mr F. S. Mullaly † to consult the deity before starting on depredations. Two flowers, the one red and the other white, are placed before the idol, a symbol of their god Kalla Alagar. The white flower is the emblem of success. A child of tender years is told to pluck a petal of one of the two flowers, and the success of the undertaking rests upon the choice made by the child. The Pulluvan astrologers of Malabar sometimes calculate beforehand the result of a project in which they are engaged, by placing before the god two bouquets of flowers, one red, the other white, of which a child picks out one with its eyes closed. Selection of the white bouquet predicts auspicious results, of the red the reverse. In the same way, when the Kammālans (Tamil artisans) appoint their Anjivīttu Nāttāmaikkāran to preside over them, five men selected from each of the five divisions meet at the temple of the caste goddess, Kāmākshi Amman. The names of the five men are written on five slips of paper, which, together with some blank slips, are thrown before the shrine of the goddess. A child, taken at random from the assembled crowd, is made to pick up the slips, and he whose name turns up first is proclaimed Anjivīttu Nāttāmaikkāran.

Eclipses are regarded as precursors of evil, which must, if possible, be averted. Concerning the origin thereof, according to tradition in Malabar, Mr Gopal Panikkar writes as follows ‡:—

* T. M. Natesa Sastri, *Calcutta Review*, 1905, cxxi. 501.

† "Notes on the Criminal Classes of the Madras Presidency," 1892, 90.

‡ "Malabar and its Folk," Madras, 2nd. ed., 58-9.

"Tradition says that, when an eclipse takes place, Rāhu the huge serpent is devouring the sun or moon, as the case may be. An eclipse being thus the decease of one of those heavenly bodies, people must, of necessity, observe pollution for the period during which the eclipse lasts. When the monster spits out the body, the eclipse is over. Food and drink taken during an eclipse possess poisonous properties, and people therefore abstain from eating and drinking until the eclipse is over. They bathe at the end of the eclipse, so as to get rid of the pollution. Any one shutting himself up from exposure may be exempted from this obligation to take a bath."

Deaths from drowning are not unknown in Madras at times of eclipse, when Hindus bathe in the sea, and get washed away by the surf. It is said * that, before an eclipse, the people prepare their drums, etc., to frighten the giant, lest he should eat up the moon entirely. Images of snakes are offered to the deity on days of eclipse by Brāhmans on whose star day the eclipse falls, to appease the wrath of the terrible Rāhu. It is noted by Mr S. M. Natesa Sastri † that "the eclipse must take place on some asterism or other, and, if that asterism happens to be that in which any Hindu was born, he has to perform some special ceremonies to absolve himself from impending evil. He makes a plate of gold or silver, or of palm leaf, according to his means, and ties it on his forehead with Sanskrit verses inscribed on it. He sits with this plate for some time, performs certain ceremonies, bathes with the plate untied, and presents it to a Brāhman with some fee, ranging from four annas to several thousands of rupees. The belief that an eclipse is a calamity to the sun or moon is such a strong Hindu belief, that no

* Letters from Madras, 1843.

† "Hindu Feasts, Fasts, and Ceremonies," Madras, 1903, 32-3.

marriage takes place in the month in which an eclipse falls."

I gather * that, "during an eclipse, many of the people retire into their houses, and remain behind closed doors until the evil hour has passed. The time is in all respects inauspicious, and no work begun or completed during this period can meet with success; indeed, so great is the dread, that no one would think of initiating any important work at this time. More especially is it fatal to women who are pregnant, for the evil will fall upon the unborn babe, and, in cases of serious malformation or congenital lameness, the cause is said to be that the mother looked on an eclipse. Women, therefore, not only retire into the house, but, in order that they may be further protected from the evil, they burn horn shavings. The evils of an eclipse are not limited to human beings, but cattle and crops also need protection from the malignant spirits which are supposed to be abroad. In order that the cattle may be preserved, they are as far as possible taken indoors, and especially those which have young calves; and, to make assurance doubly sure, their horns are smeared with chunam (lime). The crops are protected by procuring ashes from the potter's field, which seem to be specially potent against evil spirits. With these ashes images are made, and placed on the four sides of the field. Comets, too, are looked upon as omens of evil."

When a person is about to occupy a new house, he takes particular care to see that the planet Venus does not face him as he enters it. With this star before him, he sometimes postpones the occupation, or, if he is obliged to enter, he reluctantly does so through the back-door.

On the day of the capture of Seringaptam, which, being the last day of a lunar month, was inauspicious,

* *Madras Weekly Mail*, 15th October, 1908.

the astrologer repeated the unfavourable omen to Tīpu Sultān, who was slain in the course of the battle. It is recorded* that "to different Bramins he gave a black buffalo, a milch buffalo, a male buffalo, a black she-goat, a jacket of coarse black cloth, a cap of the same material, ninety rupees, and an iron pot filled with oil; and, previous to the delivery of this last article, he held his head over the pot for the purpose of seeing the image of his face; a ceremony used in Hindostan to avert misfortune."

The time at which the address of welcome by the Madras Municipal Corporation to Sir Arthur Lawley on his taking over the Governorship of Madras was changed from 12-30 P.M. to 1 P.M. on a Wednesday, as the time originally fixed fell within the period of Rahukālam, which is an inauspicious hour on that day.

It is considered by a Hindu unlucky to get shaved for ceremonial purposes in the months of Ādi, Purattāsi, Margali, and Māsi, and, in the remaining months, Sunday, Tuesday, and Saturday should be avoided. Further, the star under which a man was born has to be taken into consideration, and it may happen that an auspicious day for being shaved does not occur for some weeks. It is on this account that orthodox Hindus are sometimes compelled to go about with unkempt chins. Even for anointing the body, auspicious and inauspicious days are prescribed. Thus, anointing on Sunday causes loss of beauty, on Monday brings increase of riches, and on Thursday loss of intellect. If a person is obliged to anoint himself on Sunday, he should put a bit of the root of oleander (*Nerium*) in the oil, and heat it before applying it. This is supposed to avert the evil influences. Similarly on Tuesday dry earth, on Thursday roots of *Cynodou Dactylon*, and on Friday ashes must be used.

* Rev. E. W. Thompson, "The Last Siege of Seringapatam," 1907.

It is considered auspicious if a girl attains puberty on a Monday, Wednesday, Thursday, or Friday, and the omens vary according to the month in which the first menstrual period occurs. Thus the month of Vaiyâsi ensures prosperity, Āni male issue, Māsi happiness, Margali well-behaved children, Punguni long life and many children. At the first menstrual ceremony of a Tiyan girl in Malabar, her aunt, or, if she is married, her husband's sister, pours gingelly (*Sesamum*) oil over her head, on the top of which a gold fanam (coin) has been placed. The oil is poured from a little cup made from a leaf of the jak tree (*Artocarpus integrifolia*), flows over the forehead, and is received with the fanam in a dish. It is a good omen if the coin falls with the obverse upwards.

If a Brāhman woman loses her tāli (marriage badge), it is regarded as a bad omen for her husband. As a Dēva-dāsi (dancing-girl) can never become a widow, the beads in her tāli are considered to bring good luck to those who wear them. And some people send the tāli required for a marriage to a Dēva-dāsi, who prepares the string for it, and attaches to it black beads from her own tāli. A Dēva-dāsi is also deputed to walk at the head of Hindu marriage processions. Married women do not like to do this, as they are not proof against evil omens, which the procession may come across, and it is believed that Dēva-dāsis, to whom widowhood is unknown, possess the power of warding off the effects of unlucky omens. It may be remarked, *en passant*, that Dēva-dāsis are not at the present day so much patronised at Hindu marriages as in former days. Much is due in this direction to the progress of enlightened ideas, which have of late been strongly put forward by Hindu social reformers. General Burton narrates * how a civilian of the old school built a house at

* "An Indian Olio," 98.

Bhavāni, and established a *corps de ballet*, i.e., a set of nautch girls, whose accomplishments extended to singing *God Save the King*, and this was kept up by their descendants, so that, when he visited the place in 1852, he was "greeted by the whole party, bedizened in all their finery, and squalling the National Anthem." With this may be contrasted a circular from a modern European official, which states that "during my jamabandy (land revenue settlement) tour, people have sometimes been kind enough to arrange singing or dancing parties, and, as it would have been discourteous to decline to attend what had cost money to arrange, I have accepted the compliment in the spirit in which it was offered. I should, however, be glad if you would let it be generally known that I am entirely in accord with what is known as the anti-nautch movement in regard to such performances."

It was unanimously decided, in 1905, by the Executive Committee of the Prince and Princess of Wales' reception committee, that there should be no performance by nautch girls at the entertainment to their Royal Highnesses at Madras.

The marriage ceremonies of Ārē Dammaras (Marāthi-speaking acrobats) are supervised by an old Basavi woman, and the marriage badge is tied round the bride's neck by a Basavi (public woman dedicated to the deity).

When a marriage is contemplated among the Idaiyans (Tamil shepherds) of Coimbatore, the parents of the prospective bride and bridegroom go to the temple, and throw before the idol a red and white flower, each wrapped in a betel leaf. A small child is then told to pick up one of the leaves. If the one selected contains the white flower, it is considered auspicious, and the marriage will be contracted. The Dēvānga weavers, before settling the marriage of a girl, consult some village goddess or the tribal goddess Chaudēswari, and watch the omens. A lizard chirping on the right is good, and on the left bad. Sometimes, red and white flowers wrapped in green leaves are thrown in front of the idol, and the omen is considered good or bad, according to the flower which a child picks up. Among the hill Urālis of Coimbatore, a flower is placed on the top of a stone or figure representing the tribal goddess, and, after worship, it is addressed in the words: "Oh! swāmil (goddess), drop the flower to the right if the marriage is going to be propitious, and to the left if otherwise." Should the flower remain on the image without falling either way, it is greeted as a very happy omen. When a marriage is in contemplation among the Agamudaiyans (Tamil cultivators), some close relations of the young man proceed to some distance northward, and wait for omens. If these are auspicious, they are satisfied. Some, instead of so doing, go to a temple, and seek the omens either by placing flowers on the idol, and watching the directions in which they fall, or by picking up a flower from a large number strewn in front of the idol. If the flower picked up, and the one thought of, are of the same colour, it is regarded as a good omen. Among the Gudigāras (wood-carvers) of South Canara, the parents of the couple go to a temple, and receive from the priest some flowers which have been used in worship. These are counted, and, if their number is even, the match is arranged. At a marriage among the Malaiālis of the Kollaimalai hills, the garlands with which the bridal couple are adorned, are thrown into a well after the tāli has been tied on the bride's neck. If they float together, it is an omen that the two will love each other.

Among the Telugu Janappans (gunny-bag makers), on the day fixed for the betrothal, those assembled wait silently listening for the chirping of a lizard, which is an auspicious sign. It is said that the match is broken off if the chirping is not heard. If the omen proves auspicious, a small bundle of nine to twelve kinds of pulses and grain is given by the bridegroom's father to the father of the bride. This is preserved, and examined several days after the marriage. If the pulses and grain are in good condition, it is a sign that the newly married couple will have a prosperous career. During the marriage ceremonies of the Muhammadan Daknis or Deccanis, two big pots, filled with water, are placed near the milk-post. They are kept for forty days, and then examined. If the water remains sweet, and does not "teem with vermin," it is regarded as a good omen. The seed grains, too, which, as among many Hindu castes, were sown at the time of the wedding, should by this time have developed into healthy seedlings. At a Rona (Oriya cultivator) wedding, the Dēsāri who officiates ties to the ends of the cloths of the bridal couple a new cloth, to which a quarter-anna piece is attached, betel leaves and areca nuts, and seven grains of rice. Towards the close of the marriage rites on the third day, the rice is examined, to see if it is in a good state of preservation, and its condition is regarded as an omen for good or evil.

On the occasion of a wedding among the Badagas of the Nīlgiris, a procession goes before dawn on the marriage day to the forest, where two sticks of *Mimusops hexandra* are collected, to do duty as the milk-posts. The early hour is selected, to avoid the chance of coming across inauspicious objects. At the close of the Agamudaiyan marriage ceremonies, the twig of *Erythrina indica* or *Odina wodier*, of which the milk-post was made, is planted. If it takes root and grows, it is regarded as a favourable omen. At a Palli (Tamil cultivator) wedding two lamps, called kuda vilakku (pot light) and alankara vilakku (ornamental light), are placed by the side of the milk-post. The former consists of a lighted wick in an earthenware tray placed on a pot. It is considered an unlucky omen if it goes out before the conclusion of the ceremonial.

Prior to the betrothal ceremony of the Kammas (Telugu cultivators), a near relation of the future bridegroom proceeds with a party to the home of the future bride. On the way thither, they look for omens, such as the crossing of birds in an auspicious direction. Immediately on the occurrence of a favourable omen, they burn camphor, and break a cocoanut, which must split in two with clean edges. One half is sent to the would-be bridegroom, and the other taken to the bride's house. When this is reached, she demands the sagunam (omen) cocoanut. If the first cocoanut does not split properly, others are broken till the desired result is obtained.

In the Telugu country, the services of a member of the Bōya caste are required if a Brāhman wishes to perform Vontigadu, a ceremony by which he hopes to induce favourable auspices, under which to celebrate a marriage. The story has it that Vontigadu was a destitute Bōya, who died of starvation. On the morning of the day on which the ceremony, for which favourable auspices are required, is performed, a Bōya is invited to the house. He is given a present of gingelly (*Sesamum*) oil, wherewith to anoint himself. This done, he returns, carrying in his hand a dagger, on the point of which a lime has been stuck. He is directed to the cowshed, and there given a good meal. After finishing the meal, he steals from the shed, and dashes out of the house, uttering a piercing yell, and waving his dagger. He on no account looks behind him. The inmates of the house follow for some distance, throwing water wherever he has trodden. By this means, all possible evil omens for the coming ceremony are done away with.

A curious mock marriage ceremony is celebrated among Brāhmans, when an individual marries a third wife. It is believed that a third marriage is very inauspicious, and that the bride will become a widow. To prevent this mishap, the man is made to marry the arka plant (*Calotropis gigantea*), which grows luxuriantly in waste-lands, and the real marriage thus becomes the fourth. The bridegroom, accompanied by a Brāhman priest and another Brāhman, repairs to a spot where this plant is growing. It is decorated with a cloth and a piece of string, and symbolised into the sun. All the ceremonies, such as making hōmam (sacred fire), tying the tāli (marriage badge), etc., are performed as at a regular marriage, and the plant is cut down. On rathasapthami day, an orthodox Hindu should bathe his head and shoulders with arka leaves in propitiation of Surya (the sun). The leaves are also used during the worship of ancestors by some Brāhmans. Among the Tangalān Paraiyans, if a young man dies before he is married, a ceremony called kannikazhital (removing bachelorhood) is performed. Before the corpse is laid on the bier, a garland of arka flowers is placed round its neck, and balls of mud from a gutter are laid on the head, knees, and other parts of the body. In some places, a variant of the ceremony consists in the erection of a mimic marriage booth, which is covered with leaves of the arka plant, flowers of which are placed round the neck as a garland. Adulterers were, in former times, seated on a donkey, with their face to the tail, and marched through the village. The public disgrace was enhanced by placing a garland of the despised arka leaves on their head.

Uppiliyan women convicted of immorality are said to be garlanded with arka flowers, and made to carry a basket of mud round the village. A Konga Vellāla man, who has been found guilty of undue intimacy with a widow, is readmitted to the caste by being taken to the village common, where he is beaten with an arka stick, and by providing a black sheep for a feast. When a Kuruvikkāran man has to submit to trial by ordeal, seven arka leaves are tied to his palms, and a piece of red-hot iron is placed thereon. His innocence is established, if he is able to carry it while he takes seven long strides. The juice of the arka plant is a favourite agent in the hands of suicides.

At a Brāhman wedding the bridegroom takes a blade of the sacred dharba grass, passes it between the eyebrows of the bride and throws it away saying, "With this grass I remove the influence of any bad mark thou mayest possess, which is likely to cause widowhood."

There is a Tamil proverb relating to the selection of a wife, to the effect that curly hair gives food, thick hair brings milk, and very stiff hair destroys a family. As a preliminary to marriage among the Kurubas (Canarese shepherds), the bridegroom's father observes certain curls (suli) on the head of the proposed bride. Some of these are believed to forebode prosperity, and others misery to the family into which the girl enters by marriage. They are, therefore, very cautious in selecting only such girls as possess curls of good fortune. One of the good curls is the bāshingam on the forehead, and bad ones are the pēyanākallu at the back of the head, and the edirsuli near the right temple.* By the Pallis (Tamil cultivators) a curl on the forehead is considered as an indication that the girl will become a widow, and one

* 'Manual of the North Arcot District" 1895, i. 223-4.

on the back of the head portends the death of the eldest brother of her husband. By the Tamil Maravans, a curl on the forehead resembling the head of a snake is regarded as an evil omen.

A woman, pregnant for the first time, should not see a temple car adorned with figures of a lion, or look at it when it is being dragged along with the image of the god seated in it. If she does, the tradition is that she will give birth to a monster.

In some places, before a woman is confined, the room in which her confinement is to take place is smeared with cow-dung, and, in the room at the outer gate, small wet cow-dung cakes are stuck on the wall, and covered with margosa (*Melia Azadirachta*) leaves and cotton seeds. These are supposed to have a great power in averting evil spirits, and preventing harm to the newly-born babe or the lying-in woman.* In the Telugu country, it is the custom among some castes, *e.g.*, the Kāpus and Gamallas, to place twigs of *Balanites Roxburghii* or *Calotropis gigantea* (arka) on the floor or in the roof of the lying-in chamber. Sometimes a garland of old shoes is hung up on the door-post of the chamber. A fire is kindled, into which pieces of old leather, hair, nails, horns, hoofs, and bones of animals are thrown, in the belief that the smoke arising therefrom will protect the mother and child against evil spirits. Among some classes, when a woman is pregnant, her female friends assemble, pile up before her door a quantity of rice-husk, and set fire to it. To one door-post they tie an old shoe, and to the other a bunch of tulsi (*Ocimum sanctum*), in order to prevent the entry of any demon. A bitch is brought in, painted, and marked in the way that the women daily mark their own foreheads. Incense is burnt, and an

* S. M. Natesa Sastri, "Ind. Ant.," 1889, xviii. 287.

oblation placed before it. The woman then makes obeisance to it, and makes a meal of curry and rice, on which cakes are placed. If there is present any woman who has not been blessed with children, she seizes some of the cakes, in the hope that, by so doing, she may ere long have a child.* In some places, when a woman is in labour, her relations keep on measuring out rice into a measure close to the lying-in room, in the belief that delivery will be accelerated thereby. Sometimes a gun is fired off in an adjacent room with the same object, and I have heard of a peon (orderly), whose wife was in labour, borrowing his master's gun, to expedite matters.

Some Hindus in Madras believe that it would be unlucky for a newly-married couple to visit the museum, as their offspring would be deformed as the result of the mother having gazed on the skeletons and stuffed animals.

Twins are sometimes objects of superstition, especially if they are of different sexes, and the male is born first. The occurrence of such an event is regarded as foreboding misfortune, which can only be warded off by marrying the twins to one another, and leaving them to their fate in the jungle. Cases of this kind have, however, it is said, not been heard of within recent times.

There is a proverb that a child born with the umbilical cord round the body will be a curse to the caste. If a child is born with the cord round its neck like a garland, it is believed to be inauspicious for its uncle, who is not allowed to see it for ten days, or even longer, and then a propitiatory ceremony has to be performed. By the Koravas the birth of a child with the cord round its neck is believed to portend the death of the father or maternal uncle. This unpleasant effect is warded off by

* Rev. J. Cain, "Ind. Ant.," 1875, iv. 198.

the father or the uncle killing a fowl, and wearing its entrails round his neck, and afterwards burying them along with the cord. In other castes it is believed that a child born with the cord round its neck will be a curse to its maternal uncle, unless a gold or silver string is placed on the body, and the uncle sees its image reflected in a vessel of oil. If the cord is entwined across the breast, and passes under the armpit, it is believed to be an unlucky omen for the father and paternal uncle. In such cases, some special ceremony, such as looking into a vessel of oil, is performed. I am informed by the Rev. S. Nicholson that, if a Māla (Telugu Pariah) child is born with the cord round its neck, a cocoanut is immediately offered. If the child survives, a cock is offered to the gods on the day on which the mother takes her first bath. When the cord is cut, a coin is placed over the navel for luck. The dried cord is highly prized as a remedy for sterility. The placenta is placed by the Mālas in a pot, in which are nīm (*Melia Azadirachta*) leaves, and the whole is buried in some convenient place, generally the backyard. If this was not done, dogs or other animals might carry off the placenta, and the child would be of a wandering disposition.

The birth of a Korava child on a new moon night is believed to augur a notorious thieving future for the infant. Such children are commonly named Venkatigādu after the god at Tirupati.* The birth of a male child on the day in which the constellation Rohini is visible portends evil to the maternal uncle; and a female born under the constellation Moolam is supposed to carry misery with her to the house which she enters by marriage.

Dōmb children in Vizagapatam are supposed to be

* F. Fawcett, "Note on the Koravas," 1908.

born without souls, and to be subsequently chosen as an abode by the soul of an ancestor. The coming of the ancestor is signalised by the child dropping a chicken bone which has been thrust into its hand, and much rejoicing follows among the assembled relations.

By some Valaiyans (Tamil cultivators), the naming of infants is performed at the Aiyanar temple by any one who is under the influence of inspiration. Failing such a one, several flowers, each with a name attached to it, are thrown in front of the idol. A boy, or the priest, picks up one of the flowers, and the infant receives the name which is connected with it. In connection with the birth ceremonies of the Koyis of the Godāvari district, the Rev. J. Cain writes * that, on the seventh day, the near relatives and neighbours assemble together to name the child. Having placed it on a cot, they put a leaf of the mowha tree (*Bassia*) in its hand, and pronounce some name which they think suitable. If the child closes its hand over the leaf, it is regarded as a sign that it acquiesces, but, if the child rejects the leaf or cries, they take it as a sign that they must choose another name, and so throw away the leaf, and substitute another leaf and name, until the child shows its approbation.

It is noted,† in connection with the death ceremonies of the Kondhs, that, if a man has been killed by a tiger, purification is made by the sacrifice of a pig, the head of which is cut off with a tangi (axe) by a Pāno, and passed between the legs of the men in the village, who stand in a line astraddle. It is a bad omen to him, if the head touches any man's legs. According to another account, the head of the decapitated pig is placed in a

* "Ind. Ant.," 1876, v. 358.

† "Manual of the Ganjam District," 1882, 71-2.

stream, and, as it floats down, it has to pass between the legs of the villagers. If it touches the legs of any of them, it forebodes that he will be killed by a tiger.

The sight of a cat, on getting out of bed, is extremely unlucky, and he who sees one will fail in all his undertakings during the day. "I faced the cat this morning," or "Did you see a cat this morning?" are common sayings when one fails in anything. The Paraiyans are said to be very particular about omens, and, if, when a Paraiyan sets out to arrange a marriage with a certain girl, a cat or a valiyan (a bird) crosses his path, he will give up the girl. I have heard of a superstitious European police officer, who would not start in search of a criminal, because he came across a cat.

House dogs should, if they are to bring good luck, possess more than eighteen visible claws. If a dog scratches the wall of a house, it will be broken into by thieves; and, if it makes a hole in the ground within a cattle-shed, the cattle will be stolen. A dog approaching a person with a bit of shoe-leather augurs success; with flesh, gain; with a meaty bone, good luck; with a dry bone, death. If a dog enters a house with wire or thread in its mouth, the master of the house must expect to be put in prison. A dog barking on the roof of a house during the dry weather portends an epidemic, and in the wet season a heavy fall of rain. There is a proverb "Like a dying dog climbing the roof," which is said of a person who is approaching his ruin. The omen also signifies the death of several members of the family, so the dog's ears and tail are cut off, and rice is steeped in the blood. A goat which has climbed on to the roof is treated in like manner, dragged round the house, or slaughtered. At the conclusion of the first menstrual ceremony of a Kāppiliyan (Canarese farmer) girl, some food is placed near the entrance to the house, which a dog is allowed to eat. While so doing, it receives a severe beating. The more noise it makes, the better is the omen for the girl having a large family. If the animal does not howl, it is supposed that the girl will bear no children.

The sight of a jackal is very lucky to one proceeding on an errand. Its cry to the east and north of a village foretells something good for the villagers, whereas the cry at midday means an impending calamity. If a jackal cries towards the south in answer to the call of another jackal, some one will be hung; and, if it cries towards the west, some one will be drowned. A bachelor who sees a jackal running may expect to be married shortly. If the offspring of a primipara dies, it is sometimes buried in a place where jackals can get at it. It is believed that, if a jackal does not make a sumptuous meal off the corpse, the woman will not be blessed with more children. The corpses of the Koramas of Mysore are buried in a shallow grave, and a pot of water is placed on the mound raised over it. Should the spot be visited during the night by a pack of jackals, and the water drunk by them to slake their thirst after feasting on the dead body, the omen is accepted as a proof that the liberated spirit has fled to the realms of the dead, and will never trouble man, woman, child, or cattle.

When a person rises in the morning, he should not face or see a cow's head, but should see its hinder parts. This is in consequence of a legend that a cow killed a Brāhman by goring him with its horns. In some temples, a cow is made to stand in front of the building with its tail towards it, so that any one entering may see its face. It is said that, if a cow voids urine at the time of purchase, it is considered a very good omen, but, if she passes dung, a bad omen. The hill Kondhs will not cut the crops with a sickle having a serrated edge, such as is used by the Oriyas, but use a straight-edged knife. The crops, after they have been cut, are threshed by hand, and not with the aid of cattle. The serrated sickle is not used, because it produces a sound like that of cattle grazing, which would be unpropitious. If cattle were used in threshing the crop, it is believed that the earth-god would feel insulted by the dung and urine of the animals.

A timber merchant at Calicut in Malabar is said to have spent more than a thousand rupees in propitiating the spirit of a deceased Brāhman under the following circumstances. He had built a new house, and, on the morning after the kutti pūja (house-warming) ceremony, his wife and children were coming to occupy it. Just as they were entering the grounds, a cow ran against one of the children, and knocked it down. This augured evil, and, in a few days, the child was attacked by smallpox. One child after another caught the disease, and at last the man's wife also contracted it. They all recovered, but the wife was laid up with some uterine disorder. An astrologer was sent for, and said that the site on which the house was built was once the property of a Brāhman, whose spirit still haunted it, and must be appeased. Expensive ceremonies were performed by Brāhmans for a fortnight. The house was sold to a Brāhman priest for a nominal price. A gold image of the deceased Brāhman was made, and, after the purification ceremonies had been carried out, taken to the sacred shrine at Rāmēsvaram, where arrangements were made to have daily worship performed to it. The house, in its purified state, was sold back by the Brāhman priest. The merchant's wife travelled by train to Madras, to undergo treatment at the Maternity Hospital. The astrologer predicted that the displeasure of the spirit would be exhibited on the way by the breaking of dishes and by furniture catching fire—a strange prediction, because the bed on which the woman was lying caught fire by a spark from the engine. After the spirit had been thus propitiated, there was peace in the house.

It is noted * that, in the middle of the threshold of nearly all the gateways of the ruined fortifications round the Bellary villages may be noticed a roughly carved cylindrical or conical stone, something like a lingam. This is the boddu-rāyi, literally the navel-stone, and so the middle stone. It was planted there when the fort was first built, and is affectionately regarded as being the boundary of the village site. Once a year, in May, just before the sowing season commences, a ceremony takes place in connection with it. Reverence is first made to the bullocks of the village, and in the evening they are driven through the gateway past the boddu-rāyi, with tom-toms, flutes, and other kinds of music. The Barike (village servant) next does pūja (worship) to the stone, and then a string of mango leaves is tied across the gateway above it. The villagers now form sides, one party trying to drive the bullocks through the gate, and the other trying to keep them out. The greatest uproar and confusion naturally follow, and, in the midst of the turmoil, some bullock or other eventually breaks through the guardians of the gate, and gains the village. If that first bullock is a red one, the red grains on the red soil will flourish in the coming season. If he is white, white crops, such as cotton and white cholam, will prosper. If he is red and white, both kinds will do well.

* "Gazetteer of the Bellary District," 1904, i. 61.

Various Oriya castes worship the goddess Lakshmi on Thursdays, in the month of November, which are called Lakshi varam, or Lakshmi's day. The goddess is represented by a basket filled with grain, whereon some place a hair-ball which has been vomited by a cow. The ball is called gāya panghula, and is usually one or two inches in diameter. The owner of a cow which has vomited such a ball, regards it as a propitious augury for the prosperity of his family. A feast is held on the day on which the ball is vomited, and, after the ball has been worshipped, it is carefully wrapped up, and kept in a box, in which it remains till it is required for further worship. Some people believe that the ball continues to grow year by year, and regard this as a very good sign. Bulls are said not to vomit the balls, and only very few cows do so.

"Throughout India," Mr J. D. E. Holmes writes,* "but more especially in the Southern Presidency, among the native population, the value of a horse or ox principally depends on the existence and situation of certain hair-marks on the body of the animal. These hair-marks are formed by the changes in the direction in which the hair grows at certain places, and, according to their shape, are called a crown, ridge, or feather mark. The relative position of these marks is supposed to indicate that the animal will bring good luck to the owner and his relatives. There is a saying that a man may face a rifle and escape, but he cannot avoid the luck, good or evil, foretold by hair-marks. So much are the people influenced by these omens that they seldom keep an animal with unlucky marks, and would not allow their mares to be covered by a stallion having unpropitious marks."

It is recorded by Bishop Whitehead † that "we went to see the Mahārāja (of Mysore) at his stables, and

* *Madras Agricult. Bull.*, 1900, ii. No. 42.

† *Madras Dioc. Mag.*, 1908.

he showed us his fine stud of horses. Among them was the State horse, which is only used for religious ceremonies, and is ridden only by the Mahārāja himself. It is pure white, without spot or blemish, and has the five lucky marks. This horse came from Kathiawar, and is now about twenty years old. The Mahārāja is trying to get another, to replace it when it dies. But it is not easy to get one with the unusual points required."

Two deaths occurring in a family in quick succession, were once believed to be the result of keeping an unlucky horse in the stable. I have heard of a Eurasian police officer, who attributed the theft of five hundred rupees, his official transfer to an unhealthy district, and other strokes of bad luck, to the purchase of a horse with unlucky curls. All went well after he had got rid of the animal.

From a recent note on beliefs about the bull,* I gather that "Manu enjoins a grihasta or householder to always travel with beasts which are well broken in, swift, endowed with lucky marks, and perfect in colour and form, without urging them much with the goad. Marks are accounted lucky if they appear in certain forms, and at certain spots. One of these marks is usually known as sudi in Telugu, and suli in Tamil. A sudi is nothing but a whorl or circlet of hair, a properly formed sudi being perfectly round in form, and nearly resembling the sudivalu, the chakrayudha of Vishnu, which is a short circular weapon commonly known as the discus of Vishnu. Every ox should have at least two of these circlets or twists of hair, one on the face, and one on the back, right about its centre. Two curls may occur on the face, but they should not be one above the other, in which case they are known

* *Madras Weekly Mail*, 7th October 1909.

as kodē mel kodē, or umbrella above umbrella. The purchaser of such a bull, it is believed, will soon have some mishap in his house. Some, however, hold that this curl is not really so bad as it is supposed to be. If the curls are side by side, they are accounted lucky. In that case they are known as damāra suli, or double kettle-drum circlet, from the kettle-drums placed on either side of Brāhmani bulls in temple processions. It is sometimes known as the kalyāna (marriage) suli, because such a kettle-drum is often used in marriage processions. A curl on the hump is held to be a very good one, bringing prosperity to the purchaser. It is known as the kirita suli, or the crown circlet. The dewlaps should have a curl on either side, or none. A curl on only one side is described as not lucky. On the back of the animal, a curl must be perfectly round. If it is elongated, and stretches on one side, it is known as the pādai suli, or the bier circlet. Kattiri suli, or the scissor circlet, is found usually in the region of the belly, and is an unlucky sign. On the body is sometimes found the pūrān suli, the circlet named after the centipede from its supposed resemblance to it. On the legs is often found the velangu suli, or chain circlet, from its being like a chain bound round the legs. Both these are said to be bad marks, and bulls having them are invariably hard to sell. Attempts at erasure of unlucky marks are frequently noticed, for the reason that an animal with a bad mark is scarcely, if ever, sold to advantage. One of the most common and most effective ways of erasing an unlucky mark is to brand it pretty deep, so that the hair disappears, and the curl is no more observable. Animals so branded are regarded with considerable suspicion, and it is often difficult to secure purchasers for them."

The following are some of the marks on horses and cattle recorded by Mr Holmes: *—

(*a*) Horses

1. Deobund (having control over evil spirits), also termed dēvuman or dēvumani, said by Muhammadans to represent the Prophet's finger, and by Hindus to represent a temple bell. This mark is a ridge, one to three inches long, situated between the throat and counter along the line of the trachea. It is the most lucky mark a horse can possess. It is compared to the sun, and, therefore, when it is present, none of the evil stars can shine, and all unlucky omens are overruled.

2. Khorta-gad (peg-driver), or khila-gad, is a ridge of hair directed downwards on one or both hind-legs. It is said that no horse in the stable will be sold, so long as a horse with this mark is kept.

3. Badi (fetter), a ridge of hair directed upwards on one or both forearms on the outer side, and said to indicate that the owner of the animal will be sent to jail.

4. Thanni (teat). Teat-like projections on the sheath of the male are considered unlucky.

(*b*) Cattle

5. Bhashicam suli is a crown on the forehead above the line of the eyes, named after the chaplet worn by bride and bridegroom during the marriage ceremony. If the purchaser be a bachelor or widower, this mark indicates that he will marry soon. If the purchaser be a married man, he will either have the misfortune to

* *Loc. cit.*

lose his wife and marry again, or the good fortune to obtain two wives.

6. Mukkanti suli. Three crowns on the forehead, arranged in the form of a triangle, said to represent the three eyes of Siva, of which the one on the forehead will, if opened, burn up all things within the range of vision.

7. Pādai suli. Two ridges of hair on the back on either side of the middle line, indicating that the purchaser will soon need a coffin.

8. Tattu suli. A crown situated on the back between the points of the hips, indicating that any business undertaken by the purchaser will fail.

9. A bullock with numerous spots over the body, like a deer, is considered very lucky.

The following quaint omen is recorded by Bishop Whitehead.* At a certain village, when a pig is sacrificed to the village goddess Angalamman, its neck is first cut slightly, and the blood allowed to flow on to some boiled rice placed on a plantain leaf, and then the rice soaked in its own blood is given to the pig to eat. If the pig eats it, the omen is good, if not, the omen is bad; but, in any case, the pig has its head cut off by the pūjāri (priest).

If a Brāhmani kite (*Haliastur indus*), when flying, is seen carrying something in its beak, the omen is considered very auspicious. The sight of this bird on a Sunday morning is also auspicious, so, on this day, people may be seen throwing pieces of mutton or lumps of butter to it.†

If an owl takes refuge in a house, the building is at once deserted, the doors are closed, and the house is

* *Madras Museum Bull.*, 1907, v., No. 3, 173.

† Many of the bird superstitions here recorded were published in an article in the *Madras Mail.*

not occupied for six months, when an expiatory sacrifice must be performed. Brāhmans are fed, and the house can only be re-entered after the proper hour has been fixed upon. This superstition only refers to a thatched house; a terraced house need not be vacated.* Ill-luck will follow, should an owl sit on the housetop, or perch on the bough of a tree near the house. One screech forebodes death; two screeches forebode success in any approaching undertaking; three, the addition of a girl to the family by marriage; four, a disturbance; five, that the hearer will travel. Six screeches foretell the coming of guests; seven, mental distress; eight, sudden death; and nine signify favourable results. A species of owl, called pullu, is a highly dreaded bird. It is supposed to cause all kinds of illness to children, resulting in emaciation. At the sound of the screeching, children are taken into a room, to avoid its furtive and injurious gaze. Various propitiatory ceremonies are performed by specialists to secure its good-will. Amulets are worn by children as a preventive against its evil influences. To warn off the unwelcome intruder, broken pots, painted with black and white dots, are set up on housetops. In the Bellary district, the flat roofs of many houses may be seen decked with rags, fluttering from sticks, piles of broken pots, and so forth. These are to scare away owls, which, it is said, sometimes vomit up blood, and sometimes milk. If they sit on a house and bring up blood, it is bad for the inmates; if milk, good. But the risk of the vomit turning out to be blood is apparently more feared than the off chance of its proving to be milk is hoped for, and it is thought best to be on the safe side, and keep the owl at a distance.† The Kondhs

* "Manual of the Cuddapah District," 1875, 293.

† "Gazetteer of the Bellary District," 1904, i. 61.

believe that, if an owl hoots over the roof of a house, or on a tree close thereto, a death will occur in the family at an early date. If the bird hoots close to a village, but outside it, the death of one of the villagers will follow. For this reason, it is pelted with stones, and driven off. The waist-belt of a Koraga, whom I saw at Udipi in South Canara, was made of owl bones.

Should a crow come near the house, and caw in its usual rapid raucous tones, it means that calamity is impending. But, should the bird indulge in its peculiar prolonged guttural note, happiness will ensue. If a crow keeps on cawing incessantly at a house, it is believed to foretell the coming of a guest. The belief is so strong that some housewives prepare more food than is required for the family. There is also an insect called virunthoo poochee, or guest insect. If crows are seen fighting in front of a house, news of a death will shortly be heard. In some places, if a crow enters a house, it must be vacated for not less than three months, and, before it can be re-occupied, a purification ceremony must be performed, and a number of Brāhmans fed. Among the poorer classes, who are unable to incur this expense, it is not uncommon to allow a house which has been thus polluted to fall into ruins.* In Malabar, there is a belief that ill-luck will result if, on certain days, a crow soils one's person or clothes. The evil can only be removed by bathing with the clothes on, and propitiating Brāhmans. On other days, the omen is a lucky one. On srādh (memorial) days, pindams (balls of cooked rice) are offered to the crows. If they do not touch them, the ceremony is believed not to have been properly performed, and the wishes of the dead man are not satisfied. If the crows, after repeated trials, fail to eat the rice, the celebrant makes up his mind

* "Manual of the Cuddapah District," 1875, 293.

to satisfy these wishes, and the crows are then supposed to relish the balls. On one occasion, my Brāhman assistant was in camp with me on the Palni hills, the higher altitudes of which are uninhabited by crows, and he had perforce to march down to the plains, in order to perform the annual ceremony in memory of his deceased father. On another occasion, a Brāhman who was staying on the Palni hills telegraphed to the village of Periakulam for two crows, which duly arrived confined in a cage. The srādh ceremony was performed, and the birds were then set at liberty. On the last day of the death ceremonies of the Oddēs (navvies), some rice is cooked, and placed on an arka (*Calotropis gigantea*) leaf as an offering to the crows. The arka plant, which grows luxuriantly on waste lands, is, it may be noted, used by Brāhmans for the propitiation of rishis (sages) and pithrus (ancestors).* For seven days after the death of a Paniyan of Malabar, a little rice gruel is placed near the grave by the Chemmi (priest), who claps his hands as a signal to the evil spirits in the vicinity, who, in the shape of a pair of crows, are supposed to partake of the food, which is hence called kāka conji, or crow's gruel. On the third day after the death of a Bēdar (Canarese cultivator), a woman brings to the graveside some luxuries in the way of food, which is mixed up in a winnowing tray into three portions, and placed in front of three stones set over the head, abdomen, and legs of the deceased, for crows to partake of. On the sixth day after the death of a Korava, the chief mourner kills a fowl, and mixes its blood with rice. This he places, with betel leaves and areca nuts, near the grave. If it is carried off by crows, everything is considered to have been settled satisfactorily. When a jungle Urāli has been excommunicated from his caste, he must kill a sheep or

* *See* Thurston, "Ethnographic Notes in Southern India," 1907, 44-7.

goat before the elders, and mark his forehead with its blood. He then gives a feast to the assembly, and puts part of the food on the roof of his house. If the crows eat it, he is received back into the caste. A native clerk some time ago took leave in anticipation of sanction, on receipt of news of a death in his family at a distant town. His excuse was that his elder brother had, on learning that his son had seen two crows *in coitu*, sent him a post-card stating that the son was dead. The boy turned out to be alive, but the card, it was explained, was sent owing to a superstitious belief that, if a person sees two crows engaged in sexual congress, he will die unless one of his relations sheds tears. To avert this catastrophe, false news as to the death are sent by post or telegraph, and subsequently corrected by a letter or telegram announcing that the individual is alive. A white (albino) crow, which made its appearance in the city of Madras a fews years ago, caused considerable interest among the residents of the locality, as it was regarded as a very good omen.

Among some classes in Mysore, there is a belief that, if a death occurs in a house on Tuesday or Friday, another death will speedily follow unless a fowl is tied to one corner of the bier. The fowl is buried with the corpse. Those castes which do not eat fowls replace it by the bolt of the door.* Among the Tamils, if a burial takes place on a Saturday, a fowl must be buried or burnt, or another death will shortly occur in the family. There is a Tamil proverb that a Saturday corpse will not go alone. When a fowl is sacrified to the deity by the jungle Paliyans of the Palni hills, the head ought to be severed at one blow, as this is a sign of the satisfaction of the god for the past, and of protection for the future. Should the head still hang, this would be a bad omen, foreboding calamities for the

* J. S. F. Mackenzie, "Ind. Ant.," 1873, ii. 68.

ensuing year.* An interesting rite in connection with pregnancy ceremonies among the Oddēs (navvies) is the presentation of a fowl or two to the pregnant woman by her maternal uncle. The birds are tended with great care, and, if they lay eggs abundantly, it is a sign that the woman will be prolific.

By some it is considered unlucky to keep pigeons about a dwelling-house, as they are believed, on account of their habit of standing on one leg, to lead to poverty. The temple or blue-rock pigeon is greatly venerated by Natives, who consider themselves highly favoured if the birds build in their houses. Should a death occur in a house where there are tame pigeons, all the birds will, it is said, at the time of the funeral, circle thrice round the loft, and leave the locality for ever. House sparrows are supposed to possess a similar characteristic, but, before quitting the house of mourning, they will pull every straw out of their nests. Sparrows are credited with bringing good luck to the house in which they build their nests. For this purpose, when a house is under construction, holes are left in the walls or ceiling, or earthen pots are hung on the walls by means of nails, as an attractive site for nesting. One method of attracting sparrows to a house is to make a noise with rupees as in the act of cointing out coins.

There are experts who are able to interpret the significance of the chirping of lizards, which, *inter alia*, foretells the approach of a case of snake-bite, and whether the patient will die or not. The fall of a lizard on different parts of the body is often taken as an omen for good or evil, according as it alights on the right or left side, hand or foot, head or shoulders. A Native of Cochin foretold from the chirping of a lizard that a robbery would take

* Rev. F. Dahmen, "Anthropos," 1908, iii. 28.

place at a certain temple. In accordance with the prophecy, the temple jewels were looted, and the prophet was sent to prison under suspicion of being an accomplice of the thieves, but subsequently released. The hook-swinging ceremony is said * to be sometimes performed after the consent of the goddess has been obtained. If a lizard is heard chirping on the right, it is regarded as a sign of her consent. It is believed that the man who is swung suffers no pain if the cause is a good one, but excruciating agony if it is a bad one.

If an "iguana" (*Varanus*) enters a house, misfortune is certain to occur within a year, unless the house is shut up for six months. The appearance of a tortoise in a house, or in a field which is being ploughed, is inauspicious. In the Cuddapah district, a cultivator applied for remission of rent, because one of his fields had been left waste owing to a tortoise making its appearance in it. If, under these circumstances, the field had been cultivated, the man, his wife, or his cattle, would have died. It was pointed out that, as the tortoise was one of Vishnu's incarnations, it should have been considered as an honour that the animal visited the field; but the reply was that a tortoise would be honoured in the water, but not on the land.†

The sight of two snakes coiled round each other in sexual congress is considered to portend some great evil. The presence of a rat-snake (*Zamenis mucosus*) in a house at night is believed to bring good fortune to the inmates. Its evil influence is in its tail, a blow from which will cause a limb to shrink in size and waste away.

In a valley named Rapuri Kanama in the Cuddapah district, there is a pond near a Siva temple to Gundheswara.

* Rev. M. Phillips, "Evolution of Hinduism," 1903, 123.

† "Manual of the Cuddapah District," 1875, 292.

Those desirous of getting children, wealth, etc., should go there with a pure heart, bathe in the pond, and then worship at the temple. After this, they should take a wild pine-apple leaf, and place it on the border of the pond. If their wishes are to be granted, a crab rises from the water, and bites the leaf in two. If their wishes will not be granted, the crab rises, but leaves the leaf untouched. If, however, the person has not approached the pond with a pure heart, he will be set upon by a swarm of bees, which live in the vicinity, and will be driven off.*

If the nest of a clay-building insect is found in a house, the birth of a child is foretold; if a mud nest, of a male child; if a nest made of jungle lac, of a girl.†

* "Manual of the Cuddapah District," 1875, 288.
† "Gazetteer of the Tanjore District," 1906, i. 66.

II

ANIMAL SUPERSTITIONS

1. Mammals

There is a belief that the urine of a wild monkey (langūr) called kondamuccha, which it discharges in a thick stream, possesses the power of curing rheumatic pains, if applied to the affected part with a mixture of garlic. Some of the poorer classes in the villages of Kurnool obtain a sale even for stones on which this monkey has urinated, and hill people suffering from chronic fever sometimes drink its blood.* I am informed by Mr A. Ff. Martin, that he has seen a Muduvar on the Travancore hills much pulled down by fever seize an expiring black monkey (*Semnopithecus johni*), and suck the blood from its jugular vein. Childless Muduvar couples are dieted to make them fruitful, the principal diet for the man being plenty of black monkey. The flesh of the black monkey (Nīlgiri langūr) is sold in the Nīlgiri bazaars as a cure for whooping-cough. When Savara (hill tribe in Ganjam) children are seriously ill and emaciated, offerings are said by Mr G. V. Ramamurthi Pantulu to be made to monkeys, not in the belief that the illness is caused by them, but because the sick child, in its wasted condition, has the attenuated figure of these animals. The offerings consist of rice and

* "Manual of the Kurnool District," 1886, 114.

other articles of food, which are placed in baskets suspended from branches of trees in the jungle.

Some years ago, a drinking fountain was erected at the Madras Museum, in which the water issued from the mouth of a lion. It entirely failed in its object, as the Native visitors would not use it, because the animal was represented in the act of vomiting.

I am informed by Mr C. Hayavadana Rao that the Bēpāris, who are traders and carriers between the hills and plains in the Vizagapatam Agency tracts, regard themselves as immune from the attacks of tigers, if they take certain precautions. Most of them have to pass through places infested with these beasts, and their favourite method of keeping them off is as follows. As soon as they encamp at a place, they level a square bit of ground, and light fires in it, round which they pass the night. It is their firm belief that the tiger will not enter the square, from fear lest it should become blind, and eventually be shot. Mr Hayavadana Rao was once travelling towards Malkangiri from Jeypore, when he fell in with a party of Bēpāris thus encamped. At that time the villages about Malkangiri were being ravaged by a notorious man-eater. In connection with man-eating tigers, Mr S. M. Fraser narrates * that, in Mysore, a man-eater was said to have attacked parties bearing corpses to the burning-ground.

"The acquisition," he writes, "of such a curious taste may perhaps be explained by the following passage in a letter from the Amildar. It is a custom among the villagers here not to burn or bury the dead bodies of pregnant females, but to expose them in the neighbouring jungles to be eaten by vultures and wild beasts. The body is tied to a tree, in a sitting posture, and a pot of water is

* *Journ. Bombay Nat. Hist. Soc.*, 1902, xiv., No. 2, 388-91.

put close by. Not long ago some cowherd boys came across the dead body of a woman tied to a tree, and noticed the foot-prints of a tiger round it, but the body was untouched. The boys cut the rope binding the body, which fell to the ground, and the next day the corpse was found eaten away by the tiger."

The village of Hulikal, or tiger's stone, on the Nīlgiris is so called because in it a Badaga once killed a notorious man-eater. The spot where the beast was buried is shown near the Pillaiyar (Ganēsa) temple, and is marked by three stones. It is said that there was formerly a stone image of the slain tiger thereabouts.* When a tiger enters the dwelling of a Savara (hill tribe in Ganjam) and carries off an inmate, the village is said to be deserted, and sacrifices are offered to some spirits by the inhabitants. It is noted by Mr F. Fawcett † that the Savaras have names for numerals up to twelve only. This is accounted for by a story that, long ago, some Savaras were measuring grain in a field, and, when they had completed twelve measures, a tiger pounced on them, and devoured them. So, ever after, they have not dared to have a numeral above twelve for fear of a tiger repeating the performance. In the Vizagapatam district, a ballad is sung by the Dāsaris (a mendicant caste) about the goddess Yerakamma, who is reputed to have been the child of Dāsari parents, and to have had the possession of second sight foretold by a Yerukala fortune-teller. She eventually married, and one day begged her husband not to go to his field, as she was sure he would be killed by a tiger if he did. He went notwithstanding, and was slain as she had foreseen. She killed herself by committing sati (suttee, or burning

* "Gazetteer of the Nilgiris," 1908, i. 328.

† *Journ. Anthrop. Soc., Bombay*, i. 241-2.

of the living widow) on the spot where her shrine still stands. The Muduvars are said by Mr Martin to share with other jungle folk the belief that, if any animal is killed by a tiger or leopard so as to lie north and south, it will not be eaten by the beast of prey. Nor will it be revisited, so that sitting over a "kill" which has fallen north and south, in the hope of getting a shot at the returning tiger or leopard, is a useless proceeding. The Billava toddy-drawers believe that, if the spathe of the palm tree is beaten with the bone of a buffalo which has been killed by a tiger, the yield of toddy will, if the bone has not touched the ground, be greater than if an ordinary bone is used.

I once received an application for half a pound of tiger's fat, presumably for medicinal purposes. The bones of tigers and leopards ground into powder, and mixed with their fat, gingelly (*Sesamum*) oil, and a finely powdered blue stone, make an ointment for the cure of syphilitic sores. The bones of a leopard or hyæna, ground into powder and made into a paste with ox-gall and musk, are said to be a useful ointment for application to rheumatic joints. The addition of the fat of tigers or leopards makes the ointment more effective. I am told that when, on one occasion, a European shot a tiger, the Natives were so keen on securing some of the fat, that the shikāris (hunters) came to him to decide as to the proper distribution among themselves and the camp servants.

The leopard is looked upon as in some way sacred by the hill Kondhs. They object to a dead leopard being carried through their villages, and oaths are taken on a leopard's skin.

Writing in 1873, Dr Francis Day states* that "at

* "Report on the Sea Fisheries of India and Burma," 1873, lxxvi.

Cannanore (in Malabar), the Rājah's cat appears to be exercising a deleterious influence on one branch at least of the fishing, viz., that for sharks. It appears that, in olden times, one fish daily was taken from each boat as a perquisite for the Rājah's cat, or the poocha meen (cat-fish) collection. The cats apparently have not augmented so much as the fishing boats, so this has been converted into a money payment of two pies a day on each successful boat."

In connection with cats, there is a tradition that a Jōgi (Telugu mendicant) bridegroom, before tying the bottu (marriage badge) on his bride's neck, had to tie it by means of a string dyed with turmeric round the neck of a female cat. People sometimes object to the catching of cats by Jōgis for food, as the detachment of a single hair from the body of a cat is considered a heinous offence. To overcome the objection, the Jōgi says that he wants the animal for a marriage ceremony. On one occasion, I saw a Mādiga (Telugu Pariah) carrying home a bag full of kittens, which he said he was going to eat. Some time ago, some prisoners, who called themselves Billaikāvus (cat-eaters), were confined in the Vizagapatam jail. I am informed that these people are Māla Paidis, who eat cat flesh.

The gun with which a wolf has been shot falls under some evil influence, and it is said not to shoot straight afterwards. Hence some shikāris (hunters) will not shoot at a wolf.

The hyæna is believed to beat to death, or strangle with its tail, those whom it seizes. The head of a hyæna is sometimes buried in cattle-sheds, to prevent cattle disease. Its incisor teeth are tied round the loins of a woman in labour, to lessen the pains.*

* "Manual of the Kurnool District," 1886, 115.

There is a belief that, when a bear seizes a man, it tickles him to death.* Bears are supposed, owing to the multilobulated external appearance of the kidneys, to gain an additional pair of these organs every year of their life. They are believed to collect ripe wood-apples (*Feronia elephantum*) during the season, and store them in a secure place in the forest. After a large quantity has been collected, they remove the rind, and heap together all the pulp. They then bring honey and the petals of sweet-smelling flowers, put them on the heap of pulp, thresh them with their feet and sticks in their hands, and, when the whole has become a consistent mass, feast on it. The Vēdans (hunters) watch them when so engaged, drive them off, and rob them of their feast, which they carry off, and sell as karadi panchamritham, or bear delicacy made of five ingredients. The ordinary ingredients of panchamritham are slices of plantain (banana) fruits, jaggery (crude sugar) or sugar, cocoanut scrapings, ghī (clarified butter), honey, and cardamom seeds.

It is believed that the flesh or blood of some animals, which have certain organs largely developed, will cure disease of corresponding organs in the human subject. Thus, the flesh of the jackal, which is credited with the possession of very powerful lungs, is said to be a remedy for asthma.

By the jungle Paliyans of the Palni hills, the following device is adopted to protect themselves from the attacks of wild animals, the leopard in particular. Four jackals' tails are planted in four different spots, chosen so as to include the area in which they wish to be safe from the brute. Even if a leopard entered the magic square,

* M. J. Walhouse, "Ind. Ant.," 1876, v. 23.

it could do the Paliyan no harm, as its mouth is locked.*

There is a belief that the urine of wild dogs (*Cyon dukhunensis*) is extremely acrid, and that they sprinkle with it the bushes through which they drive their prey (deer and wild pigs), and then rush upon the latter, when blinded by the pungent fluid. According to another version, they jerk the urine into their victim's eyes with their tails.

The Koyis of the Godāvari district are said by the Rev. J. Cain † to hold in reverence the Pāndava brothers, Arjuna and Bhīma, and claim descent from the latter by his marriage with a wild woman of the woods. The wild dogs or dhols are regarded as the dūtas or messengers of the brothers, and they would on no account kill a dhol, even though it should attack their favourite calf. They even regard it as imprudent to interfere with these dūtas, when they wish to feast upon their cattle. The long black beetles, which appear in large numbers at the beginning of the hot weather, are called by the Koyis the Pāndava flock of goats.

At a sale of cattle, the vendor sometimes takes a small quantity of straw in his hand, and, putting some cow-dung on it, presents it to the purchaser.‡ The five products of the cow, known as pānchagavyam — milk, curds, butter, urine, and fæces—are taken by Hindus to remove pollution from confinement, a voyage across the seas, and other causes. It is on record § that the Tanjore Nayakar, having betrayed Madura and suffered for it, was told by his Brāhman advisers that he had better

* Rev. F. Dahmen, "Anthropos," 1908, iii. 30.

† "Ind. Ant.," 1876, v. 359.

‡ H. J. Stokes, "Ind. Ant.," 1874, iii. 90.

§ J. S. Chandler, *Calcutta Review*, July, 1903, cxvii. 28.

be born again. So a colossal cow was cast in bronze, and the Nayakar shut up inside. The wife of his Brāhman guru (religious preceptor) received him in her arms, rocked him on her knees, and caressed him on her breast, and he tried to cry like a baby. It is recorded by Frazer * that, when a Hindu child's horoscope portends misfortune or crime, he is born again from a cow thus. Being dressed in scarlet, and tied on a new sieve, he is passed between the hind-legs of a cow forward through the fore-legs, and again in the reverse direction, to simulate birth. The ordinary birth ceremonies are then gone through, and the father smells his son as a cow smells her calf.

Tradition runs to the effect that, at the time of the separation of Rāmēsvaram island from the mainland, the cows became prisoners thereon. Not being able, like the cows of Cape Cod, which are fed on herrings' heads, to adapt themselves to a fish diet, they became gradually converted into diminutive metamporphosed cows, which may still be seen grazing on the shore. The legend is based on the fancied resemblance of the horned coffer-fishes (*Ostracion cornutus*), which are frequently caught by the fishermen, to cattle. Portions of the skulls of cats and dogs, which are sometimes picked up on the beach, also bear a rude resemblance to the skull of a cow, the horns being represented by the zygoma.

A story is told at Cochin that the beautiful blue and white tiles from Canton, which adorn the floor of the synagogue of the White Jews, were originally intended for the Durbar hall of a former Rāja of Cochin. But a wily Jew declared that bullock's blood must have been used in the preparation of the glaze, and offered to take

* "Totemism," 1887, 33.

them off the hands of the Rāja, who was only too glad to get rid of them.

The afterbirths (placentæ) of cattle are tied to a tree which yields a milky juice, in the belief that the cow will thereby give a better yield of milk.

There is a custom among the Tellis (Oriya oil-pressers) that, if a cow dies with a rope round its neck, or on the spot where it is tethered, the family is under pollution until purification has been effected by means of a pilgrimage, or by bathing in a sacred river. The Holodia section of the Tellis will not rear male calves, and do not castrate their bulls. Male calves are disposed of by sale as speedily as possible

If the jungle Paliyans of Tinnevelly come across the carcase of a cow or buffalo near a stream, they will not go near it for a long time. They absolutely refuse to touch leather, and one of them declined to carry my camera box, because he detected that it had a leather strap.

The Bākudas of South Canara will not carry a bedstead, unless the legs are first taken off, and it is said that this objection rests upon the supposed resemblances between the four-legged cot and the four-legged ox. In like manner, the Koragas have a curious prejudice against carrying any four-legged animal, dead or alive. This extends to anything with four legs, such as a chair, table, etc., which they cannot be prevailed on to lift, unless one leg is removed. As they work as coolies, this is said sometimes to cause inconvenience.*

Among the Sembaliguda Gadabas of Vizagapatam, there is a belief that a piece of wild buffalo horn, buried in the ground of the village, will avert or cure cattle disease.†

The jungle Kādirs believe that their gods occasionally

* M. J. Walhouse, *Journal Anthrop. Inst.*, 1874, iv. 376.

† H. D. Taylor, "Madras Census Report," 1891.

reside in the body of a "bison" (*Bos gaurus*), and have been known to worship a bull shot by a sportsman.

The goddess Gāngadēvi is worshipped by the Kēvutos (fishing caste) of Ganjam at the Dasara festival, and goats are sacrificed in her honour. In the neighbourhood of the Chilka lake, the goats are not sacrificed, but set at liberty, and allowed to graze on the Kālikadēvi hill. There is a belief that animals thus dedicated to the goddess do not putrify when they die, but dry up.

The Tiyans (toddy-drawers) of Malabar carry, tucked into the waist-cloth, a bone loaded with lead at both ends, which is used for tapping the flower-stalk of the palm tree to bring out the juice. A man once refused to sell one of these bones to Mr F. Fawcett at any price, as it was the femur of a sāmbar (*Cervus unicolor*), which possessed such virtue that it would fetch juice out of any tree. Deer's horn, ground into a fine paste, is said to be an excellent balm for pains and swellings. It is sometimes made into a powder, which is mixed with milk or honey, and produces a potion which is supposed to aid the growth of stunted women.*

A Yānādi shikāri (hunter) has been known, when skinning a black buck (antelope) shot by a European, to cut out the testicles, and wrap them up in his loin-cloth, to be subsequently taken as an aphrodisiac. Antelope horn, when powdered and burnt, is said to drive away mosquitoes, and keep scorpions away. A paste made with antelope horn is used as an external application for sore throat. Antelope and chinkāra (Indian gazelle) horns, if kept in grain baskets, are said to prevent weevils from attacking the grain.

The Gadabas of Vizagapatam will not touch a horse, as they are palanquin-bearers, and have the same objection

* *Madras Mail*, 26th January, 1906.

to the rival animal that a cab-driver has to a motor-car. In South Canara, none but the lowest Pariah will rub a horse down. If a Malai Vellāla of Coimbatore touches one of these animals, he has to perform a religious ceremonial for the purpose of purification.

The members of the elephant sept of the Oriya Haddis, when they see the foot-prints of an elephant, take some of the dust from the spot, and make a mark on the forehead with it. They also draw the figure of an elephant, and worship it, when they perform srādh and other ceremonies. Wild elephants are said to be held in veneration by the jungle Kādirs, whereas tame ones are believed to have lost the divine element.*

When cholera breaks out in a Kondh village, all males and females smear their bodies from head to foot with pig's fat liquefied by heat, and continue to do so until a few days after the disappearance of the dread disease. During this time they do not bathe, lest the smell of the fat should be washed away.

Some women rub the blood of the small garden-bat, which has well-developed ears, into the artificially dilated lobes of their ears, so as to strengthen them. The wings of bats are highly prized as a hairwash. They are crushed, and mixed with cocoanut oil, and other ingredients. The mixture is kept underground in a closed vessel for three months, and then used to prevent the hair from falling out or turning grey.† The Paniyans of Malabar are said to eat land-crabs for a similar purpose.

The common striped or palm-squirrel (*Sciurus palmarum*) was, according to a legend, employed by Rāma to assist the army of monkeys in the construction of the bridge to connect Rāmēsvaram island with Ceylon, whither Rāvana

* L. K. Anantha Krishna Iyer, "Cochin Tribes and Castes," 1909, i. 22.

† *Madras Mail*, 26th January, 1906.

had carried off his wife Sīta. The squirrel helped the monkeys by rolling in the sand on the shore, so as to collect it in its hairy coat, and then depositing it between the piled up stones, so as to cement them together. Seeing it fatigued by its labours, Rāma sympathetically stroked its back with the three middle fingers of his right hand, marks of which still persist in the squirrels at the present day. There is a further legend that, once upon a time, one of the gods, having compassion on the toddy-drawers because their life was a hard one, and because they were constantly exposed to danger, left at the foot of a palmyra tree some charmed water, the value of which was that it saved from injury any one falling from a height. A toddy-drawer, however, got drunk, and, forgetting to drink the elixir, went home. When he returned, he found that a squirrel had drunk it, and vowed vengeance on it. And that is why every toddy-drawer will always kill a squirrel, and also why the squirrel, from whatever height it may fall, comes to no harm.* In a note on the Pariah caste in Travancore, the Rev. S. Mateer narrates † a legend that the Shānāns (Tamil toddy-drawers) are descended from Adi, the daughter of a Pariah woman at Karuvur, who taught them to climb the palm tree, and prepared a medicine which would protect them from falling from the high trees. The squirrels also ate some of it, and enjoy a similar immunity. There is a Tamil proverb that, if you desire to climb trees, you must be a Shānān. The story was told by Bishop Caldwell of a Shānān who was sitting upon a leaf-stalk at the top of a palmyra palm in a high wind, when the stalk gave way, and he came down to the ground quite safely, sitting on the

* S. P. Rice, "Occasional Essays on Native South Indian Life," 1901, 211.

† *Journ. Roy. Asiat. Soc.*, 1884, xvi. 181.

leaf, which served the purpose of a natural parachute. Woodpeckers are called Shānāra kurivi by bird-catchers, because they climb trees like Shānāns.

There is a legend that, before the Kāliyūga began, the Pāndavas lived on the Nīlgiris. A kind of edible truffle (*Mylitta lapidescens*) is known as little man's bread on these hills. The Badaga legendary name for it is Pāndva-unna-buthi, or dwarf bundle of food,* *i.e.*, food of the dwarfs, who are supposed to have built the pāndu kūlis or kistvaens. Being so small, they called in the black-naped hare (*Lepus nigricollis*) to plough their fields. The black patches on their necks are the inherited mark of the yoke. The blood of the hare is administered to children suffering from cough.

Brāhmans use a porcupine quill for parting their wives' hair in a ceremony connected with the period of gestation known as sīmantam. It is said † that among the Nāmbūtiri Brāhmans, the quill should have three white marks on it. The quills of porcupines are sold by Jōgis (Telugu mendicants) to goldsmiths, for use as brushes.

There is a tradition among the fishing folk of Rāmēsvaram island that a box of money was once found in the stomach of a dugong (*Halicore dugong*), and an official is consequently invited to be present at the examination of the stomach contents, so that the possessors of the carcase may not be punished under the Treasure Trove Act for concealing treasure. The fat of the dugong is believed to be efficacious in the treatment of dysentery, and is administered in the form of sweetmeats, or used instead of ghī (clarified butter) in the preparation of food.

* Report, Govt. Botanical Gardens, Nīlgiris, 1903.

† "Gazetteer of Malabar," 1908, i. 163.

2. Birds

The following story is current concerning the sacred vultures of Tirukazhukunram. The Ashtavasus, or eight gods who guard the eight points of the compass, did penance, and Siva appeared in person before them. But, becoming angry with them, he cursed them, and turned them into vultures. When they asked for forgiveness, Siva directed that they should remain at the temple of Vedagiri Iswara. One pair of these birds still survives, and come to the temple daily at noon for food. Two balls of rice cooked with ghī (clarified butter) and sugar, which have been previously offered to the deity, are placed at a particular spot on the hill. The vultures, arriving simultaneously, appropriate a ball apiece. The temple priests say that, every day, one of the birds goes on a pilgrimage to Benares, and the other to Rāmēsvaram. It is also said that the pair will never come together, if sinners are present at the temple.

When a person is ill, his family sometimes make a vow that they will ofter a few pounds of mutton to the Brāhmani kite (*Haliastur indus*, Garuda pakshi) on the patient's recovery. It is believed that, should the offering be acceptable, the sick person will speedily get better, and the bird will come to demand its meat, making its presence known by sitting on a tree near the house, and crying plaintively. The shadow of a Brāhmani kite falling on a cobra is said to stupefy the snake. The Kondhs do not consider it a sin to kill this bird, which is held in veneration throughout Southern India. A Kondh will kill it for so slight an offence as carrying off his chickens.

The crow is believed to possess only one eye, which moves from socket to socket as occasion demands. The

SACRED VULTURES, TIRUKAZHUKUNRAM.

To face p. 86.

belief is founded on the legend that an Asura, disguised as a crow, while Rāma was sleeping with his head on Sīta's lap in the jungles of Dandaka, pecked at her breasts, so that blood issued therefrom. On waking, Rāma, observing the blood, and learning the cause of it, clipped a bit of straw, and, after infusing it with the Brahma astra (miraculous weapon), let it go against the crow Asura, who appealed to Rāma for mercy. Taking pity on it, Rāma told the Asura to offer one of its eyes to the weapon, and saved it from death. Since that time, crows are supposed to have only one eye. The Kondhs will not kill crows, as this would be a sin amounting to the killing of a friend. According to their legend, soon after the creation of the world, there was a family consisting of an aged man and woman, and four children, who died one after the other in quick succession. Their parents were too infirm to take the necessary steps for their cremation, so they threw the bodies away on the ground at some distance from their home. God appeared to them in their dreams one night, and promised that he would create the crow, so that it might devour the dead bodies. Some Koyis believe that hell is the abode of an iron crow, which feeds on all who go there. There is a legend in the Kavarathi Island of the Laccadives, that a Māppilla tangal (Muhammadan priest) once cursed the crows for dropping their excrement on his person, and now there is not a crow on the island.

It is believed that, if a young crow-pheasant is tied by an iron chain to a tree, the mother, as soon as she discovers the captive, will go and fetch a certain root, and by its aid break the chain, which, when it snaps, is converted into gold.

In some Kāpu (Telugu cultivator) houses, bundles of ears of rice may be seen hung up as food for sparrows, which are held in esteem. The hopping of sparrows is said to resemble the gait of a person confined in fetters, and there is a legend that the Kāpus were once in chains, and the sparrows set them at liberty, and took the bondage on themselves. Native physicians prescribe the flesh and bones of cock sparrows for those who have lost their virility. The birds are cleaned, and put in a mortar, together with other medicinal ingredients. They are pounded together for several hours, so that the artificial heat produced by the operation converts the mixture into a pulpy mass, which is taken in small doses. The flesh of quails and partridges is also believed to possess remedial properties.

A west coast housewife, when she buys a fowl, goes through a mystic ritual to prevent it from getting lost. She takes it thrice round the fireplace, saying to it: "Roam over the country and the forest, and come home safe again." Some years ago, a rumour spread through the Koyi villages that an iron cock was abroad very early in the morning, and upon the first village in which it heard one or more cocks crow it would send a pestilence, and decimate the village. In one instance, at least, this led to the immediate extermination of all the cocks in the village.

The Indian roller (*Coracias indica*), commonly called the blue jay, is known as pāla-pitta or milk bird, because it is supposed that, when a cow gives little milk, the yield will be increased if a few of the feathers of this bird are chopped up, and given to it along with grass.

The fat of the peacock, which moves gracefully and easily, is supposed to cure stiff joints. Peacock's feathers are sold in the bazaar, and the burnt ashes are used as a cure for vomiting.

The deposit of white magnesite in the "Chalk Hills" of the Salem district is believed to consist of the bones of the mythical bird Jatayu, which fought Rāvana, to rescue Sīta from his clutches.

3. Reptiles and Batrachians.

It is recorded by Canter Visscher* that, "in the mountains and remote jungles of this country (Malabar), there is a species of snake of the shape and thickness of the stem of a tree, which can swallow men and beasts entire. I have been told an amusing story about one of these snakes. It is said that at Barcelore a chego (Chogan) had climbed up a cocoanut tree to draw toddy or palm wine, and, as he was coming down, both his legs were seized by a snake which had stretched itself up alongside the tree with its mouth wide open, and was sucking him in gradually as he descended. Now, the Indian, according to the custom of his country, had stuck his teifermes (an instrument not unlike a pruning knife), into his girdle with the curve turned outwards; and, when he was more than half swallowed, the knife began to rip up the body of the snake so as to make an opening, by which the lucky man was most unexpectedly able to escape. Though the snakes in this country are so noxious to the natives, yet the ancient veneration for them is still maintained. No one dares to injure them or to drive them away by violence, and so audacious do they become that they will sometimes creep between people's legs when they are eating, and attack their bowls of rice, in which case retreat is necessary until the monsters have satiated themselves, and taken their departure."

Another snake story, worthy of the Baron Münchausen, is recorded in Taylor's "Catalogue raisonné of Oriental Manuscripts." †

* Letters from Malabar, Translation, Madras, 1862.

† 1862, iii. 464.

"The Coya (Koyi) people eat snakes. About forty years since a Brāhman saw a person cooking snakes for food, and, expressing great astonishment, was told by the forester that these were mere worms; that, if he wished to see a serpent, one should be shown him; but that, as for themselves, secured by the potent charms taught them by Ambikēsvarer, they feared no serpents. As the Brāhman desired to see this large serpent, a child was sent with a bundle of straw and a winnowing fan, who went, accompanied by the Brāhman, into the depths of the forest, and, putting the straw on the mouth of a hole, commenced winnowing, when smoke of continually varying colours arose, followed by bright flame, in the midst of which a monstrous serpent having seven heads was seen. The Brāhman was speechless with terror at the sight, and, being conducted back by the child, was dismissed with presents of fruits."

It is stated by Mr Gopal Panikkar * that, "people believe in the existence inside the earth of a precious stone called manikkakkallu. These stones are supposed to have been made out of the gold, which has existed in many parts of the earth from time immemorial. Certain serpents of divine nature have been blowing for ages on these treasures of gold, some of which dwindle into a small stone of resplendent beauty and brightness called manikkam. The moment their work is finished, the serpents are transformed into winged serpents, and fly up into the air with the stones in their mouths."

According to another version of this legend,† "people in Malabar believe that snakes guard treasure. But silver they will have none. Even in the case of gold, the snakes are said to visit hidden treasure for twelve years occasionally, and, only when they find that the

* "Malabar and its Folk," Madras, 2nd ed., 59.

† C. Karunakara Menon, *Calcutta Review*, July, 1901.

treasure is not removed in the meantime, do they begin to guard it. When once it has begun to watch, the snake is said to be very zealous over it. It is said to hiss at it day and night. This constant application is believed to diminish its proportions, and to make it assume a smaller appearance. In time, in the place of the pointed tail, the reptile is said to get wings, and the treasure, by the continuous hissing, to assume the form of a precious stone. When this is done, the snake is said to fly with its precious acquisition. So strong is this belief that, when a comet appeared some ten years ago, people firmly believed that it was the flight of the winged serpent with the precious stone."

Natives, when seeking for treasure, arm themselves with a staff made from one of the snake-wood trees, in the belief that the snakes which guard the treasure will retire before it.

In Malabar, it is believed that snakes wed mortal girls, and fall in love with women. When once they do so, they are said to be constantly pursuing them, and never to leave them, except for an occasional separation for food. The snake is said never to use its fangs against its chosen woman. So strong is the belief, that women in Malabar would think twice before attempting to go by themselves into a bush.*

There is a temple in Ganjam, the idol in which is said to be protected from desecration at night by a cobra. When the doors are being shut, the snake glides in, and coils itself round the lingam. Early in the morning, when the priest opens the door, it glides away, without attempting to harm any of the large number of spectators, who never fail to assemble.†

* C. Karunakara Menon, *Calcutta Review*, July, 1901.

† *Madras Mail*, 22nd July, 1905.

The town of Nāgercoil in Travancore derives its name from the temple dedicated to the snake-god (nāga kovil), where many stone images of snakes are deposited. There is a belief that snake-bite is not fatal within a mile of the temple.

The safety with which snake-charmers handle cobras is said to be due to the removal of a stone, which supplied their teeth with venom, from under the tongue or behind the hood. This stone is highly prized as a snake poison antidote. It is said to be not unlike a tamarind stone in size, shape, and appearance; and is known to be genuine if, when it is immersed in water, bubbles continue to rise from it, or if, when put into the mouth, it gives a leap, and fixes itself to the palate. When it is applied to the punctures made by the snake's poison fangs, it is said to stick fast and extract the poison, falling off of itself as soon as it is saturated. After the stone drops off, the poison which it has absorbed is removed by placing it in a vessel of milk which becomes darkened in colour. A specimen was submitted to Faraday, who expressed his belief that it was a piece of charred bone, which had been filled with blood, and then charred again.*

There is, in Malabar, a class of people called mantravādis (dealers in magical spells), who are believed to possess an hereditary power of removing the effects of snake poison by repeating mantrams, and performing certain rites. If a house is visited by snakes, they can expel them by reciting such mantrams on three small pebbles, and throwing them on to the roof. In cases of snake-bite, they recite mantrams and wave a cock over the patient's body from the head towards the feet. Sometimes a number of cocks have to be sacrificed before

* *Vide*, Yule and Burnell, "Hobson-Jobson," ed. 1903, 874-9.

the charm works. The patient is then taken to a tank (pond) or well, and a number of pots of water are emptied over his head, while the mantravādi utters mantrams. There are said to be certain revengeful snakes, which, after they have bitten a person, coil themselves round the branches of a tree, and render the efforts of the mantravādi ineffective. In such a case, he, through the aid of mantrams, sends ants and other insects to harass the snake, which comes down from the tree, and sucks the poison from the punctures which it has made.

In the early part of the last century, a certain Tanjore pill had a reputation as a specific against the bite of mad dogs, and of the most poisonous snakes.*

The following note on a reputed cure for snake poisoning, used by the Oddēs (navvies), was communicated to me by Mr Gustav Hàller.

"A young boy, who belonged to a gang of Oddēs, was catching rats, and put his hand into a bamboo bush, when a cobra bit him, and clung to his finger when he was drawing his hand out of the bush. I saw the dead snake, which was undoubtedly a cobra. I was told that the boy was in a dying condition, when a man of the same gang said that he would cure him. He applied a brown pill to the wound, to which it stuck without being tied. The man dipped a root into the water, and rubbed it on the lad's arm from the shoulder downwards. The arm, which was benumbed, gradually became sensitive, and at last the fingers could move, and the pill dropped off. The moist root was rubbed on to the boy's tongue, and into the corner of the eyes, before commencing operations. The man said that a used pill is quite efficacious, but should be well washed to get rid of the poison. In the manufacture of the pills, five leaves of a creeper are dried, and ground to powder.

* *Asiatic Journal*, ii. 381.

The pill must be inserted for nine days between the bark and cambium of a margosa tree (*Melia Azadirachta*) during the new moon, when the sap ascends."

The creeper referred to is *Tinospora cordifolia* (gul bēl), and the roots are apparently those of the same climbing shrub. There is a widespread belief that gul bēl growing on a margosa tree is more efficacious as a medicine than that which is found on other kinds of trees.

In cases of snake-bite, the Dommara snake-charmers place over the seat of the bite a black stone, which is said to be composed of various drugs mixed together and burnt. It is said to drop off, as soon as it has absorbed all the poison. It is then put into milk or water to extract the poison, and the fluid is thrown away as being dangerous to life if swallowed. The Mandulas (wandering medicine men) use as an antidote against snake-bite a peculiar wood, of which a piece is torn off, and eaten by the person bitten.* Among the Vīramushtis (professional mendicants), there is a subdivision called Nāga Mallika (*Rhinacanthus communis*), the roots of which are believed to cure snake-bite. The jungle Paliyans of the Palni hills are said † to carry with them certain leaves, called naru valli vēr, which they believe to be a very efficient antidote to snake-bite. As soon as one of them is bitten, he chews the leaves, and also applies them to the punctures. The Kudumi medicine men of Travancore claim to be able to cure snake-bite by the application of certain leaves ground into a paste, and by exercising their magical powers. The Telugu Tottiyans are noted for their power of curing snake-bites by means of mystical incantations, and the original inventor of this mode

* Bishop Whitehead, *Madras Diocesan Magazine*, July, 1906.

† Rev. F. Dahmen, "Anthropos," 1908, iii. 22.

of treatment has been deified under the name of Pāmbalamman.

The jungle Yānādis are fearless in catching cobras, which they draw out of their holes without any fear of their fangs. They claim to be under the protection of a charm, while so doing. A correspondent writes that a cobra was in his grounds, and his servant called in a Yānādi to dislodge it. The man caught it alive, and, before killing it, carefully removed the poison-sac with a knife, and swallowed it as a protection against snake-bite.

The Nāyādis of Malabar, when engaged in catching rats in their holes, wear round the wrist a snake-shaped metal ring, to render them safe against snakes which may be concealed in the hole.

A treatment for cobra-bite is to take a chicken, and make a deep incision into the beak at the basal end. The cut surface is applied to the puncture made by the snake's fangs, which are opened up with a knife. After a time the chicken dies, and, if the patient has not come round, more chicken must be applied until he is out of danger. The theory is that the poison is attracted by the blood of the chicken, and enters it. The following treatment for cobra bite is said * to be in vogue in some places :—

"As soon as a person has been bitten, a snake-charmer is sent for, who allures the same or another cobra whose fangs have not been drawn to the vicinity of the victim, and causes it to bite him at as nearly as possible the same place as before. Should this be fulfilled, the bitten man will as surely recover as the snake will die. It is believed that, if a person should come across two cobras together, they will give him no quarter. To avoid being pursued

* *Madras Mail*, 26th January, 1906.

by them, he takes to his heels, after throwing behind some garment, on which the snakes expend their wrath. When they have completed the work of destruction, the pieces to which the cloth has been reduced, are gathered together, and preserved as a panacea for future ills."

A fisherman, who is in doubt as to whether a water-snake which has bitten him is poisonous or not, sometimes has resort to a simple remedy. He dips his hands into the mud, and eats several handfuls thereof.*

The fragrant inflorescence of *Pandanus fascicularis* is believed to harbour a tiny snake, which is more deadly than the cobra. Incautious smelling of the flowers may, it is said, lead to death.

The earth-snake (*Typhlops braminus*) is known as the ear-snake, because it is supposed to enter the ear of a sleeper, and cause certain death.

The harmless tree-snake (*Dendrophis pictus*) is more dreaded than the cobra. It is believed that, after biting a human being, it ascends the nearest palmyra palm, where it waits until it sees the smoke ascending from the funeral pyre of the victim. The only chance of saving the life of a person who has been bitten is to have a mock funeral, whereat a straw effigy is burnt. Seeing the smoke, the deluded snake comes down from the tree, and the bitten person recovers.

The green tree-snake (*Dryophis mycterizans*) is said to have a habit of striking at the eyes of people, to prevent which a rag is tied round the head of the snake, when it is caught. Another, and more curious belief is that a magical oil can be prepared from its dead body. A tender cocoanut is opened at one end, and the body of the snake is put into the cocoanut, which, after being closed, is buried in a miry place, and allowed to remain

* *Madras Mail*, 26th January, 1906.

there until the body decays, and the water in the cocoanut becomes saturated with the products of decomposition. When this has taken place, the water is taken out, and used as oil for a lamp. When a person carries such a lamp lighted, his body will appear to be covered all over by running green tree-snakes, to the great dismay of all beholders.*

For the following note on beliefs concerning the green tree-snake (*Dryophis*), I am indebted to Dr N. Annandale. A recipe for making a good curry, used by women who are bad cooks, is to take a tree-snake, and draw it through the hands before beginning to make the curry. To cure a headache, kill a tree-snake, and ram cotton seed and castor-oil down its throat, until the whole body is full. Then bury it, and allow the seeds to grow. Take the seeds of the plants that spring up, and separate the cotton from the castor seeds. Ram them down the throat of a second snake. Repeat the process on a third snake, and make a wick from the cotton of the plant that grows out of its body, and oil from the castor plants. If you light the wick in a lamp filled with the oil, and take it outside at night, you will see the whole place alive with green tree-snakes. Another way of performing the same experiment is to bore a hole in a ripe cocoanut, put in a live tree-snake, and stop the hole up. Then place the cocoanut beneath a cow in a cowshed for forty days, so that it is exposed to the action of the cow's urine. A lamp fed with oil made from the cocoanut will enable you to see innumerable tree-snakes at night.

The bite of the sand-snake (*Eryx Johnii*) is believed to cause leprosy and twisting of the hands and feet. An earth-snake, which lives at Kodaikānal on the Palni

* M. Upendra Pai, *Madras Christian Coll. Mag.*, 1895., xiii., No. 1, 29.

hills, is credited with giving leprosy to any one whose skin it licks. In the treatment of leprosy, a Russell's viper (*Vipera russellii*) is stuffed with rice, and put in an earthen pot, the mouth of which is sealed with clay. The pot is buried for forty days, and then exhumed. Chickens are fed with the rice, and the patient is subsequently fed on the chickens. The fat of the rat-snake (*Zamenis mucosus*) is used as an external application in the treatment of leprosy. An old woman, during an epidemic of cholera at Bezwāda, used to inject the patients hypodermically with an aqueous solution of cobra venom.

Mischievous children, and others, when they see two persons quarrelling, rub the nails of the fingers of one hand against those of the other, and repeat the words "Mungoose and snake, bite, bite," in the hope that thereby the quarrel will be intensified, and grow more exciting from the spectator's point of view.

When a friend was engaged in experiments on snake venom, some Dommaras (jugglers) asked for permission to unbury the corpses of the snakes and mungooses for the purpose of food.

If a snake becomes entangled in the net of a Bestha fisherman in Mysore when it is first used, the net is rejected, and burnt or otherwise disposed of.

There is a widespread belief among children in Malabar, that a lizard (*Calotes versicolor*) sucks the blood of those whom it looks at. As soon, therefore, as they catch sight of this creature, they apply saliva to the navel, from which it is believed that the blood is extracted.

A legend is recorded by Dr Annandale,* in accordance with which every good Muhammadan should kill the

* *Mem. Asiat. Soc.*, Bengal, 1906, i., No. 10.

blood-sucker (lizard), *Calotes gigas*, at sight, because, when some fugitive Muhammadans were hiding from their enemies in a well, one of these animals came and nodded its head in their direction till their enemies saw them.

A similar legend about another lizard is described as existing in Egypt. Dr Annandale further records that the Hindus and Muhammadans of Ramnād in the Ramnād district regard the chamæleon (*Chamæleon calcaratus*) as being possessed by an evil spirit, and will not touch it, lest the spirit should enter their own bodies. I have been told that the bite of a chamæleon is more deadly than that of a cobra.

There is a popular belief that the bite of the Brahmini lizard (*Mabuia carinata*), called aranai in Tamil, is poisonous, and there is a saying that death is instantaneous if aranai bites. The same belief exists in Ceylon, and Mr Arthur Willey informs me that deaths attributed to the bite of this animal are recorded almost annually in the official vital statistics. I have never heard of a case of poisoning by the animal in question. There is a legend that, "when the cobra and the arana were created, poison was supplied to them, to be sucked from a leaf. The arana sucked it wholesale, leaving only the leaf smeared over with poison for the cobra to lap poison from; thereby implying that the cobra is far less venomous than the arana. Thus people greatly exaggerate the venomous character of the arana." *

It has already been noted (p. 73) that, when Savara children are emaciated from illness, offerings are made to monkeys. Blood-suckers are also said to be propitiated, because they have filamentous bodies. A blood-sucker

* T. K. Gopal Panikkar, "Madras and its Folk," Madras, 2nd ed., 65-6.

is captured, small toy arrows are tied round its body, and a piece of cloth is tied round its head. Some drops of liquor are then poured into its mouth, and it is set at liberty.

The Marātha Rājas of Sandūr belong to a family called Ghorpade, which name is said to have been earned by one of them scaling a precipitous fort by clinging to an "iguana" (*Varanus*), which was crawling up it. The flesh of the "iguana" is supposed to be possessed of extraordinary invigorating powers, and a meal off this animal is certain to restore the powers of youth. Its bite is considered very dangerous, and it is said that, when it has once closed its teeth on human flesh, it will not reopen them, and the only remedy is to cut out the piece it has bitten.* This animal and the crocodile are believed to proceed from the eggs laid by one animal. They are laid and hatched near water, and, of the animals which come out of them, some find their way into the water, while others remain on land. The former become crocodiles, and the latter "iguanas." The flesh of the crocodile is administered as a cure for whooping-cough.

It is popularly believed that, if a toad falls on a pregnant woman, the child that is to be born will die soon after birth. The only remedy is to capture the offending toad, and fry it in some medicinal oil, which must be administered to the child in order to save it from death.†

4. Fishes

It is recorded ‡ that "Matsya gundam (fish pool) is a curious pool in the Machēru (fish river) near the village of Matam, close under the great Yendrika hill.

* "Manual of the Cuddapah District," 1875, 293-4.

† *Madras Mail*, 26th January, 1906.

‡ "Gazetteer of the Vizagapatam District," 1907, i. 286.

The pool is crowded with mahseer (*Barbus tor*) of all sizes. These are wonderfully tame, the bigger ones feeding fearlessly from one's hand, and even allowing their backs to be stroked. They are protected by the Mādgole zamindars, who on several grounds venerate all fish. Once, the story goes, a Brinjāri caught one, and turned it into curry, whereon the king of the fish solemnly cursed him, and he and all his pack-bullocks were turned into rocks, which may be seen there to the present day. At Sivarātri, a festival occurs at the little thatched shrine near by, the priest at which is a Bagata (Telugu freshwater fisher), and part of the ritual consists in feeding the sacred fish. The Mādgole zamindars claim to be descended from the rulers of Matsya Dēsa. They are installed on a stone throne shaped like a fish, display a fish on their banners, and use a figure of a fish as a signature. Some of their dependents wear ear-rings shaped like a fish."

A tank at Coondapoor contained a species of fish locally known as the flower-fish, which was especially reserved for the table of Tīpu Sultan, being fat and full of blood.* The sacred fish at Tirupparankunram near Madura are said to have been sages in a bygone age, and it is believed to be very meritorious to look at them. They are said to appear on the surface of the water only if you call out "Kāsi Visvanātha." But it is said that a handful of peas thrown into the pool is more effective. The Ambalakkārans (Tamil cultivators) admit that they are called Valaiyans, but repudiate any connection with the caste of that name. They explain the appellation by a story that, when Siva's ring was swallowed by a fish in the Ganges, one of their ancestors invented the first net (valai) made in the world.

* "Manual of the South Canara District," 1895, ii. 242.

Some Natives will not eat the murrel fish (*Ophiocephalus striatus*), owing to its resemblance to a snake. Some Halēpaiks (Canarese toddy-drawers) avoid eating a fish called Srinivāsa, because they fancy that the streaks on the body bear a resemblance to the Vaishnavite sectarian mark (nāmam). Members of the Vamma gōtra of the Janappans (Telugu traders) abstain from eating the bombadai fish, because, when some of their ancestors went to fetch water in a marriage pot, they found a number of this fish in the water collected in the pot.

When a new net is used for the first time by the Besthas of Mysore, the first fish which is caught is cut, and the net is smeared with its blood. One of the meshes of the net is burnt, after incense has been thrown into the fire.

5. Invertebrates

The Sahavāsis of Mysore are described * as "immigrants, like the Chitpāvanas. Sahavāsi means co-tenant or associate, and the name is said to have been earned by the community in the following manner. In remote times, a certain Brāhman came upon hidden treasure, but, to his amazement, the contents appeared in his eyes to be all live scorpions. Out of curiosity, he hung one of them outside his house. A little while after, a woman of inferior caste, who was passing by the house, noticed it to be gold, and, upon her questioning him about it, the Brāhman espoused her, and by her means was able to enjoy the treasure. He gave a feast in honour of his acquisition of wealth. He was subsequently outcasted for his mésalliance with the low caste female, while those who ate with him were put under a ban, and thus acquired the nickname."

* "Mysore Census Report," 1891, part i. 235.

It is commonly said that the scorpion has great reverence for the name of Ganēsa, because it is supposed that when, on seeing a scorpion, one cries out "Pilliyar annai" (in the name of Ganēsa), the scorpion will suddenly stop; the truth of the matter being that any loud noise arrests the movements of the animal.*

At the temple of Kolaramma at Kolar in Mysore, a pit under the entrance is full of scorpions, and the customary offerings are silver scorpions. The village goddess at Nangavaram in the Trichinopoly district is called Sattāndi Amman, and her idol represents her in the act of weaving a garland of scorpions. It is generally supposed that no scorpion can live in this village, and that the sacred ashes from Sattāndi Amman's shrine are a specific for scorpion stings. People sometimes carry some of the ashes about with them, in case they should be stung.† At Royachoti in the Cuddapah district, a festival is held on the occasion of the god going hunting. The idol Vīrabudra is carried to a mantapam outside the town, and placed on the ground. Beneath the floor of the mantapam there is a large number of scorpions. Whilst the god is taking his rest, the attendants catch these scorpions, and hold them in their hands without being stung. As long as the god remains in the mantapam, the scorpions do not sting, but, directly he leaves it, they resume their poisonous propensities.‡ The peon (attendant) in the zoological laboratory of one of the Madras colleges would put his hand with impunity into a jar of live scorpions, of which he believed that only a pregnant female would sting him with hurt. Lieutenant-

* S. K. Sundara Charlu, *Indian Review*, 1905, vi., No. 6, 421.
† "Gazetteer of the Trichinopoly District," 1907, i. 283.
‡ "Manual of the Cuddapah District," 1875, 288.

Colonel D. D. Cunningham records* the case of a certain Yōgi (religious mendicant), who was insusceptible to the stings of scorpions, "which would fix their stings so firmly into his fingers that, when he raised and shook his hand about, they remained anchored and dangling by their tails, whilst neither then nor afterwards did he show the slightest sign of pain or inconvenience. The immunity may possibly have been the result of innate idiosyncratic peculiarity in the constitution of the performer, or more probably represented the outcome of artificial exemption acquired at the expense of repeated inoculations with the virus, and corresponding development of its antitoxin."

A sweeper man, who had a mole on his back in shape somewhat resembling a scorpion, believed himself to be immune against scorpion sting, and would confidently insert the poison spine of a live scorpion into his skin. In a letter to a medical officer, a Native wrote, that, when a pregnant woman is stung by a scorpion, the child which is in the womb at the time of such stinging, when delivered, does not suffer from the sting of a scorpion, if ever it is stung during its lifetime. Some families keep in their homes small pots called thēlkodukku undi (scorpion sting vessels), and occasionally drop therein a copper coin, which is supposed to secure immunity against scorpion sting. The Sakuna Pakshi mendicants of Vizagapatam have a remedy for scorpion sting in the root of a plant called thēlla visari (scorpion antidote), which they carry about with them on their rounds. The root should be collected on a new-moon day which falls on a Sunday. On that day, the Sakuna Pakshi bathes, cuts off his loin-cloth, and goes stark-naked to a selected spot,

* "Plagues and Pleasures of Life in Bengal," 1907, 196-8.

where he gathers the roots. If a supply thereof is required, and the necessary combination of moon and day is not forthcoming, the roots should be collected on a Sunday or Wednesday. In cases of scorpion sting, Dommara medicine-men rub up patent boluses with human milk or juice of the milk-hedge plant (*Euphorbia Tirucalli*), and apply them to the parts. Among quaint remedies for scorpion sting may be noted, sitting with an iron crowbar in the mouth, and the application of chopped lizard over the puncture. The excrement of lizards fed on scorpions, and the undigested food in the stomach of a freshly killed goat, dried and reduced to powder, are also believed to be effective remedies. There is a belief that scorpions have the power of reviving, even after being completely crushed into pulp. We are, therefore, warned not to rest secure till the animal has actually been cremated.

The whip-scorpion *Thelyphonus* is believed to be venomous, some Natives stating that it stings like a scorpion, others that it ejects a slimy fluid which burns, and produces blisters. The caudal flagellum of *Thelyphonus*, of course, possesses no poison apparatus.

When the umbilical cord of a Kondh baby sloughs off, a spider is burnt in the fire, and its ashes are placed in a cocoanut shell, mixed with castor-oil, and applied by means of a fowl's feather to the navel.

The eggs of red ants, boiled in margosa (*Melia Azadirachta*) oil, are said to be an invaluable remedy for children suffering from asthma.

If a house is infested by mosquitoes, or the furniture and bedding by bugs, the names of a hundred villages or towns should be written on a piece of paper. Care must be taken that all the names end in uru, kōttai, palayam, etc. The paper is fastened to the ceiling or bed-post, and relief from the pests will be instantaneous.*

The Oriya Haddis, on the evening of the tenth day after a death, proceed to some distance from the house, and place food and fruits on a cloth spread on the ground. They then call the dead man by his name, and eagerly wait till some insect settles on the cloth. As soon as this happens, the cloth is folded up, carried home, and shaken over the floor close to the spot where the household gods are kept, so that the insect falls on the sand spread on the floor. A light is then placed on the sanded floor, and covered with a new pot. After some time, the pot is removed, and the sand examined for any marks which may be left on it.

A devil, in the disguise of a dung-beetle of large size, is believed to haunt the house wherein a baby has been newly born, and the impact of the insect against the infant will bring about its instant death.

The following case was brought to my notice by the Chemical Examiner to Government. In Malabar, a young man, apparently in good health, walked home with two other men after a feast, chewing betel. Arriving at his home, he retired to rest, and was found dead in the morning. Blood was described as oozing out of his eyes. It was given out that the cause of death was an insect, which infests betel leaves, and is very poisonous. The belief in death from chewing or swallowing the veththilai or vettila poochi (betel insect) is a very general one, and is so strong that, when a person suffers from giddiness, after chewing betel, he is afraid that he has partaken of the poisonous insect. Native gentlemen take particular care to examine every betel leaf, wipe it with a cloth, and smear chunam (lime) over it, before chewing.

* *Madras Mail*, 26th January, 1906.

The poochi is called by Gundert* vettila pāmpu or moorkhan (snake), or vettila thēl (scorpion). It has been described† as "a poisonous creature, which lives adhering to the betel leaf. Its presence cannot be easily detected, and many deaths occur among persons who are in the habit of carelessly chewing betel. The poison passes into the system through the moisture of the mouth, and death ensues within an hour and a half. It generally inhabits the female leaf, *i.e.*, the leaf that opens at night. The following symptoms are seen when a person is affected with the poison :—exhaustion, delirium, copious perspiration, and change of colour of the skin. Treatment :—administer internally the juice of the leaves of a tree called arippēra. Make the patient suck the milk of the breast of a woman, whose baby is more than eighty days old."

A perichæte earthworm was sent to me from Malabar as a specimen of vettila poochi, with a note to the effect that, when it is accidentally chewed, the chief symptom is drawing in of the tongue, and consequent death from suffocation. The antidote was said to be salt and water, and the leaves of the goa (guava) tree. From South Canara, Mr H. Latham sent me a planarian worm, about two inches in length, which is believed to be the vettila poochi. His camp boy told him of a case in which death was said to have resulted from eating one of these animals cooked with some jak fruit.

A few years ago, a scare arose in connection with an insect, which was said to have taken up its abode in imported German glass bangles, which compete with the indigenous industry of the Gāzula bangle-makers. The insect was reported to lie low in the bangle till it

* "Malayālam Dictionary," 1872, 983.

† Kērala Chintamani.

was purchased, when it would come out and nip the wearer, after warning her to get her affairs in order before succumbing. A specimen of a broken bangle, from which the insect was said to have burst forth, was sent to me. But the insect was not forthcoming.

As a further example of the way in which the opponents of a new industry avail themselves of the credulity of the Native, I may cite the recent official introduction of the chrome-tanning industry in Madras. In connection therewith, a rumour spread more or less throughout the Presidency that the wearing of chrome-tanned boots or sandals gave rise to leprosy, blood poisoning, and failure of the eyesight.

III

THE EVIL EYE

THE objection which a high caste Brāhman has to being seen by a low caste man when he is eating his food is based on a belief allied to that of the evil eye. The Brāhmanical theory of vision, as propounded in the sacred writings, and understood by orthodox pandits, corresponds with the old corpuscular theory. The low caste man being in every respect inferior to the Brāhman, the matter or subtle substance proceeding from his eye, and mixing with the objects seen by him, must of necessity be inferior and bad. So food, which is seen by a low caste man, in virtue of the *radii perniciosi* which it has received, will contaminate the Brāhman. This, it has been pointed out,* is "a good illustration of the theory propounded by Mr E. S. Hartland at the York meeting of the British Association (1906), that both magic and religion, in their earliest forms, are based on the conception of a transmissible personality, the mana of the Melanesian races."

A friend once rode accidentally into a weaver's feast, and threw his shadow on their food, and trouble arose in consequence. On one occasion, when I was in camp at Coimbatore, the Oddēs (navvies) being afraid of my evil eye, refused to fire a new kiln of bricks for the new

* *Nature*, 18th October, 1906.

club chambers, until I had taken my departure. On another occasion, I caught hold of a ladle, to show my friend Dr Rivers what were the fragrant contents of a pot, in which an Oddē woman was cooking the evening meal. On returning from a walk, we heard a great noise proceeding from the Oddē men who had meanwhile returned from work, and found the woman seated apart on a rock, and sobbing. She had been excommunicated, not because I touched the ladle, but because she had afterwards touched the pot. After much arbitration, I paid up the necessary fine, and she was received back into her caste.

The following passage occurred in an official document, which was sent to Sir M. E. Grant Duff, when he was Governor of Madras.* The writer was Mr Andrew, C.S.

"Sir C. Trevelyan visited Walajapet many years ago. When there, he naturally asked to see the cloths, carpets, etc. (which are manufactured there). Soon after (owing to the railway of course), trade began to diminish, and to this day, I hear that even the well-to-do traders think it was owing to the visit, as they believe that, if a great man takes particular notice of a person or place, ill-luck will follow. A month ago, I was walking near Ranipet, and stopped for a minute to notice a good native house, and asked whose it was, etc. A few hours after, the house took fire (the owner, after his prayers upstairs, had left a light in his room), and the people in the town think that the fire was caused by my having noticed the house. So, when His Excellency drove through Walajapet last July, the bazaar people did not show their best cloths, fearing ill-luck would follow, but also because they thought he would introduce their trade in carpets, etc., into the Central Jail, Vellore, and so ruin them."

* Grant Duff, "Notes from an Indian Diary, 1881-1886."

In villages, strangers are not allowed to be present, when the cows are milked. Sudden failure of milk, or blood-stained milk, are attributed to the evil eye, to remove the influence of which the owner of the affected cow resorts to the magician. When the hill Kondhs are threshing the crop, strangers may not look on the crop, or speak to them, lest their evil eye should be cast on them. If a stranger is seen approaching the threshing-floor, the Kondhs keep him off by signalling with their hands, without speaking.

In Malabar, a mantram, which is said to be effective against the potency of the evil eye, runs as follows:—"Salutation to thee, O God! Even as the moon wanes in its brightness at the sight of the sun, even as the bird chakora (crow-pheasant) disappears at the sight of the moon, even as the great Vasuki (king of serpents) vanishes at the sight of the chakora, even as the poison vanishes from his head, so may the potency of his evil eye vanish with thy aid."* In Malabar, fear of the evil eye is very general. At the corner of the upper storey of almost every Nāyar house near a road or path is suspended some object, often a doll-like hideous creature, on which the eye of the passers-by may rest.†

"A crop," Mr Logan writes,‡ "is being raised in a garden visible from the road. The vegetables will never reach maturity, unless a bogey of some sort is set up in their midst. A cow will stop giving milk, unless a conch (*Turbinella rapa*) shell is tied conspicuously about her horns. [Māppilla cart-drivers tie black ropes round the neck, or across the faces of their bullocks.] When a

* L. K. Anantha Krishna Iyer, "The Cochin Tribes and Castes," 1909, i. 166.

† F. Fawcett, *Madras Museum Bull.*, 1901, iii., No 3, 309.

‡ Malabar, 1887, i. 175.

house or shop is being built, there surely is to be found exposed in some conspicuous position an image, sometimes of extreme indecency, a pot covered with cabalistic signs, a prickly branch of cactus, or what not, to catch the evil eye of passers-by, and divert their attention from the important work in hand."

Many of the carved wooden images recall forcibly to mind the Horatian satire:—"Olim truncus eram. . . . Obscenoque ruber porrectus ab inguine palus.

For the following note on the evil eye in Malabar, I am indebted to Mr S. Appadorai Iyer.

"It is not the eye alone that commits the mischief, but also the mind and tongue. Man is said to do good or evil through the mind, word and deed, *i.e.*, manasa, vācha, and karmana. When a new house is being constructed, or a vegetable garden or rice-field are in a flourishing condition, the following precautions are taken to ward off the evil eye:—

"(*a*) In Buildings

"1. A pot with black and white marks on it is suspended mouth downwards.

"2. A wooden figure of a monkey, with pendulous testicles, is suspended.

"3. The figure of a Malayāli woman, with protuberant breasts, is suspended.

"(*b*) In Gardens and Fields

"1. A straw figure, covered with black cloth daubed with black and white dots, is placed on a long pole. If the figure represents a male, it has pendent testicles, and, if a female, well developed breasts. Sometimes, male and female figures are placed together in an embracing posture.

EVIL EYE FIGURES, MALABAR.

To face p. 112.

"2. Pots, as described above, are placed on bamboo poles.

"3. A portion of the skull of a bull, with horns attached, is set up on a long pole.

"The figures, pots, and skulls, are primarily intended to scare away crows, stray cattle, and other marauders, and secondly to ward off the evil eye. Instances are quoted, in which handsome buildings have fallen down, and ripe fruits and grain crops have withered through the influence of the eye, which has also been held responsible for the bursting of a woman's breasts."

In Madras, human figures, made of broken bricks and mortar, are kept permanently in the front of the upstairs verandah. Some years ago, Sir George Birdwood recorded the flogging, by order of the Police Magistrate of Black Town (now George Town), Madras, of a Hindu boy for exhibiting an indecent figure in public view. What he had explicitly done was to set up, in accordance with universal custom, a phallic image before a house that was in course of erection by a Hindu gentleman, who was first tried under the indictment, but was acquitted, he, the owner, not having been the person who had actually exhibited the image.*

Monstrous Priapi, made in straw, with painted clay pots for heads, pots smeared with chunam (lime) and studded with black dots, or palmyra palm fruits coated with chunam, may often be seen set up in the fields, to guard the ripening crop. In a note on the Tamil Paraiyans, the Rev A. C. Clayton writes as follows: †

"Charms, in the form of metal cylinders, are worn to avoid the baneful influence of the evil eye. To prevent

* D'Alviella, "The Migration of Symbols," 1894, introduction; and *Times* (London), 3rd September, 1891.

† *Madras Museum Bull.*, 1906, v., No. 2, 86-7.

this from affecting the crops, Paraiyans put up scarecrows in their fields. These are usually small broken earthen pots, whitewashed or covered with spots of whitewash, or even adorned with huge clay noses and ears, and made into grotesque faces. For the same reason, more elaborate figures, made of mud and twigs in human shape, are sometimes set up."

The indecent figures carved on temple cars, are intended to avert the evil eye. During temple or marriage processions, two huge human figures, male and female, made of bamboo wicker-work, are carried in front for the same purpose. At the buffalo races in South Canara, which take place when the first crop has been gathered, there is a procession, which is sometimes headed by two dolls represented *in coitu* borne on a man's head. At a race meeting near Mangalore, one of the devil-dancers had the genitalia represented by a long piece of cloth and enormous testicles.

Sometimes, in case of illness, a figure is made of rice-flour paste, and copper coins are stuck on the head, hands, and abdomen thereof. It is waved in front of the sick person, taken to a place where three roads or paths meet, and left there. At other times, a hole is made in a gourd (*Benincasa cerifera* or *Lagenaria vulgaris*), which is filled with turmeric and chunam, and waved round the patient. It is then taken to a place where three roads meet, and broken.

At a ceremony performed in Travancore when epidemic disease prevails, an image of Bhadrakāli is drawn on the ground with powders of five colours, white, yellow, black, green, and red. At night, songs are sung in praise of that deity by a Tīyattunni and his followers. A member of the troupe then plays the part of Bhadrakāli in the act of murdering the demon Darika, and, in conclusion, waves

EVIL EYE FIGURES SET UP IN FIELDS.

To face p. 114.

a torch before the inmates of the house, to ward off the evil eye, which is the most important item in the whole ceremony. The torch is believed to be given by Siva, who is worshipped before the light is waved.

In cases of smallpox, a bunch of nīm (*Melia Azadirachta*) is sometimes moved from the head to the feet of the sick person, with certain incantations, and then twisted and thrown away.

The sudden illness of children is often attributed to the evil eye. In such cases, the following remedies are considered efficacious :—

(1) A few sticks from a new unused broom are set fire to, waved several times round the child, and placed in a corner. With some of the ashes the mother makes a mark on the child's forehead. If the broom burns to ashes without making a noise, the women cry : "Look at it. It burns without the slightest noise. The creature's eyes are really very bad." Abuse is then heaped on the person whose eyes are supposed to have an evil influence.

(2) Some chillies, salt, human hair, nail-cuttings, and finely powered earth from the pit of the door-post are mixed together, waved three times in front of the child, and thrown onto the fire. Woe betide the possessor of the evil eye, if no pungent, suffocating smell arises when it is burning.

(3) A piece of burning camphor is waved in front of the child.

(4) Balls of cooked rice, painted red, black, and white (with curds), are waved before the child.

Loss of appetite in children is attributed by mothers to the visit of a supposed evil person to the house. On that person appearing again, the mother will take a little sand or dust from under the visitor's foot, whirl it round the head of the child, and throw it on the hearth. If the suspected person is not likely to turn up again, a handful of cotton-seed, chillies, and dust from the middle of the street, is whirled round the child's head, and thrown on the hearth. If the chillies produce a strong smell, the evil eye has been averted. If they do not do so, the suspect is roundly abused by the mother, and never again admitted to the house.

Matrons make the faces of children ugly by painting two or three black dots on the chin and cheeks, and painting the eyelids black with lamp-black paste. It is a good thing to frighten any one who expresses admiration of one's belongings. For example, if a friend praises your son's eyes, you should say to him, "Look out! There is a snake at your feet." If he is frightened, the evil eye has been averted. It is said* that "you will cause mortal offence to a Hindu lady, should you remark of her child 'What a nice baby you have,' or 'How baby has grown since I saw him last.' She makes it a rule to speak deprecatingly of her child, and represents it as the victim of non-existent ailments, so that your evil eye shall not affect it. But, should she become aware that, in spite of her precautions, you have defiled it with your admiration, she will lose no time in counteracting the effect of drishtidosham. One of the simplest methods adopted for this purpose is to take a small quantity of chillies and salt in the closed palm, and throw it into the fire, after waving it thrice round the head of the child, to the accompaniment of incantations. If no pungent odour is apparent, it is an indication that the dosham has been averted."

At the Sakalathi festival of the Badagas of the Nīlgiris, a cake is made, on which are placed a little rice and butter. Three wicks steeped in castor-oil are put in

* *Madras Mail*, 26th January, 1906.

it, and lighted. The cake is then waved round the heads of all the children of the house, taken to a field, and thrown thereon with the words "Sakalathi has come." At the Sūppidi ceremony, which every Nāttukōttai Chetti (Tamil banker) youth has to perform before marriage, the young man goes to the temple. On his return home, and at the entrance of Nāttukōttai houses which he passes, rice-lamps are waved before him.

The custom of making a "wave offering" * at puberty and marriage ceremonies is very widespread. Thus, when a Tangalān Paraiyan girl attains puberty, she is bathed on the ninth day, and ten small lamps of flour paste, called drishti māvu vilakku, are put on a sieve, and waved before her. Then coloured water (ārati or ālām,) and burning camphor, are waved in front of her. At the puberty ceremonies of the Tamil Maravans, the girl comes out of seclusion on the sixteenth day, bathes, and returns to her house. At the threshold, her future husband's sister is standing, and averts the evil eye by waving betel leaves, plantains, cooked flour paste, a vessel filled with water, and an iron measure containing rice with a style stuck in it.

At a Palli (Tamil cultivator) wedding, water coloured with turmeric and chunam (ārati) is waved round the bride and bridegroom. Later on, when the bride is about to enter the home of the bridegroom, coloured water and a cocoanut are waved in front of the newly married couple. At a marriage among the Pallans (Tamil cultivators), when the contracting couple sit on the dais, coloured water, or balls of coloured rice with lighted wicks, are waved round them. Water is poured into their hands from a vessel, and sprinkled over their heads. The vessel is then waved before them. During a Kōliyan

* Leviticus, viii. 29.

(Tamil weaver) wedding coloured water, into which leaves of *Bauhinia variegata* are thrown, are waved. At a marriage among the Khatris (weavers), when the bridegroom arrives at the house of the bride, her mother comes out, and waves coloured water, and washes his eyes with water. At a Tangalān Paraiyan wedding, during a ceremony for removing the evil eye, a pīpal (*Ficus religiosa*) leaf is held over the foreheads of the bridal couple, with its tail downwards, and all the close relations pour milk over it, so that it trickles over their faces. During a marriage among the Sembadavans (Tamil fishermen), the bride and bridegroom go through a ceremony called sige kazhippu, with the object of warding off the evil eye, which consists in pouring a few drops of milk on their foreheads from a fig or betel leaf. At a Kāpu (Telugu cultivator) wedding, the Ganga idol, which is kept in the custody of a Tsākala (washerman), is brought to the marriage house. At the entrance thereto, red-coloured food, coloured water, and incense, are waved before it. During a marriage among the Balijas (Telugu traders), the bridegroom is stopped at the entrance to the room in which the marriage pots are kept by a number of married women, and has to pay a small sum for the ārati (coloured water), which is waved by the women. At a Bilimagga (weaver) wedding in South Canara, the bridegroom's father waves incense in front of a cot and brass vessel, and lights and ārati water are waved before the bridegroom.

At a royal marriage in Travancore, in 1906, a bevy of Nāyar maidens, quaintly dressed, walked in front of the Rāni's palanquin. They were intended as Drishti Pariharam, to ward off the evil eye.

Sometimes, in Malabar, when a person is believed to be under the influence of a devil or the evil eye, salt,

IMPRESSIONS OF HAND ON WALL OF HOUSE.

To face p. 119.

chillies, tamarinds, oil, mustard, cocoanut, and a few pice (copper coins), are placed in a vessel, waved round the head of the affected individual, and given to a Nāyādi,* whose curse is asked for. There is this peculiarity about a Nāyādi's curse, that it always has the opposite effect. Hence, when he is asked to curse one who has given him alms, he complies by invoking misery and evil upon him. The terms used by him for such invocations are attupo or mutinjupo (to perish), adimondupo (to be a slave), etc.†

During one of my tours, a gang of Yerukalas absolutely refused to sit on a chair, and I had perforce to measure their heads while they squatted on the ground. To get rid of my evil influence, they subsequently went through the ceremony of waving red-coloured water and sacrificing fowls.

During a marriage among the Mādigas (Telugu Pariahs), a sheep or goat is sacrificed to the marriage pots. The sacrificer dips his hand in the blood of the animal, and impresses the blood on his palms on the wall near the door leading to the room in which the pots are kept. This is said to avert the evil eye. Among the Telugu Mālas, a few days before a wedding, two marks are made, one on each side of the door, with oil and charcoal, for the same purpose. At Kadūr, in the Mysore Province, I once saw impressions of the hand on the walls of Brāhman houses. Impressions in red paint of a hand with outspread fingers may be seen on the walls of mosques and Muhammadan buildings.‡

When cholera, or other epidemic disease, breaks out,

* The Nāyādis are a polluting class, whose approach within 300 feet is said to contaminate a Brāhman.

† L. K. Anantha Krishna Iyer, "The Cochin Tribes and Castes," 1909, i. 55-6.

‡ M. J. Walhouse, *Journ. Anthrop. Inst.*, 1890, xix. 56.

Muhammadans leave the imprint of the hand dipped in sandal paste on the door. When a Tamil Paraiyan dies, an impression of the dead man's palm is sometimes taken in cow-dung, and stuck on the wall.*

The failure of a criminal expedition of the Koravas is said by Mr F. Fawcett,† to be "generally attributed to the evil eye, or the evil tongue, whose bad effects are evinced in many ways. If the excursion has been for house-breaking, the house-breaking implement is often soldered at its sharp end with panchalokam (five metals), to counteract the effect of the evil eye. The evil tongue is a frequent cause of failure. It consists in talking evil of others, or harping on probable misfortunes. There are various ways of removing its unhappy effects. A mud figure of a man is made on the ground, and thorns are placed over the mouth. This is the man with the evil tongue. Those who have suffered walk round it, crying out and beating their mouths; the greater the noise, the better the effect. Cutting the neck of a fowl half through and allowing it to flutter about, or inserting a red hot splinter in its anus to madden it with pain, are considered to be effective, while, if a cock should crow after its neck has been cut, calamities are averted."

* "Gazetteer of the Tanjore District," 1906, i. 89.

† "Note on the Koravas," 1908.

IV

SNAKE WORSHIP

VERY closely connected with the subject of vows and votive offerings is that of the worship of snakes, to which vows are made and offerings dedicated.

In a note on serpent worship in Malabar,* it is stated that "even to-day some corner of the garden of every respectable tarawad † is allotted for snakes. Here a few trees are allowed to grow wild, and under them, on a masonry platform, one or more sculptured granite stones representing hooded serpents (cobras) are consecrated and set up. The whole area is held sacred, and a mud lamp is lighted there every evening with religious regularity. I have seen eggs, milk, and plantains offered in the evening, after the lamp has been lit, at these shrines, to invoke the serpent's aid on particular occasions. Such is the veneration in which these shrines are held that Cherumars (agrestic serfs) and other low caste aborigines, who are believed to pollute by their very approach, are absolutely interdicted from getting within the precincts. Should, however, any such pollute the shrine, the resident snake or its emissary is said to apprise the owner of the defilement by creeping to the very threshold of his house, and remaining there until the Karanavan,‡ or other

* *Madras Standard*, 2nd June, 1903.

† A tarawad means a family, consisting of all the descendants in the female line of one common female ancestor.

‡ The senior male in a tarawad or tarwad.

managing member of the family promises to have it duly purified by a Brāhman."

Concerning snake worship in Malabar, Mr C. Karunakara Menon writes * as follows:—

"The existence of snake groves is said to owe its origin to Srī Parasurāma. [According to tradition, Parasurāma was an avatar of Vishnu, who destroyed the Kshatriya Rājas, and retired to Gokarnam in Canara. He called on Varuna, the god of water, to give him some land. Varuna caused the sea to recede, and thus the land called Kērala (including Malabar) came into existence. Brāhmans were brought from Northern India to colonise the new country, but they ran away from fear of the snakes, of which it was full. Parasurāma then brought in a further consignment of Brāhmans from the north, and divided the country into sixty-four Brāhmanical colonies.] Parasurāma advised that a part of every house should be set apart for snakes as household gods. The (snake) groves have the appearance of miniature reserved forests, as they are considered sacred, and there is a strong prejudice against cutting down trees therein. The groves contain a snake king and queen made of granite, and a tower-like structure, made of laterite,† for the sacred snakes. Snakes were, in olden days, considered a part of the property. [Transfer deeds made special mention of the family serpent as one of the articles sold along with the freehold.]

"When a snake is seen inside, or in the neighbourhood of the house, great care is taken to catch it without giving it the least pain. Usually a stick is placed gently on its head, and the mouth of an earthenware pot is shown to it. When it is in, the pot is loosely covered with a cocoanut shell, to allow of free breathing. It is then taken to a secluded spot, the pot is destroyed, and the

* See *Calcutta Review*, July, 1901, cxiii. 21-5.

† Laterite is a reddish geological formation, found all over Southern India.

snake set at liberty. It is considered to be polluted by being caught in this way, and holy water is sometimes poured over it. Killing a snake is considered a grievous sin, and even to see a snake with its head bruised is believed to be a precursor of calamities. Pious Malayālis (natives of Malabar), when they see a snake killed in this way, have it burnt with the full solemnities attendant on the cremation of a high-caste Hindu. The carcase is covered with a piece of silk, and burnt in sandalwood. A Brāhman is hired to observe pollution for some days, and elaborate funeral oblations are offered to the dead snake."

In Travancore there was formerly a judicial ordeal by snake-bite. The accused thrust his hand into a mantle, in which a cobra was wrapped up. If it bit him, he was declared guilty, if not innocent.

In connection with snake worship in Malabar, Mr Upendra Pai gives the following details.* Among snakes none is more dreaded than the cobra (*Naia tripudians*), which accordingly has gathered round it more fanciful superstitions than any other snake. This has led to cobra worship, which is often performed with a special object in view. In some parts of the country, every town or village has its images of cobras rudely carved on stone. These cobra stones, as they are termed, are placed either on little platforms of stone specially erected for them, or at the base of some tree, preferably a holy fig.† On the fifth day of the lunar month Shravana, known as the Nāgarapanchami—that is, the fifth day of the nāgas or serpents—these stones are first washed;

* *Madras Christian Coll. Mag.*, 1895, xiii., No. 1, 24-5.

† The pīpal or aswatha (*Ficus religiosa*). Many villages have such a tree with a platform erected round it, on which are carved figures of the elephant god Ganēsa, and cobras. Village panchāyats (councils) are often held on this platform.

then milk, curds, ghee (clarified butter), and cocoanut water, are poured over them. Afterwards they are decorated with flowers, and offerings are made to them. The cobra stone is also worshipped at other times by those who have no male children, in order to obtain such. But to establish new images of cobras in suitable places is regarded as a surer method of achieving this object. For this certain preliminary ceremonies have to be gone through, and, when once the image has been established, it is the duty of the establisher to see that it is properly worshipped at least once a year, on the Nāgarapanchami day. The merit obtained is proportionate to the number of images thus worshipped, so that pious people, to obtain a great deal of merit, and at the same time to save themselves the expense of erecting many stone images, have several images drawn, each on a tiny bit of a thin plate of gold or silver. These images are handed over to some priest, to be kept along with other images, to which daily worship is rendered. In this way, great merit is supposed to be obtained. It is also believed that such worship will destroy all danger proceeding from snakes. The cobra being thus an object of worship, it is a deadly sin to kill or maim it. For the cobra is in the popular imagination a Brāhman, and there is no greater sin than that of killing a Brāhman. Accordingly, if any one kills a cobra, he is sure to contract leprosy, which is the peculiar punishment of those who have either killed a cobra, or have led to the destruction of its eggs by digging in or ploughing up soil which it haunts, or setting on fire jungle or grass in the midst of which it is known to live and breed.

In a note on snake worship, Mr R. Kulathu Iyer writes as follows: *—

* *Indian Patriot*, 13th January, 1908.

PRAYING FOR OFFSPRING BEFORE LINGAM, SNAKE-STONES, AND FIGURE OF GANĒSA.

To face p. 124.

"In Travancore there is a place called Mannarsala, which is well known for its serpent worship. It is the abode of the snake king and queen, and their followers. The grove and its premises cover about 16 acres. In the middle of this grove are two small temples dedicated to the snake king and queen. There are also thousands of snakes of granite, representing the various followers of the king and queen. Just to the northern side of the temple there is a house, the abode of the Nampiathy,* who performs pooja (worship) in the temple. In caste he is lower in grade than a Brāhmin. The temple has paddy (rice) fields and estates of its own, and also has a large income from various sources. There is an annual festival at this temple, known as Ayilyam festival, which is celebrated in the months of Kanny and Thulam (September and October). A large number of people assemble for worship with offerings of gold, silver, salt, melons, etc. The sale proceeds of these offerings after a festival would amount to a pretty large sum. On the day previous to the Ayilyam festival, the temple authorities spend something like three thousand rupees in feeding the Brāhmins. A grand feast is given to nearly three thousand Brāhmins at the house of the Nampiathy. On the Ayilyam day, all the serpent gods are taken in procession to the illam (house of the Nampiathy) by the eldest female member of the house, and offerings of neerumpalum (a mixture of rice-flour, turmeric, ghee, water of tender cocoanuts, etc.), boiled rice, and other things, are made to the serpent gods. It is said that the neerumpalum mixture would be poured into a big vessel, and kept inside a room for three days, when the vessel would be found empty. It is supposed that the serpents drink the contents. As regards the origin of this celebrated grove, Mr S. Krishna Iyer, in one of his contributions to the *Calcutta Quarterly Review*, says that 'the land from Avoor on the south to Alleppy on the north was the site of the Khandava forest

* Elayads, Ilayatus, or Nambiyatiris, are priests at most of the snake groves on the west coast.

celebrated in the Mahabaratha; that, when Arjuna set fire to it, the serpents fled in confusion and reached Mannarasalay, and there prayed to the gods for protection; that thereupon the earth around was miraculously cooled down, and hence the name mun-l-ari-l-sala, the place where the earth was cooled. After the serpents found shelter from the Khandava fire, an ancestress of the Nambiathy had a vision calling upon her to dedicate the groves and some land to the Nāga Rāja (snake king), and build a temple therein. These commands were obeyed forthwith, and thenceforward the Nāga Rāja became their family deity.' In the 'Travancore State Manual,' Mr Nagam Iyer, referring to Mannarsala, says that 'a member of this Mannarsala illam married a girl of the Vettikod illam, where the serpents were held in great veneration. The girl's parents, being very poor, had nothing to give in the way of dowry, so they gave her one of the stone idols of the serpent, of which there were many in the house. The girl took care of this idol, and worshipped it regularly. Soon she became pregnant, and gave birth to a male child and a snake. The snake child grew up, and gave rise to a numerous progeny. They were all removed to a spot where the present kavu (grove) is. In this kavu there are now four thousand stone idols representing snake gods.' Such is the origin of this celebrated grove of Central Travancore."

On the bank of the river separating Cranganore from the rest of the Native State of Cochin is the residence of a certain Brāhman called the Pāmpanmekkat (snake guardian) Nambūdri, who has been called the high priest of serpent worship. It is recorded * by Mr Karunakara Menon that, "a respectable family at Angadipuram (in Malabar) sold their ancestral house to a supervisor in the Local Fund P. W. D. (Public Works Department). He cut down the snake grove, and planted it up. Some members

* *Calcutta Review*, July, 1901, cxiii. 21.

of the vendor's family began to suffer from some cutaneous complaint. As usual the local astrologer was called in, and he attributed the ailment to the ire of the aggrieved family serpents. These men then went to the Brāhmin house of Pampu Mekat. This Namboodri family is a special favourite of the snakes. When a new serpent grove has to be created, or if it is found necessary to remove a grove from one place to another, the ritual is entirely in the hands of these people. When a family suffers from the wrath of the serpents, they generally go to this Namboodri house. The eldest woman of the house would hear the grievances of the party, and then, taking a vessel full of gingelly (*Sesamum*) oil, and looking into it, would give out the directions to be observed in satisfying the serpents."

Concerning the Pāmpanmekkat Nambūdri, Mr Gopal Panikkar writes * that, "it is said that this Nambūdri household is full of cobras, which find their abode in every nook and corner of it. The inmates can scarcely move about without placing their feet upon one of these serpents. Owing to the magic influence of the family, the serpents cannot and will not injure them. The serpents are said to be always at the beck and call of the members of this Nambūdri family, and render unquestioned obedience to their commands. They watch and protect the interests of the family in the most zealous spirit."

It is said † that, "every year the Nambūdri receives many offerings in the shape of golden images of snakes, for propitiating the serpent god to ward off calamity, or to enlist its aid in the cure of a disease, or for the attainment of a particular object. It is well known that the Nambūdri has several hundreds of these images and other valuable

* "Malabar and its Folk," Madras, 2nd ed., 150.

† *Madras Standard*, 2nd June, 1903.

offerings, the collection of centuries, amounting in value to over a lakh of rupees. This aroused the cupidity of a gang of dacoits (robbers), who resolved some years ago to ease the Nambūdri of a great portion of this treasure. On a certain night, armed with lathies (sticks), slings, torches, and other paraphernalia, the dacoits went to the illam, and, forcibly effecting an entrance, bound the senior Nambutri's hands and feet, and threw him on his breast. This precaution taken, the keys of the treasure-room were demanded, the alternative being further personal injury. To save himself from further violence, the keys were surrendered. The dacoits secured all the gold images, leaving the silver ones severely alone, and departed. But, directly they went past the gate of the house, many snakes chased them, and, in the twinkling of an eye, each of the depredators had two snakes coiled round him, others investing the gang, and threatening, with uplifted hoods and hisses, to dart at them. The dacoits remained stunned and motionless. Meantime, the authorities were communicated with, and the whole gang was taken into custody. It is said that the serpents did not budge an inch until after the arrival of the officers."

Other marvellous stories of the way in which the snakes carry out their trust are narrated.

A section of Ambalavāsis or temple servants in Malabar, called Tēyyambādis, the members of which dance and sing in Bhagavati temples, perform a song called Nāgapāttu (song in honour of snakes) in private houses, which is supposed to be effective in procuring offspring.*

In many houses of the Tiyans of Malabar, offerings are made annually to a bygone personage named Kunnath Nāyar, and to his friend and disciple, Kunhi Rāyan, a Māppilla (Muhammadan). According to the legend, the

* "Gazetteer of Malabar," 1908, i. 112.

PULLUVAN AND POT-DRUM.

To face p. [illegible]

Nāyar worshipped the kite until he obtained command and control over all the snakes in the land. There are Māppilla devotees of Kunnath Nāyar and Kunhi Rāyan, who exhibit snakes in a box, and collect alms for a snake mosque near Manarghāt at the foot of the Nīlgiri hills. A class of snake-charmers in Malabar, called Kuravan, go about the country exhibiting snakes. It is considered to be a great act of piety to purchase these animals, and set them at liberty. The vagrant Kakkalans of Travancore, who are said to be identical with the Kakka Kuravans, are unrivalled at a dance called pāmpātam (snake dance).

The Pulluvans of Malabar are astrologers, medicine-men, and priests and singers in snake groves. According to a legend * they are descended from a male and female servant, who were exiled by a Brāhman in connection with the rescuing by the female of a snake which escaped when the Gāndava forest was set on fire by Agni, the god of fire. Another legend records how a five-hooded snake fled from the burning forest, and was taken home by a woman, and placed in a room. When her husband entered the room, he found an ant-hill, from which the snake issued forth, and bit him. As the result of the bite, the man died, and his widow was left without means of support. The snake consoled her, and devised a plan, by which she could maintain herself. She was to go from house to house, and cry out, "Give me alms, and be saved from snake-poisoning." The inmates would give alms, and the snakes, which might be troubling them, would cease to annoy. For this reason, the Pulluvas, when they go with their pot-drum (pulluva kudam) to a house, are asked to play, and sing songs which are acceptable to the snake gods, in return for which they receive a present of money. A Pulluvan and his wife preside at

* *See* "Men and Women of India," February, 1906.

the ceremony called Pāmban Tullal, which is carried out with the object of propitiating the snake gods. Concerning this ceremony, Mr L. K. Anantha Krishna Iyer writes as follows * :—

"A pandal (booth) supported by four poles driven into the ground is put up for the purpose, and the tops of the poles are connected with a network of strings, over which a silk or red cloth is spread to form a canopy. The pandal is well decorated, and the floor below it is slightly raised and smoothed. A hideous figure of the size of a big serpent is drawn in rice-flour, turmeric (*Curcuma longa*), kuvva (*Curcuma angustifolia*), powdered charcoal, and a green powder. These five powders are essential, for their colours are visible on the necks of serpents. Some rice is scattered on the floor and on the sides, and ripe and green cocoanuts are placed on a small quantity of rice and paddy (unhusked rice) on each side. A pūja for Ganapathi (the elephant god) is performed, to see that the whole ceremony terminates well. A good deal of frankincense is burned, and a lamp is placed on a plate, to add to the purity, sanctity, and solemnity of the occasion. The members of the house go round the pandal as a token of reverence, and take their seats close by. It often happens that the members of several neighbouring families take part in the ceremony. The women, from whom devils have to be cast out, bathe and take their seats on the western side, each with a flower-pod of the areca palm. The Pulluvan, with his wife or daughter, begins his shrill musical tunes (on serpents), vocal and instrumental alternately. As they sing, the young female members appear to be influenced by the modulation of the tunes and the smell of the perfumes. They gradually move their heads in a circle, which soon quickens, and the long locks of hair are soon let loose. These movements appear to keep time with the Pulluvan's music. In their unconscious state, they beat upon the

* "The Cochin Tribes and Castes," 1909, i. 153-4.

floor, and wipe off the figure drawn. As soon as this is done, they go to a serpent grove close by, where there may be a few stone images of serpents, before which they prostrate themselves. They now recover their consciousness, and take milk, water of the green cocoa-nut, and plantain fruits, and the ceremony is over."

In connection with the Pāmban Tullal, Mr Gopal Panikkar writes* that "sometimes the gods appear in the bodies of all these females, and sometimes only in those of a select few, or none at all. The refusal of the gods to enter into such persons is symbolical of some want of cleanliness in them; which contingency is looked upon as a source of anxiety to the individual. It may also suggest the displeasure of these gods towards the family, in respect of which the ceremony is performed. In either case, such refusal on the part of the gods is an index of their ill-will or dissatisfaction. In cases where the gods refuse to appear in any one of those seated for the purpose, the ceremony is prolonged until the gods are so propitiated as to constrain them to manifest themselves. Then, after the lapse of the number of days fixed for the ceremony, and, after the will of the serpent gods is duly expressed, the ceremonies close."

Sometimes, it is said, it may be considered necessary to rub away the figure as many as one hundred and one times, in which case the ceremony is prolonged over several weeks. Each time that the snake design is destroyed, one or two men, with torches in their hands, perform a dance, keeping step to the Pulluvan's music. The family may eventually erect a small platform or shrine in a corner of their grounds, and worship at it annually. The snake deity will not, it is believed, manifest himself if any of the persons or articles required

* "Malabar and its Folk," Madras, 2nd ed., 147-8.

for the ceremony are impure, *e.g.*, if the pot-drum has been polluted by the touch of a menstruating female. The Pulluvan, from whom a drum was purchased for the Madras Museum, was very reluctant to part with it, lest it should be touched by an impure woman. In addition to the pot-drum, the Pulluvans play on a lute with snakes painted on the reptile skin, which is used in lieu of parchment. The skin, in a specimen which I acquired, is apparently that of the big lizard *Varanus bengalensis*. The lute is played with a bow, to which a metal bell is attached.

In the "Madras Census Report," 1871,* Surgeon-Major Cornish states that there is a place near Vaisarpadi, close to Madras, in which the worship of the living snakes draws crowds of votaries, who make holiday excursions to the temple, generally on Sundays, in the hope of seeing the snakes, which are preserved in the temple grounds; and, he adds, probably as long as the desire of offspring is a leading characteristic of the Indian people, so long will the worship of the serpent, or of snake-stones, be a popular cult. He describes further how, at Rajahmundry in the Telugu country, he came across an old ant-hill by the side of a public road, on which was placed a stone representing a cobra, and the ground all round was stuck over with pieces of wood carved very rudely in the shape of a snake. These were the offerings left by devotees at the abode taken up by an old snake, who would occasionally come out of his hole, and feast on the eggs and ghī (clarified butter) left for him by his adorers. Around this place he saw many women who had come to pray at the shrine. If they chanced to see the cobra, the omen was interpreted favourably, and their prayers for progeny would be granted.

* Vol. i. 105.

Concerning snake worship in the Tamil country, Mr W. Francis writes as follows*:—

"A vow is taken by childless wives to instal a serpent (nāgapratishtai), if they are blessed with offspring. The ceremony consists in having a figure of a serpent cut in a stone slab, placing it in a well for six months, giving it life (prānapratishtai) by reciting mantrams and performing other ceremonies over it, and then setting it up under a pīpal tree (*Ficus religiosa*), which has been married to a margosa (*Melia Azadirachta*). Worship, which consists mainly in going round the tree 108 times, is then performed to it for the next forty-five days. Similar circumambulations will also bring good luck in a general way, if carried out subsequently."

It is further recorded by Mr F. R. Hemingway† that, "Brāhmans and the higher Vellālans think that children can be obtained by worshipping the cobra. Vellālans and Kallans perform the worship on a Friday. Among the Vellālans, this is generally after the Pongal festival. The Vellālans make an old woman cry aloud in the backyard that a sacrifice will be made to the cobra next day, and that they pray it will accept the offering. At the time of sacrifice, cooked jaggery (crude sugar) and rice, burning ghī in the middle of rice-flour, and an egg, are offered to the cobra, and left in the backyard for its acceptance. The Pallis annually worship the cobra by pouring milk on an ant-hill, and sacrificing a fowl near it. Valaiyans, Pallans, and Paraiyans sacrifice a fowl in their own backyards."

In the Tamil country, children whose birth is attributed to a vow taken by childless mothers to offer a snake cut on a stone slab, sometimes have a name bearing reference

* "Gazetteer of the South Arcot District," 1906, i. 102.

† "Gazetteer of the Tanjore District," 1906, i. 70.

to snakes given to them, *i.e.*, Sēshāchalam,* Sēshamma, Nāgappa, or Nāgamma. Nāga, Nāgasa, or Nāgēswara, occurs as the name of a totemistic exogamous sept or gōtra of various classes in Ganjam and Vizagapatam. In the Odiya caste of farmers in Ganjam, members of the Nāgabonso sept claim to be descendants of Nāgamuni, the serpent rishi. Nāgavadam (cobra's hood) is the name of a subdivision of the Tamil Pallis, who wear an ornament called nāgavadam, representing a cobra, in the dilated lobes of the ears.

Ant (*i.e.*, white-ant, *Termes*) hills, which have been repeatedly referred to in this chapter, are frequently inhabited by cobras, and offerings of milk, fruit, and flowers are consequently made to them on certain ceremonial occasions. Thus it is recorded,† by the Rev. J. Cain that when he was living in Ellore Fort in the Godāvari district, in September, 1873, "a large crowd of people, chiefly women and children, came in, and visited every white-ant hill, poured upon each their offerings of milk, flowers, and fruit, to the intense delight of all the crows in the neighbourhood. The day was called the Nāgula Chaturdhi—Chaturdhi, the fourth day of the eighth lunar month—and was said to be the day when Vāsuki, Takshakā, and the rest of the thousand Nāgulu were born to Kasyapa Brahma by his wife Kadruva.‡ The other chief occasions when these ant-hills are resorted to are when people are affected with earache or pains in the eye, and certain skin diseases. They visit the ant-hills, pour out milk, cold rice, fruit, etc., and carry away part of the earth, which they apply to the

* Sēsha or Adisēsha is the serpent, on which Vishnu is often represented as reclining.

† "Ind. Ant.," 1876, v. 188.

‡ *See* the Skanda Purāna.

troublesome member, and, if they afterwards call in a Brāhman to repeat a mantra or two, they feel sure the complaint will soon vanish. Many parents first cut their children's hair near one of these hillocks, and offer the first fruits of the hair to the serpents residing there."

The colossal Jain figure of Gomatēsvara, Gummatta, or Gomata Rāya, at Srāvana Belgola in Mysore,* is represented as surrounded by white-ant hills, from which snakes are emerging, and with a climbing plant twining itself round the legs and arms.

On the occasion of the snake festival in the Telugu country, the Bōya women worship the Nāgala Swāmi (snake god) by fasting, and pouring milk into the holes of white-ant hills. By this a double object is fulfilled. The ant-hill is a favourite dwelling of the cobra, and was, moreover, the burial-place of Valmīki, from whom the Bōyas claim to be descended. Valmīki was the author of the Rāmāyana, and is believed to have done penance for so long in one spot that a white-ant hill grew up round him. On the Nāgarapanchami day, Lingāyats worship the image of a snake made of earth from a snake's hole with offerings of milk, rice, cocoanuts, flowers, etc. During the month Aswija, Lingāyat girls collect earth from ant-hills, and place it in a heap at the village temple. Every evening they go there with wave-offerings, and worship the heap. At the Dipāvali festival,† the Gamallas (Telugu toddy-drawers) bathe in the early morning, and go in wet clothes to an ant-hill, before which they prostrate themselves, and pour a little water into one of the holes. Round the hill they wind five turns of cotton thread, and return home. Sub-

* Other colossal statues of Gummatta are at Karkal and Vēnūr or Yēnūr in South Canara.

† The feast of lights (dipa, lights, avali, a row).

sequently they come once more to the ant-hill with a lamp made of flour paste. Carrying the light, they go three or five times round the hill, and throw split pulse (*Phaseolus Mungo*) into one of the holes. On the following morning they again go to the hill, pour milk into it, and snap the threads wound round it.

The famous temple of Subramanya in South Canara is said to have been in charge of the Subramanya Stānikas (temple servants), till it was wrested from them by the Shivalli Brāhmans. In former times, the privilege of sticking a golden ladle into a heap of food piled up in the temple on the Shasti day is said to have belonged to the Stānikas. They also brought earth from an ant-hill on the previous day. Food from the heap, and some of the earth, are received as sacred articles by devotees who visit the sacred shrine.

At the Smasanākollai festival in honour of the goddess Ankalamma at Malayanūr, some thousands of people congregate at the temple. In front of the stone idol is a large ant-hill, on which two copper idols are placed, and a brass vessel is placed at the base of the hill, to receive the various offerings.

At a wedding among the nomad Lambādis, the bride and bridegroom pour milk into an ant-hill, and offer cocoanuts, milk, etc., to the snake which lives therein. During the marriage ceremonies of the Dandāsis (village watchmen in Ganjam), a fowl is sacrificed at an ant-hill. At a Bēdar (Canarese cultivator) wedding, the earth from an ant-hill is spread near five water-pots, and on it are scattered some paddy (unhusked rice) and dhāl (*Cajanus indicus*) seeds. The spot is visited later on, and the seeds should have sprouted.

V

VOWS, VOTIVE AND OTHER OFFERINGS

In addition to the observance of penances and fasting, Hindus of all castes, high and low, make vows and offerings to the gods, with the object of securing their good-will or appeasing their anger. By the lower castes, offerings of animals—fowls, sheep, goats, or buffaloes—are made, and the gods whom they seek to propitiate are minor deities, *e.g.*, Ellamma or Muneswara, to whom animal sacrifices are acceptable.* The higher castes usually perform vows to Venkatēswara of Tirupati, Subramanya of Palni, Vīrarāghava of Tiruvallur, Tirunārayana of Mēlkote, and other celebrated gods. But they may, if afflicted with serious illness, at times, as at the leaf festival at Periyapalayam (p. 148), seek the good offices of minor deities.

"A shrine," Mr F. Fawcett writes,† "to which the Malayālis (inhabitants of Malabar), Nāyars included, resort is that of Subramaniya at Palni in the north-west of the Madura district. Not only are vows paid to this shrine, but men, letting their hair grow for a year after their father's death, proceed to have it cut there. The plate shows an ordinary Palni pilgrim. The arrangement which he is carrying is called a kāvadi (portable shrine). There

* See Bishop Whitehead, "The Village Deities of Southern India," *Madras Museum Bull.*, 1907, v. No. 3.

† *Ibid.*, 1901, iii. No. 3, 270-1.

are two kinds of kāvadi, a milk kāvadi containing milk, and a fish kāvadi containing fish. The vow may be made in respect of either, each being appropriate to certain circumstances. [Miniature silver kāvadis, and miniature crowns, are sometimes offered by pilgrims to the god.] When the time comes near for the pilgrim to start for Palni, he dresses in reddish-orange clothes, shoulders his kāvadi, and starts out. Together with a man ringing a bell, and perhaps one with a tom-tom, with ashes on his face, he assumes the *rôle* of a beggar. The well-to-do are inclined to reduce the beggar period to the minimum, but a beggar every votary must be, and as a beggar he goes to Palni in all humbleness and humiliation, and there he fulfils his vow, leaves his kāvadi and his hair, and a small sum of money. Though the individuals about to be noticed were not Nāyars, their cases illustrate very well the religious idea of the Nāyar as expressed under certain circumstances. It was at Guruvayūr (in Malabar) in November 1895. On a high raised platform under a peepul tree were a number of people under vows, bound for Palni. A boy of fourteen had suffered as a child from epilepsy, and seven years ago his father vowed on his behalf that, if he was cured, he would make his pilgrimage to Palni. He wore a string of beads round his neck, and a like string on his right arm. These were in some way connected with the vow. His head was bent, and he sat motionless under his kāvadi, leaning on the bar, which, when he carried it, rested on his shoulder. He could not go to Palni until it was revealed to him in a dream when he was to start. He had waited for his dream seven years, subsisting on roots (yams, etc.), and milk—no rice. Now he had had the longed-for dream, and was about to start. Another pilgrim was a man wearing an oval band of silver over the lower portion of the forehead, almost covering his eyes; his tongue protruding beyond the mouth, and kept in position by a silver skewer through it. The skewer was put in the day before, and was to be left in for forty days. He had been fasting for two years. He was much under the influence of the god, and whacking incessantly at a drum in delicious excitement. Several of the pilgrims had a handkerchief tied over the mouth, they being under a vow of silence. [At Kumbakonam in the Tanjore district, 'there is a math in honour of a recently deceased saint named Paradēsi, who attained wide fame in the district some years ago. He never spoke, and was welcomed and feasted everywhere, and was the subject of many vows. People used to promise to break cocoanuts in his presence, or clothe him with fine garments, if they obtained their desire, and such vows were believed to be very efficacious.' * At the Manjēshwar Temple in South Canara, there is a Darsana, (man who gets inspired) called the dumb Darsana, as he gives signs instead of speaking. Bishop Whitehead records † the case of a Brāhman, who had taken a vow of silence for twenty-one years, because people make so much mischief by talking. He conversed by means of signs and writing in the dust]. One poor man wore the regular instrument of silence, the mouth-lock ‡—a wide silver band over the mouth, and a skewer piercing both cheeks. He sat patiently in a tent-like affair. People fed him with milk, etc. The use of the mouth-lock is common with the Nāyars, when they assume the pilgrim's robes and set out for Palni. Pilgrims generally go in crowds under charge of a priestly guide, one who, having made a certain number of journeys to the shrine, wears a peculiar sash and other gear."

In connection with kāvadis, it may be noted that, at the time of the annual migration of the sacred herd of cattle belonging to the Kāppiliyans (Canarese farmers in the Madura district) to the hills, the driver is said to carry a pot of fresh-drawn milk within a kāvadi. On the day on which the return journey to the Kambam

* "Gazetter of the Tanjore District," 1906, i. 219.

† *Madras Dioc. Mag.*, November, 1910.

‡ *See* Fawcett, Note on the Mouth-lock Vow, *Journ. Anthrop. Soc., Bombay*, i. 97-102.

valley is commenced, the pot is opened, and the milk is said to be found in a hardened state. A slice thereof is cut off, and given to each person who accompanied the herd to the hills. It is believed that the milk would not remain in good condition, if the sacred herd had been in any way injuriously affected during its sojourn there. The usual vow performed at the shrine of Dandāyudhapāni or Subramanya near Settikulam in the Trichinopoly district is to carry milk, sugar, flour, etc., in a kāvadi, and offer it to the god.* A case is recorded † from Ceylon, in which a man who was about to proceed with a kāvadi to a shrine was held by several men, while a blow with the palm of the hand caught him in the middle of the back, to numb the pain created by the forcing of sharp iron hooks into the fleshy part of the back.

Reference has been made (p. 137) to the offering of hair by devotees at the Palni shrine. When people are prevented from going to a temple at the proper time, hair is sometimes removed from their children's head, sealed up in a vessel, and put into the receptacle for offerings when the visit to the temple is paid. In cases of dangerous sickness, the hair is sometimes cut off, and offered to a diety.

"The sacrifice of locks," Mr A. Srinivasan writes, "is meant to propitiate deceased relations, and the deity which presides over life's little joys and sorrows. It is a similar intention that ,has dictated the ugly disfigurement of widows. We meet with the identical fact and purpose in the habit of Telugu Brāhmans and non-Brāhmans in general, sacrificing their whole locks of hair to the goddess Ganga of Prayaga, to the god Venkatēsa of Tirupati, and other local gods. The Brāhman ladies of the south have

* "Gazetteer of the Trichinopoly District," 1907, i. 289.

† *Scottish Standard Bearer*, November 1907.

more recently managed to please Ganga and other gods with just one or two locks of hair."

Sometimes, in performance of a vow, Patnūlkāran (Madura weaver) boys are taken to the shrine at Tirupati for the tonsure ceremony.* Married couples desirous of offspring make a vow that, if a child be granted to them, they will perform the ceremony of the first shaving of its head at the temple of the god who fulfils their desire.† It is said‡ that Alagarkōvil in the Madura district is such a favourite place for carrying out the first shaving of the heads of children, that the right to the locks presented to the shrine is annually sold by auction.

Writing in 1872, Mr Breeks remarked § that "about Ootacamund, a few Todas have latterly begun to imitate the religious practices of their native neighbours, and my particular friend Kinniaven, after an absence of some days, returned with a shaven head from a visit to the temple of Siva at Nanjengudi" (in Mysore).

A Toda who came to see me had his hair hanging down in long tails reaching below the shoulders. He had, he said, let it grow long because his wife, though married five years, had borne no child. A child had, however, recently been born, and he was going to sacrifice his locks as a thank-offering at the Nanjengōd temple. By the Badagas of the Nīlgiris, the fire-walking ceremony is celebrated to propitate the deity Jeddayaswāmi, to whom vows are made. In token thereof, they grow one twist or plait of hair, which is finally cut off as an offering to Jeddayaswāmi.

* The Patnulkārans claim to be Saurāshtra Brāhmans.

† "Gazetteer of the Tanjore District," 1906, i. 71.

‡ "Gazetteer of the Madura District," i. 86.

§ "Primitive Tribes of the Nilagiris," 1873, 17.

By some Gavaras (a cultivating caste) of Vizagapatam, special reverence is paid to the deity Jagganāthaswāmi of Orissa, whose shrine at Puri is visited by some, while others take vows in the name of the god. On the day of the car festival at Puri, local car festivals are held in Gavara villages, and women carry out the performance of their vows. A woman, for example, who is under a vow, in order that she may be cured of illness or bear children, takes a big pot of water, and, placing it on her head, dances frantically before the god, through whose influence the water which rises out of the pot falls back into it, instead of being spilt. The class of Vaishnavite mendicants called Dāsari claims descent from a wealthy Sūdra,* who, having no offspring, vowed that, if he was blessed with children, he would devote one to the service of the deity. He subsequently had many sons, one of whom he named Dāsan, and placed entirely at the service of the god. Dāsan forfeited all claim to his father's estate, and his descendants are therefore all beggars.† In a note on the Dāsaris of Mysore,‡ it is stated that "they become Dāsas or servants dedicated to the god at Tirupati by virtue of a peculiar vow, made either by themselves or their relatives at some moment of anxiety or danger, and live by begging in his name. Among certain castes (*e.g.*, Banajiga, Tigala, and Vakkaliga), the custom of taking a vow to become a Dāsari prevails. In fulfilment of that vow, the person becomes a Dāsari, and his eldest son is bound to follow suit."

It may be noted that, in the Canarese country, a custom obtains among the Bēdars and some other castes, under which a family which has no male issue must dedicate

* Sūdra is the fourth traditional caste of Manu.

† "Manual of the North Arcot District," 1895, i. 242.

‡ *Mysore Census Report*, 1901, part i. 519.

one of its daughters as a Basavi.* The girl is taken to the temple, and married to the god, a tāli (marriage badge) and toe-rings being put on her. Thenceforward she becomes a public woman, except that she should not consort with any one of lower caste than herself. It may be added that a Basavi usually lives faithfully with one man, and she works for her family as hard as any other woman.

Married couples, to whom offspring is born after the performance of a vow, sometimes name it after the deity whose aid has been invoked, such as Srinivāsa at Tirupati, Lakshminarasimha at Sholingūr, or some other local god or goddess. At Negapatam, some Hindus make vows to the Mīrān (Muhammadan saint) of Nāgur, and name their child after him. The name thus given is not, however, used in every-day life, but abandoned like the ceremonial name given prior to the Hindu upanāyana ceremony. In the Telugu country, the poorer classes of Hindus sometimes promise that, if a son is born to them, they will call him after a Muhammadan Fakir, and, consequently, it is far from uncommon to find a Hindu named Fakirgadu or Fakirappa, with a Hindu termination to a Muhammadan commencement.†

It has been noted (p. 138) that some pilgrims to the shrine at Palni have a skewer piercing both cheeks. It is recorded by Bishop Whitehead ‡ that "devotees go to the shrine of Durgamma at Bellary with silver pins about six inches long thrust through their cheeks, and with a lighted lamp in a brass dish on their head. On arriving before the shrine, they place the lamp on the ground, and the pin is removed, and offered to the goddess."

* Basavi, *see* article "Dēva-dāsi" in my "Castes and Tribes of Southern India," 1909, ii. 125-53.

† "Manual of the Cuddapah District, 1875, 283.

‡ *Madras Museum Bull.*, 1907, v. No. 3, 149.

The Bishop was told that the object of this ceremony is to enable the devotee to come to the shrine with a concentrated mind.

A common form of vow made to Māriamman at Pāppakkālpatti in the Trichinopoly district is a promise to stick little iron skewers into the body. In performance of vows, the Sēdans and Kaikōlans (weaver castes) pierce some part of the body with a spear. The latter thrust a spear through the muscles of the abdomen in honour of their god Sāhā-nayanar at Ratnagiri.

At the annual festival of the goddess Gangamma at Tirupati, a Kaikōlan devotee dances before the goddess, and, when he is worked up to the proper pitch of frenzy, a metal wire is passed through the middle of his tongue. It is believed that the operation causes no pain or bleeding, and the only remedy adopted is the chewing of margosa (*Melia Azadirachta*) leaves and some kunkumam (red powder) of the goddess. If, during a temple car procession, the car refuses to move, the Vīramushtis (Lingāyat mendicants), who are guardians of the idol, cut themselves with their swords until it is set in motion. There is a proverb that the Siva Brāhman (temple priest) eats well, whereas the Vīramushti hurts himself with the sword, and suffers much. The Vīramushtis are said, in former days, to have performed a ceremony called pāvadam. When an orthodox Lingāyat was insulted, he would swallow his lingam, and lie flat on the ground in front of the house of the offender, who had to collect some Lingāyats, and send for a Vīramushti. He had to arrive accompanied by a pregnant Vīramushti woman, priests of Draupadi, Pachaiamman, and Pothurāja temples, some individuals from the nearest Lingāyat mutt, and others. Arrived at the house, the pregnant woman would sit down in front of the person lying on the ground.

With his sword the Vīramushti man then made cuts in his scalp and chest, and sprinkled the recumbent man with the blood. He would then rise, and the lingam would come out of his mouth. Mondi mendicants, when engaged in begging, cut the skin of the thighs with a knife, lie down and beat their chest with a stone, vomit, roll in the dust or mud, and throw ordure into the houses of those who will not contribute alms. It was noted, in a recent report of the Banganapalle State, that an inām (grant of rent-free land) was held on condition of the holder "ripping open his stomach" at a certain festival.

A vow performed in honour of the village goddess at Settikulam in the Trichinopoly district is for the votaries. male and female, to fling themselves on heaps of thorns before her. This vow is generally fulfilled by those cured of disease. It is called mullu padagalam, or bed of thorns.* At the annual fire-walking festival at Nuvagode in Ganjam, the officiating priest sits on a seat of sharp thorns. It is noticed† by the missionary Gloyer that, on special occasions, some Dōmbs in Vizagapatam fall into a frenzied state, in which they cut their flesh with sharp instruments, or pass long, thin iron bars through the tongue and cheeks, during which operation no blood must flow. For this purpose, the instruments are rubbed over with some blood-congealing material. They also affect sitting on a sacred swing, armed with long iron nails. Mr G. F. Paddison informs me that he once saw a villager in the Vizagapatam district sitting outside the house, while groans proceeded from within. He explained that he was ill, and his wife was swinging on nails with their points upwards, to cure him.

* "Gazetteer of the Trichinopoly District," 1907, i. 289.

† Jeypore, Breklum, 1901.

In the Tanjore district, persons afflicted with disease promise that, if they are cured, they will brand their bodies, go round a temple a certain number of times by rolling over and over in the dust, and offer a pregnant goat by stabbing it through the womb. Sometimes vows of self-mortification are taken in anticipation of relief. Such are undertaking to go without salt in one's food, or to eat without using the hands, until a cure is effected.* At Palni in the Madura district, there is an annual feast at the Māriamman temple, at which people, in performance of a vow, carry in their bare hands earthen pots with a bright fire blazing inside them. They are said to escape burns by the favour of the goddess, but it is whispered that immunity is sometimes rendered doubly sure by putting sand or rice-husk at the bottom of the pot.† Some Dāsaris (religious mendicants) go through a performance called Panda Sērvai, which consists in beating themselves with a flaming torch all over the body. I am informed by Mr Paddison that some Dōmbs are reputed to be able to pour blazing oil all over their bodies, without suffering any hurt; and one man is said to have had a miraculous power of hardening his skin, so that any one could have a free shot at him without hurting him. In the Mēlūr tāluk of the Madura district, it is stated that women who are anxious for offspring vow that, if they attain their wish, they will go and have a cocoanut broken on their head by a priest at the temple of Sendurai.‡ At an annual festival in honour of the god Sērvarāyan on the Shevaroy hills in the Salem district, those Malayālis who wish to take a vow to be faithful to their god have to receive

* "Gazetteer of the Tanjore District," 1906, I. 72.

† "Gazetteer of the Madura District," 1906, i. 86-7.

‡ *Ibid.*, 86.

fifteen lashes on the bare back with a stout leather thong, administered by the chief priest.

The annual festival at the temple of Karamadai in the Coimbatore district is visited by about forty or fifty thousand pilgrims, belonging for the most part to the lower classes. In case of sickness or other calamity, they take a vow to perform one of the following :—

(1) To pour water at the feet of the idol inside the temple. Each devotee is provided with a goat-skin bag, or a new earthen pot. He goes to the tank, and, after bathing, fills the receptacle with water, carries it to the temple, and empties it before the idol. This is repeated a number of times according to the nature of the vow. If the vow is a life-long one, it has to be performed every year until death.

(2) To give kavalam to Dāsaris (religious mendicants). Kavalam consists of plantain fruits cut up into small slices, and mixed with sugar, jaggery (crude sugar), fried grain, or beaten rice. The Dāsaris are attached to the temple, and wear short drawers, with strings of small brass bells tied to their wrists and ankles. They appear to be possessed, and move wildly about to the beating of drums. As they go about, the devotees put some of the kavalam into their mouths. The Dāsaris eat a little, and spit out the remainder into the hands of the devotees, who eat it. This is believed to cure all disease, and to give children to those who partake of it. In addition to kavalam, some put betel leaves in the mouths of the Dāsaris, who, after chewing them, spit them into the mouths of the devotees. At night the Dāsaris carry torches made of rags, on which the devotees pour ghī (clarified butter). Some people say that, many years ago, barren women used to take a vow to visit the temple at the time of the festival, and, after offering kavalam,

have sexual intercourse with the Dāsaris. The temple authorities, however, profess ignorance of this practice.

On the last day of the Gangajatra festival at Tirupati, a figure is made of clay and straw, and placed in the tope (grove), where crowds of all classes, including Paraiyans, present food to it. Buffaloes, goats, sheep, and fowls are sacrificed, and it is said that Brāhmans, though they will not be present, send animals to be slaughtered. At the conclusion of the festivities, the image is burnt during the feast, which last over ten days, the lower orders of the people paint themselves, and indulge in much boisterous merriment. Those who have made a vow to Ganga fast for some days before the festival begins. They wear a structure made of bamboo in the form of a car, which is decorated with paper of different colours, and supported by iron nails pressed into the belly and back. They go about with this structure on their heads. Those who have been attacked by cholera, or other serious disease, make a vow to Ganga, and perform this ceremonial.

A festival, which is attended by huge crowds of Hindus of all classes, takes place annually in the month of Audi (July-August) at the village of Periyapālayam, about sixteen miles from Madras, where the goddess Māriamma is worshipped under the name of Periyapālayaththamman. According to the legend, as narrated by the Rev. A. C. Clayton,*

"there was once a Rishi (sage), who lived on the banks of the Periyapālayam river with his wife Bavāni. Every morning she used to bathe in the river, and bring back water for the use of the household. But she never took any vessel with her in which to bring the water home, for she was so chaste that she had acquired power to

* *Madras Museum Bull.*, 1906, v., No. 2, 78-9.

form a water-pot out of the dry river sand, and carry the water home in it. One day, while bathing, she saw the reflection of the face of the sky-god, Indra, in the water, and could not help admiring it. When she returned to the bank of the river, and tried to form her water-pot out of sand as usual, she could not do so, for her admiration of Indra had ruined her power, and she went home sadly to fetch a brass water-vessel. Her husband saw her carrying this to the river, and at once suspected her of unchastity, and, calling his son, ordered him to strike off her head with a sword. It was in vain that the son tried to avoid matricide. He had to obey, but he was so agitated by his feelings that, when at last he struck at his mother, he cut off not only her head, but that of a leather-dresser's wife who was standing near. The two bodies lay side by side. The rishi was so pleased with his son's obedience that he promised him any favour that he should ask, but he was very angry when the son at once begged that his mother might be restored to life. Being compelled to keep his word, he told the son that, if he put his mother's head on her trunk, she would again live. The son tried to do so, but in his haste took up the head of the leather-dresser's wife by mistake, and put it on Bavāni's body. Leather-dressers are flesh-eaters, and so it comes about that, on days when her festival is celebrated, Bavāni — now a goddess — longs for meat, and thousands of sheep, goats, and fowls, must be slain at her shrine. This legend bears marks of Brāhmanic influence. Curiously enough, the priest of this Paraiya shrine is himself a Brāhman."

The vows, which are performed at the festival at Periyapālayam, are as follows :—

(1) Wearing a garment of margosa (*Melia Azadirachta*) leaves, or wearing an ordinary garment, and carrying a lighted lamp made of rice-flour on the head.

(2) Carrying a pot decorated with flowers and margosa leaves round the temple.

(3) Going round the temple, rolling on the ground.

(4) Throwing a live fowl on to the top of the temple.

(5) Throwing a cocoanut in front, prostrating on the ground in salutation, going forward several paces and again throwing the cocoanut, and repeating the procedure till three circuits of the temple have been made.

(6) Giving offerings to the idol Parasurāma, cradle with baby made of clay or wood, etc., to bring offspring to the childless, success in a lawsuit or business transaction, and other good luck. In addition, pongal (boiled rice) has to be offered, and by some a sheep or goat is sacrificed. If a vow has been made on behalf of a sick cow, the animal is bathed in the river, clad in margosa leaves, and led round the temple. The leaf-wearing vow is resorted to by the large majority of the devotees, and performed by men, women and children. Those belonging to the more respectable classes go through it in the early morning, before the crowd has collected in its tens of thousands. The leafy garments are purchased from hawkers, who do a brisk trade in the sale thereof. The devotees have to pay a modest fee for admission to the temple precincts, and go round the shrine three or more times. Concerning the Periyapālayam festival, a recent writer observes that, "the distinctive feature is that the worshippers are clad in leaves. The devotees are bound to wear a garment made of fresh margosa twigs with their leaves. This garment is called vēpansilai. It consists of a string three or four yards long, from which depend, at intervals of two to three inches apart, twigs measuring about two feet in length, and forming a fringe of foliage. This string being wound several times round the waist, the fringe of leaves forms

a kilt or short petticoat. Men are content to wear the kilt, but women also wear round their neck a similar garment, which forms a short cloak reaching to the waist. To impress on devotees the imperative obligation imposed on them to wear the leaf garment in worshipping the goddess, it is said that a young married woman, being without children, made a vow to the goddess that, on obtaining a son, she would go on a pilgrimage to Periyapālayam, and worship her in accordance with the ancient rite. Her prayer having been answered, she gave birth to a son, and went to Periyapālayam to fulfil her vow. When, however, it was time to undress and put on the vēpansilai, her modesty revolted. Unobserved by her party, she secretly tied a cloth round her waist before putting on the vēpansilai. So attired, she went to the temple to worship. On seeing her coming, the goddess detected her deceit, and, waxing wroth, set the woman's dress all ablaze, and burnt her so severely that she died."

It is noted by Bishop Whitehead * that it was formerly the custom for women to come to the shrine of Durgamma at Bellary clad in twigs of the margosa tree. But this is now only done by children, the grown-up women putting the margosa twigs over a cloth wrapped round the loins. At a festival of the village goddess at Kudligi in the Bellary district, the procession is said by Mr F. Fawcett to be headed by a Mādiga (Telugu Pariah) naked save for a few margosa leaves. The wearing of these leaves on the occasion of festivals in honour of Māriamma is a very general custom throughout Southern India. Garments made of leaves are still worn by the females of some tribes on the west coast, *e.g.*, the Thanda Pulayans, Vettuvans, and Koragas. Concerning the Koragas, Mr Walhouse writes † that they

* *Madras Museum Bull.*, 1907, v., No. 3, 149.

† "Ind. Ant.," 1881, x. 364.

"wear an apron of twigs and leaves over the buttocks. Once this was the only covering allowed them, and a mark of their deep degradation. But now, when no longer compulsory, and of no use, as it is worn over the clothes, the women still retain it, believing its disuse would be unlucky."

"Kūvvākkam in the South Arcot district is known for its festival to Aravān (more correctly Irāvān) or Kūttāndar, which is one of the most popular feasts with Sūdras in the whole district. Aravān was the son of Arjuna, one of the five Pāndava brothers. Local traditions says that, when the great war which is described in the Mahābhārata was about to begin, the Kauravas, the opponents of the Pāndavas, to bring them success, sacrificed a white elephant. The Pāndavas were in despair of being able to find any such uncommon object with which to propitiate the gods, until Arjuna suggested that they should offer up his son Aravān. Aravān agreed to yield his life for the good of the cause, and, when eventually the Pāndavas were victorious, he was deified for the self-abnegation which had thus brought his side success. Since he died in his youth, before he had been married, it is held to please him if men, even though grown up and already wedded, come now and offer to espouse him, and men who are afflicted with serious diseases take a vow to marry him at his annual festival in the hope of thereby being cured. The festival occurs in May, and for eighteen nights the Mahābhārata is recited by a Palli (Tamil agriculturist),* large numbers of people, especially of that caste, assembling to hear it read. On the eighteenth night, a wooden image of Kūttāndar is taken to a tope (grove) and seated there. This is the signal for the sacrifice of an enormous number of fowls. Every one who comes brings one or two, and the number killed runs literally into thousands. While this is going on, all the men who have taken vows to be

* The Pallis claim to be descendants of the fire race (Agnikula) of the Kshatriyas, and that, as they and the Pāndava brothers were born of fire, they are related.

VETTUVANS WEARING LEAFY GARMENTS.

To face p. 152.

married to the deity appear before his image dressed like women, make obeisance, offer to the priest (who is a Palli by caste) a few annas, and give into his hands the tālis (marriage badge worn by women) which they have brought with them. These the priest, as representing the God, ties round their necks. The God is brought back to his shrine that night, and, when in front of the building, he is hidden by a cloth held before him. This symbolises the sacrifice of Aravān, and the men who have just been married to him set up loud lamentations at the death of their husband. Similar vows are taken and ceremonies performed, it is said, at the shrines of Kūttāndar, two miles north-west of Porto Novo, and Ādivarāhanattum (five miles north-west of Chidambaram), and, in recent years, at Tiruvarkkulam (one mile east of the latter place); other cases probably occur." *

I am informed by Mr R. F. Stoney that, in the Madura district, iron chains are hung on bābūl (*Acacia arabica*) trees, and dedicated to the rustic deity Karuppan. At Mēlūr Mr Stoney saw large masses of such chains, which are made by the village blacksmiths. They are very rough, and are furnished at one end with what is said to be a sickle, and also a spear-head. I gather further † that, in the Mēlūr tāluk, the shrine of Karuppan may usually be known by the hundreds of chains hung outside it, which have been presented to the god in performance of vows. The deity is said to be fond of bedecking himself with chains, and these offerings are usually suspended from a kind of horizontal bar made of two stone uprights supporting a slab of stone placed horizontally upon the top of them. The god is also fond of presents of clubs and swords.

"Sometimes," a recent writer states, "a big chain hangs suspended from a tree, and the village panchāyats

* "Gazetteer of the South Arcot District," 1906, i. 375-6.

† "Gazetteer of the Madura District," 1906, i. 85.

(tribunals) are held in the Aiyanar (or Sangali Karuppan) temple. The accused is made to submit to an ordeal in proof of innocence. The ordeal consists in his swearing on the chain, which he is made to touch. He has such a dread of this procedure, that, as soon as he touches the chain, he comes out with the truth, failure to speak the truth being punished by some calamity, which he believes will overtake him within a week. These chains are also suspended to the trees near the temples of village goddesses, and used by village panchāyats to swear the accused in any trial before them."

It is narrated* by Moor that he "passed a tree, on which were hanging several hundred bells. This was a superstitious sacrifice by the Bandjanahs,† who, passing this tree, are in the habit of hanging a bell or bells upon it, which they take from the necks of their sick cattle, expecting to leave behind them the complaint also. Our servants particularly cautioned us against touching these diabolical bells; but, as a few were taken for our own cattle, several accidents that happened were imputed to the anger of the deity to whom these offerings were made, who, they say, inflicts the same disorder on the unhappy bullock who carries a bell from this tree as he relieved the donor from."

At Diguvemetta in the Kurnool district, I came across a number of bells, both large and small, tied to the branches of a tamarind tree, beneath which were an image of the deity Malalamma, and a stone bull (Nandi). Suspended from a branch of the same tree was a thick rope, to which were attached heads, skulls, mandibles, thigh-bones, and feet of fowls, and the foot of a goat.

* "Narrative of Little's Detachment," 1794, 212-3.

† Lambādis or Brinjāris, who formerly acted as carriers of supplies and baggage in times of war in the Deccan.

Mr Fawcett once saw, at a Savara village in Ganjam, a gaily ornamented hut near a burning-ground. Rude figures of birds and red rags were tied to five bamboos, which were sticking up in the air about eight feet above the hut, one at each corner, and one in the centre. A Savara said that he built the hut for his dead brother, and had buried the bones in it.* It is noted by the Rev. J. Cain † that, in some places, the Lambādis fasten rags torn from some old garment to a bush in honour of Kampalamma (kampa, a thicket). On the side of a road from Bastar are several large heaps of stones, which they have piled up in honour of the goddess Guttalamma. Every Lambādi who passes the heaps is bound to place one stone on the heap, and make a salaam to it. It is further recorded by Mr Walhouse ‡ that, when going from the Coimbatore plains to the Mysore frontier, he saw a thorn-bush rising out of a heap of stones piled round it, and bearing bits of rag tied to its branches by Lambādis. In the Telugu country, rags are offered to a god named Pathalayya (Mr Rags). On the trunk-roads in the Nellore district, rags may be seen hanging from the bābūl (*Acacia arabica*) trees. These are offerings made to Pathalayya by travellers, who tear off pieces of their clothing with a vague idea that the offering thereof will render their journey free from accidents, such as upsetting of their carts, or meeting with robbers. Outside the temple of the village goddess at Ojini in the Bellary district, Mr Fawcett tells us,§ "are hung numbers of miniature cradles and bangles presented by women who have borne children, or been cured of sickness through

* *Journ. Anthrop. Soc., Bombay*, i. 253-4.

† "Ind. Ant.," 1879, viii. 219.

‡ *Ibid.*, 1880, ix. 150.

§ *Journ. Anthrop. Soc., Bombay*, ii. 272.

the intervention of the goddess. Miniature cows are presented by persons whose cows have been cured of sickness, and doll-like figures for children. One swāmi (god) there is, known by a tree hung with iron chains, hooks—anything iron; another by rags, and so on. The ingenious dhōbi (washerman), whose function is to provide torches on occasions, sometimes practises on the credulity of his countrymen by tying a few rags to a tree, which by and by is covered with rags, for the passers-by are not so stiff-necked as to ask for a sign other than a rag; and under cover of the darkness, the dhōbi makes his torch of the offerings."

On the road to the temple at Tirumala (Upper Tirupati) in the North Arcot district, the goddess Gauthala Gangamma has her abode in a margosa or āvaram (*Cassia auriculata*) tree, surrounded by a white-ant hill. Passers-by tear off a piece of their clothing, and tie it to the branches, and place a small stone at the base of the ant-hill. Occasionally cooked rice is offered, fowls are sacrificed, and their heads and legs tied to the tree. In the Madura district, bits of rag are hung on the trees in which a deity named Sāttān is believed to reside.* It is noted by Mr W. Francis † that, "in some places in the South Arcot district, for example, on the feeder road to the Olakkūr station in Tindivānam tāluk and near the eighth mile of the road from Kallakurchi to Vriddhachalam, are trees on which passers-by have hung bits of rag, until they are quite covered with them. The latter of the two cases had its origin only a few years back in the construction by some shepherd boys of a toy temple to Ganēsa formed of a few stones under the tree, to draw attention to which they hung up a rag

* "Gazetteer of the Madura District," 1906, i. 86.

† "Gazetteer of the South Arcot District," 1906, i. 102.

or two. The tree is now quite covered with bits of cloth, and beneath it is a large pile of stones, which have been added one by one by the superstitious passers-by."

It is recorded by the Abbé Dubois * that "at Palni, in Madura, there is a famous temple consecrated to the god Velayuda, whose devotees bring offerings of a peculiar kind, namely large sandals, beautifully ornamented, and similar in shape to those worn by the Hindus on their feet. The god is addicted to hunting, and these shoes are intended for his use when he traverses the jungles and deserts in pursuit of his favourite sport. Such shabby gifts, one might think, would go very little way towards filling the coffers of the priests of Velayuda. Nothing of the sort: Brahmins always know how to reap profit from anything. Accordingly the new sandals are rubbed on the ground and rolled a little in the dust, and are then exposed to the eyes of the pilgrims who visit the temple. It is clear enough that the sandals must have been worn on the divine feet of Velayuda; and they become the property of whosoever pays the highest price for such holy relics."

Mr Walhouse informs us † that the champak and other trees round the ancient shrine of the Trimurti at the foot of the Ānaimalai mountains are thickly hung with sandals and shoes, many of huge size, evidently made for the purpose, and suspended by pilgrims as votive offerings. The god of the temple at Tirumala is said to appear annually to four persons in different directions, east, west, south and north, and informs them that he requires a shoe from each of them. They whitewash their houses, worship the god, and spread rice-flour thickly on the

* "Hindu Manners, Customs, and Ceremonies" translation by H. K. Beauchamp, 1897, ii. 610.

† "Ind. Ant.," 1880, ix. 152.

floor of a room, which is locked for the night. Next morning the mark of a huge foot is found on the floor, and the shoe has to be made to fit this. When ready, it is taken in procession through the streets of the village, conveyed to Tirumala, and presented to the temple. Though the makers of the shoes have worked in ignorance of each others' work, the shoes brought from the north and south, and those from the east and west, are believed to match and make a pair. Though the worship of these shoes is chiefly meant for Paraiyans, who are prohibited from ascending the Tirupati hill, as a matter of fact all, without distinction of caste, worship them. The shoes are placed in front of the image of the god near the foot of the hill, and are said to gradually wear away by the end of the year.

"At Bēlur in the Mysore Province," Mr Lewis Rice writes,* "the god of the temple is under the necessity of making an occasional trip to the Baba Budan hills to visit the goddess. On these occasions he is said to make use of a large pair of slippers kept for the purpose in the temple. When they are worn out, it devolves upon the chucklers (leather-workers) of Channagiri and Bisvapatna, to whom the fact is revealed in a dream, to provide new ones."

In order to present the slippers, they are allowed to enter the courtyard of the temple.

On the way leading up to the temple at Tirumala, small stones heaped up in the form of a hearth, and knots tied in the leaves of young date-palms may be seen. These are the work of virgins who accompany the parties of pilgrims. The knots are tied to ensure the tying of the marriage tāli string on their necks, and the heaping up of the stones is done with a view to ensuring the

* "Mysore," 1897, ii. 350.

birth of children to them. If the girls revisit the hill after marriage and the birth of offspring, they untie the knot on a leaf, and disarrange one of the hearths. Men cause their name to be cut on rocks by the wayside, or on the stones with which the path leading to the temple is paved, in the belief that good luck will result if their name is trodden on by some pious man.

At Tirupati, a number of Balijas are engaged in the red sanders (*Pterocarpus santalinus*) wood-carving industry. Figures of deities, mythological figures, miniature temple cars, and domestic utensils, are among the articles turned out by them. Vessels made of red sanders wood carry no pollution, and can be used by women during the menstrual period, and taken back to the house without any purification ceremony. For the same reason, Sanyāsis (ascetics) use such vessels for performing worship. The carved figures are sold to pilgrims and others who visit Tirupati, and are also taken for sale to Conjeeveram, Madura, and other places, at times when important temple festivals are celebrated. Carved wooden figurines, male and female, represented in a state of nudity, are also manufactured at Tirupati, and sold to Hindus. Those who are childless perform on them the ear-boring ceremony, in the belief that, as the result thereof, issue will be born to them. Or, if there are grown-up boys or girls in a family, who remain unmarried, the parents celebrate the marriage ceremony between a pair of figurines, in the hope that the marriage of their children will speedily follow. They dress up the dolls in clothes and jewelry, and go through the ceremonial of a real marriage. Some there are who have spent as much money on a doll's wedding as on a wedding in real life.

The simplest form of offerings consists of fruits, such

as plantains and cocoanuts. Without an offering of fruit no orthodox Hindu would think of entering a temple, or coming into the presence of a Native of position. The procession of servants and retainers, each bringing a gift of a lime fruit, on New Year's Day is familiar to Anglo-Indians. By the rules of Government, framed with a view to preventing bribery, the prohibition of the receipt of presents from Native Chiefs and others does not extend to the receipt of a few flowers or fruits, and articles of inappreciable value, although even such trifling presents should be discouraged.

As a thanksgiving for recovery from illness, votive offerings frequently take the form of silver or gold representations of the part of the body affected, which are deposited in a vessel kept for the purpose at the temple. They are kept for sale in the vicinity of the temple, and must be offered by the person who has taken the vow, or on whose behalf it has been taken. When a person has been ill all over, a silver human figure, or a thin silver wire of the same length as himself, and representing him, is sometimes offered.

Of silver offerings from temples in the Tamil country, the Madras Museum possesses an extensive collection, in which are included the face, hands, feet, buttocks, tongue, larynx, navel, nose, ears, eyes, breasts, genitalia, etc.; snakes offered to propitiate the anger of serpents, snakes coiled *in coitu*, sandals, flags, umbrellas, and cocoanuts strung on a pole.

When litigation arises in Malabar in connection with the title to a house and compound (grounds) in which it stands, a vow is sometimes made to offer a silver model representing the property, if a favourable decree is obtained. Some time ago, a rich landlord offered at the temple a silver model representing the exact number of trees, house,

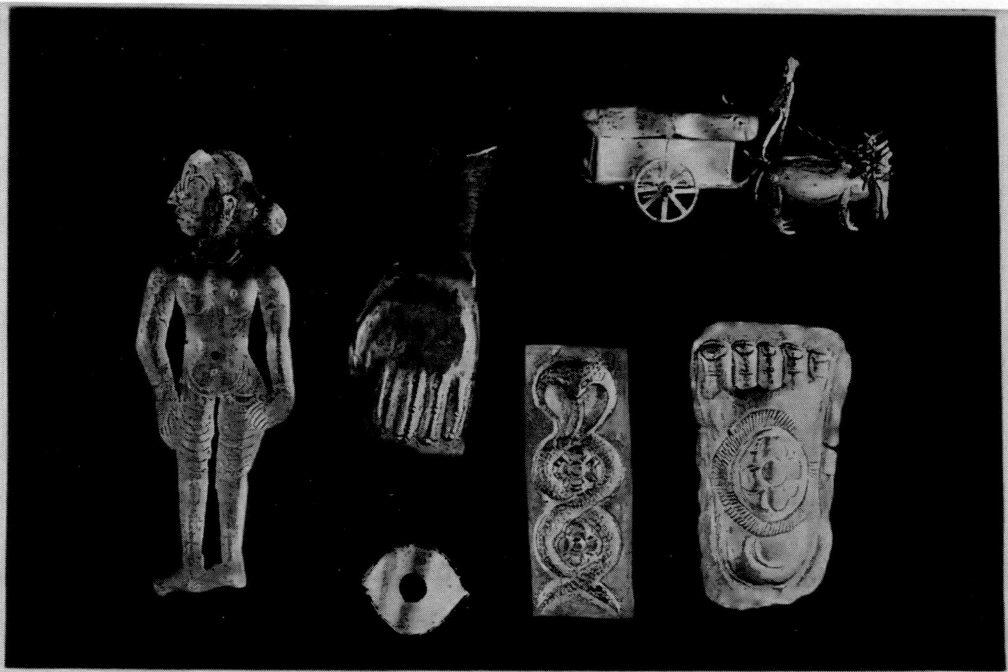

SILVER, VOTIVE OFFERINGS.

To face p. 160

well, etc., and costing several hundreds of rupees, when a suit was decided in his favour.

In connection with the temple at Guruvayūr in Malabar, Mr Fawcett writes as follows * :—

"I visited the festival on one occasion, and purchase was made of a few offerings such as are made to the temple in satisfaction of vows—a very rude representation of an infant in silver, a hand, a leg, an ulcer, a pair of eyes, and, most curious of all, a silver string which represents a man, the giver. Goldsmiths working in silver and gold are to be seen just outside the gate of the temple, ready to provide at a moment's notice the object that any person intends to offer, in case he is not already in possession of his votive offering."

A Nāyar examined by Mr Fawcett was wearing a silver ring as a vow, which was to be given up at the next festival at Kottiūr in North Malabar. Another was wearing a silver bangle. He had a wound in his arm which was long in healing, so he made a vow to the god at Tirupati (Tirumala) that, if his arm was healed, he would give up the bangle at the temple.

A few years ago, a shrine was erected at Cochin for a picture of the Virgin and Child, which attained to great celebrity for its power of working miracles. "Many stories," Mr Fawcett writes,† "of the power of the picture are current. A fisherman, who had lost his nets, vowed to give a little net, if they were found. The votive offerings, which are sometimes of copper or brass, take strange forms. There are fishes, prawns, rice, cocoanut trees, cows, etc. A little silver model of a bridge was given by a contractor, who vowed, when he found his foundations were shaky, to give it if his work should

* *Madras Museum Bull.*, 1901, iii., No. 3, 266.

† The making of a shrine, *Calcutta Review*, 1899, cviii. 173-5.

pass muster. The power of the picture is such that the votaries are not confined to the Christian community. There are among them many Hindus and Mahomedans."

In South Canara, silver rats and pigs are offered to protect the crops from destruction by these animals. Silver rice-grains are offered when children do not take their food properly, and silver sheaves of grain if the crop is abundant. At Pyka, brass or clay figures of the tiger, leopard, elephant, wild boar, and bandicoot rat, are presented at the shrine of a female bhūtha* named Poomanikunhoomani, to protect the crops and cattle from the ravages of these animals. The figures must be solid, as the bhūthas would be very angry if they were hollow. A brass figure of Sarabha, a mythological eight-legged animal, which is supposed to be the vehicle of the god Vīrabhadra, is presented as an offering to some Siva temples in South Canara in cases where a person is attacked with a form of ulcer known as Siva's ulcer. Sometimes a silver lizard is offered at temples, to counteract the evils which would result from a lizard falling on some unlucky part of the body, such as the kudumi (hair knot) of a female. The lizard, associated with the name of Siva, is regarded as sacred. It is never intentionally killed, and, if accidentally hurt or killed, an image of it in gold or silver is presented by high caste Hindus to a Siva temple.†

In Malabar, a Brāhman magician transfers the spirits of those who have died an unnatural death to images made of gold, silver, or wood, which are placed in a temple or special building erected for them. It is said by Mr F. Fawcett, "to be a sacred duty to a deceased Tiyan in

* Bhūtha, or demon worship, prevails in South Canara, where the villages have their bhūtha sthānam or demon shrine.

† "Cochin Census Report," 1901, part i. 25.

CLAY AND METAL OFFERINGS, SOUTH CANARA.

To face p. 162.

Malabar, who was of importance, for example, the head of a family, to have a silver image of him made, and arrange for it being deposited in some temple, where it will receive its share of worship, and offerings of food and water. The temples at Tirunelli in Wynād and Tirunavayi, which are among the oldest in Malabar, were generally the resting-places of these images, but now some of the well-to-do deposit them much further afield, even at Benares and Rāmēsvaram. A silver image is presented to the local Siva temple, where, for a consideration, worship is done every new moon day. On each of these days, mantrams are supposed to be repeated a thousand times. When the image has been the object of these mantrams sixteen thousand times, it is supposed to have become eligible for final deposit at Tirunavayi or elsewhere."

If a Muhammadan suffers from severe pain in the hand or foot, a vow is sometimes taken to the effect that a silver hand or foot will be taken to the grave of some saint, and put into the treasury which is kept there to meet the expenses of the annual ceremonies of the saint. At Vizagapatam * there is a celebrated Muhammadan saint, who lies buried by the Durga on the top of the hill overlooking the harbour. He is considered to be all potent over the elements of the Bay of Bengal, and many a silver dhoni (native boat) is presented at his shrine by Hindu ship-owners after a successful voyage. A suit once arose between a Kōmati boat-owner and his Muhammadan captain during settlement of the accounts. The captain stated that, during a storm off the coast of Arakan, he had vowed a purse of rupees to the saint, and had duly presented it on his return. This sum he charged to the owner of the vessel, whose sole contention was that the vow had never been discharged; the propriety

* "Gazetteer of the Vizagapatam District," 1907, i. 329.

of conciliating the saint in a hurricane he allowed. At Timmancherla in the Anantapur district there is a tomb of a holy Muhammadan named Masthan Ali, in whose honour a religious ceremony is held annually in April, which is attended by both Muhammadans and Hindus. The latter make vows at the tomb, which has a special reputation for granting offspring to the childless. The headman of the village, who is a Hindu, brings the first offerings in procession with much ceremony.*

At the annual festival at the temple at Nedamangad in Travancore, which is attended by large numbers of the lower classes, the worshippers are said by the Rev. S. Mateer † to "bring with them wooden models of cows covered, in imitation of shaggy hair, with ears of rice. Many of these images are brought, each in a separate procession from its own place. The headmen are finely dressed with cloths stained purple at the edge. The image is borne on a bamboo frame, accompanied by a drum," and carried round the temple. The Gudigars (wood-carvers) at Udipi in South Canara make life-size wooden buffaloes and large human figures as votive offerings for the Iswara Temple at Hiriadkāp, where they are set up in a row. By the Savaras of Vizagapatam, rudely carved and grotesque wooden representations of human beings, monkeys, lizards, parrots, peacocks, guns, pickaxes, daggers, etc., are dedicated to the tribal deity. They would not sell them to the district officer who acquired them on my behalf, but parted with them on the understanding that they would be worshipped by the Sirkar (Government). In like manner, the fishermen of the Ganjam coast objected to specimens of the gods which are placed in little shrines on the sea-shore being sent

* "Gazetteer of the Anantapur District," 1905, i. 164.

† "Native Life in Travancore," 1883.

to me, till they were told that it was because the Government had heard of their devotion to their gods that they wanted to have some of them in Madras. The gods, which are made in clay and wood, include Bengali Bābu riding on a black horse, who is believed to bless the fishermen, secure large hauls of fish for them, and protect them against danger when out fishing. It has been observed that this affinity between the Ganjam fishermen and the Bengali Bābu, resulting in the apotheosis of the latter, is certainly a striking example of the catholicity of hero-worship, and it would be interesting to know how long, and for what reasons the conception of protection has appealed to the followers of the piscatory industry. It was Sir George Campbell, the Lieutenant-Governor of Bengal, who compelled his Bengali officials, much against their inclination, to cultivate the art of equitation.

I am informed by Mr G. V. Ramamurthi Pantulu that the Savaras attend the markets or fairs held in the plains, or at the foot of the ghâts, to purchase salt and other articles. If a Savara is taken ill at the market or on his return thence, he attributes the illness to a spirit of the market called Biradi Sonum. The bulls which carry the goods of the Hindu merchants to the market are supposed to convey the spirit. In propitiating it, the Savara makes an image of a bull in straw, and, taking it out of his village, leaves it on the footpath, after a pig has been sacrificed. Owners of cattle take the animals when sick round the sacred hill at Tirukazhukunram in performance of a vow, in the belief that their health will be thus restored.

"A Brāhmini bull," Mr A. Srinivasan writes, "is dedicated to the god Venkatēswara of Tirupati, for the benefit of the living in fulfilment of vows. The act of dedication and release is preceded by elaborate rituals of marriage, as among men and women. The bride, which should be a heifer that has not calved, is furnished by the father-in-law of the donor. The heifer is united in holy wedlock to the bullock, after formal chanting of mantrams, by the tying of the tāli and toe-rings to the neck. In this sham marriage, the profuse ornamentation of the couple with saffron (turmeric) and red powder, the pouring of rice on their heads, and a procession through the streets with music, are conspicuous features."

I am told that, if the devotee cannot afford a live animal, a mimic representative is made in rice.

Painted hollow images are made by special families of Kusavans (potters) known as pūjāri (priest), who, for the privilege of making them, have to pay an annual fee to the headman, who spends it on a festival at the caste temple. When a married couple are anxious to have female offspring, they take a vow to offer figures of the seven virgins (Saptha Kannimar), who are represented all seated in a row. If a male or female recovers from cholera, smallpox, or other severe illness, a figure of the corresponding sex is offered. A childless woman makes a vow to offer up the figure of a baby, if she brings forth offspring. Figures of animals—cattle, horses, sheep, etc.—are offered at the temple when they recover from sickness, or are recovered after they have been stolen. Horses made of clay, painted red and other colours, are set up in the fields to drive away demons, or as a thank-offering for recovery from sickness, or any piece of good luck. The villagers erect these horses in honour of the popular deity Ayanar, the guardian deity of the fields, who is a renowned huntsman, and is believed, when, with his wives Purna and Pushkala, he visits the village at night, to mount the horses, and ride down the demons. Ayanar is said * to be the special deity of the Kusavan caste. Kusavans are generally the pūjāris at his temples, and they make the earthenware, and brick and mortar horses and images, which are placed before these buildings. The pupils of the eyes of the various images are not painted in till they are taken to the temple, where offerings of fruit, etc., are first made. Even the pupils of a series of images which were specially made for me were not painted at the potter's house, but in the verandah of the traveller's bungalow where I was staying. A very interesting account of the nētra mangalya, or ceremony of painting the eyes of images, as performed by craftsmen in Ceylon, has been published by Mr A. K. Coomaraswamy.† Therein he writes that "by far the most important ceremony connected with the building and decoration of a vihāra (temple), or with its renovation, was the actual *netra mangalya* or eye ceremonial. The ceremony had to be performed in the case of any image, whether set up in a vihāra or not. Even in the case of flat paintings it was necessary. D. S. Muhandiram, when making for me a book of drawings of gods according to the Rūpavaliya, left the eyes to be subsequently inserted on an auspicious occasion, with some simpler form of the ceremony described."

On this subject, Knox writes as follows ‡:—

"Some, being devoutly disposed, will make the image of this god (Buddha) at their own charge. For the making whereof they must bountifully reward the Founder. Before the eyes are made, it is not accounted a god, but a lump of ordinary metal, and thrown about the shop with no more regard than anything else. But, when the eyes are to be made, the artificer is to have a good gratification,

* "Gazetteer of the Madura District," 1906, i. 102.

† "Mediæval Sinhalese Art," 1908, 70-75.

‡ Philalethes, "History of Ceylon," 1817, 163.

besides the first agreed upon reward. The eyes being formed, it is thenceforward a god. And then, being brought with honour from the workman's shop, it is dedicated by solemnities and sacrifices, and carried with great state into the shrine or little house, which is before built and prepared for it."

Putting money into a receptacle (undi) as an offering to a particular deity is a very common custom. In the case of a popular god, such as the one at Tirumala, an earthen pot is sometimes replaced by a copper money-box or iron safe. In South Canara there was a well-to-do family, the members of which kept on depositing coins in the family undi, which were set apart for the Tirumala god during a number of generations. Not only in cases of sickness, but even when a member of the family went to a neighbouring village, and returned safely, a few coins were put into the undi. For some reason, the opening of the undi, and offering of its contents at Tirumala, was postponed, and, when it was finally opened, it was found to contain a miscellaneous collection of coins, current and uncurrent. When a temple is far away, and those who wish to make offerings thereat cannot, owing to the expense of the journey or other reason, go there themselves, the offerings are taken by a substitute. If the god to whom the offering is made is Srinivāsa of Tirumala, a small sum of money must be offered as compensation for not taking it in person. The god is sometimes called Vaddi Kāsulu Varu, in allusion to the money (kāsu) or interest. In some large towns, in the months of July and August, parties of devotees may be seen wandering about the streets, and collecting offerings to the god, which will be presented to him in due course. If a Kelasi (barber) in South Canara is seriously ill, he sometimes undertakes a vow to beg from door to door, and convey the money thus collected to Tirumala. In his house he keeps a small closed box with a slit in the lid, through which he drops a coin at every stroke of misfortune, and the contents are eventually sent to the holy shrine.* A few years ago, a Native complained to the police that about seven hundred rupees had been stolen from some brass pots, which he kept in a separate room of his house. The money, he stated, was dedicated to the Tirumula temple, and was kept in the pots buried in paddy (unhusked rice). He himself had put in about fifty rupees during the time that the pots had been in his charge, either as an annual contribution, or on occasions of sickness. His mother stated that it had been a custom in the family to put money into the vessel for several generations, and she had never seen the pots opened.

It is whispered that Kallan dacoits invoke the aid of their deity Alagarswāmi, when they are setting out on marauding expeditions, and, if they are successful therein, put part of their ill-gotten gains into the offertory box, which is kept at his shrine.† In this connection, the Rev. J. Sharrock states that "there is an understanding that, if their own village gods help them in their thefts, they are to have a fair share of the spoil, and, on the principle of honour among thieves, the bargain is always kept. When strange deities are met with on their thieving expeditions, it is usual to make a vow that, if the adventure turns out well, part of the spoil shall next day be left at the shrine of the god, or be handed over to the pujāri of that particular deity. They are afraid that, if this precaution be not taken, the god may make them blind, or cause them to be discovered, or

* M. Bapu Rao, *Madras Christian Coll. Mag.*, April 1894, xi.

† "Gazetteer of the Madura District," 1906, i. 286.

may go so far as to knock them down, and leave them to bleed to death."

The most popular of the Muhammadan saints who are buried at Porto Novo, where a considerable number of Marakkāyars (Muhammadans) are engaged as sailors,

"is one Mālumiyar, who was apparently in his lifetime a notable sea-captain. His fame as a sailor has been magnified into the miraculous, and it is declared that he owned ten or a dozen ships, and used to appear in command of all of them simultaneously. He has now the reputation of being able to deliver from danger those who go down to the sea in ships, and sailors setting out on a voyage, or returning from one in safety, usually put an offering in the little box kept at his darga, and these sums are expended in keeping that building lighted and whitewashed. Another curious darga in the town is that of Araikāsu Nāchiyar, or the one pie lady. Offerings to her must on no account be worth more than one pie ($\frac{1}{192}$ of a rupee); tributes in excess of that value are of no effect. If sugar for so small an amount cannot be procured, the devotee spends the money on chunam (lime) for her tomb, and this is consequently covered with a superabundance of whitewash. Stories are told of the way in which the valuable offerings of rich men have altogether failed to obtain her favour, and have had to be replaced by others of the regulation diminutive dimensions." *

The chief god of the Dōmbs of Vizagapatam is said † to be represented by a pie piece placed in or over a new earthen pot smeared with rice and turmeric powder. It is said ‡ that Muhammadans, belonging to the lower classes, consult panchāngam Brāhmans about the chances of success in their enterprises. Some of these Brāhmans

* "Gazetteer of the South Arcot District," 1906, i. 278.

† F. Fawcett, *Man*, 1901, i., No. 29, p. 37.

‡ "Madras Census Report," 1901, part i. 134.

send half the fee so obtained to the Muhammadan mosque at Nagūr near Negapatam, and will even offer sugar and flowers at that shrine, though they endeavour to excuse the act by saying that the saint was originally a Brāhman.

I once saw a Muhammadan at Tumkur in Mysore, whither he had journeyed from Hyderabad, who had a rupee tied round his arm in token of a vow that, if he returned safe from plague and other ills to his own country, he would give money in charity. When a Muhammadan falls ill, a rupee and a quarter is sometimes done up in a red cloth, and tied round the arm, to be given to the poor on recovery. Members of the poorer classes tie an anna and a quarter in like manner, after performing a fateha ceremony. Should the sickness of a Hindu be attributed to a god or goddess, a vow is made, in token whereof a copper or silver coin is wrapped up in a piece of cloth dipped in turmeric paste, and kept in the house, or tied to the neck or arm of the sick person. A cock may be waved round the head of the patient, and afterwards reared in the house, to be eventually offered up at the shrine of the deity. A Bēdar, whom I saw at Hospet in the Bellary district, had a quarter anna rolled up in cotton cloth, which he wore on the upper arm in performance of a vow.

In an account of the cock festival at Cranganore in Malabar, whereat vast numbers of cocks are sacrificed, Mr Gopal Panikkar records* that, "when a man is taken ill of any infectious disease, his relations generally pray to the goddess (at Cranganore) for his recovery, solemnly covenanting to perform what goes by the name of a thulabhāram (or thulupurushadānam) † ceremony.

* "Malabar and its Folk," Madras, 2nd ed., 133.

† Thula (scales), purusha (man), dānam (gift).

This consists in placing the patient in one of the scale-pans of a huge balance, and weighing him against gold, or, more generally, pepper (and sometimes other substances), deposited in the other scale-pan. Then this weight of the substance is offered to the goddess. This has to be performed right in front of the goddess in the temple yard."

At Mulki in South Canara there is a temple of Venkatēswara, which is maintained by Konkani Brāhmans. A Konkani Brāhman, who is attached to the temple, becomes inspired almost daily between 10 and 11 A.M., immediately after worship, and people consult him. Some time ago, a rich merchant from Gujarat consulted the inspired man as to what steps should be taken to enable his wife to be safely delivered. He was told to take a vow that he would present to the god of the temple, silver, sugar-candy, and date fruits, equal in weight to that of his wife, This he did, and his wife was delivered of a male child. The cost of the ceremonial is said to have been five thousand rupees. In the thulabhāram ceremony as performed by the Mahārājas of Travancore,* they are weighed against gold coins, called thulabhāra kāsu, specially struck for the occasion, which are divided among the priests who performed the ceremony, and Brāhmans.

The following quaint custom, which is observed at the village of Pullambadi in the Trichinopoly district, is described by Bishop Whitehead.†

"The goddess Kulanthal Amman has established for herself a useful reputation as a settler of debts. When a creditor cannot recover a debt, he writes down his claim on a scroll of palm-leaves, and offers the goddess a

* *See* Shungoony Menon, "History of Travancore," 1878, 58-72.

† *Madras Diocesan Record*, October, 1905.

part of the debt, if it is paid. The palmyra scroll is hung up on an iron spear in the compound of the temple before the shrine. If the claim is just, and the debtor does not pay, it is believed that he will be afflicted with sickness and bad dreams. In his dreams he will be told to pay the debt at once, if he wishes to be freed from his misfortunes. If, however, the debtor disputes the claim, he draws up a counter-statement, and hangs it on the same spear. Then the deity decides which claim is true, and afflicts with sickness and bad dreams the man whose claim is false. When a claim is acknowledged, the debtor brings the money, and gives it to the pūjāri, who places it before the image of Kulanthal Amman, and sends word to the creditor. The whole amount is then handed over to the creditor, who pays the sum vowed to the goddess into the temple coffers in April or May. So great is the reputation of the goddess, that Hindus come from about ten miles round to seek her aid in recovering their debts. The goddess may sometimes make mistakes, but, at any rate, it is cheaper than an appeal to an ordinary court of law, and probably almost as effective as a means of securing justice. In former times, no written statements were presented; people simply came and represented their claims by word of mouth to the deity, promising to give her a share. The custom of presenting written claims sprang up about thirty years ago, doubtless through the influence of the Civil Courts. Apparently more debts have been collected since this was done, and more money has been gathered into the treasury."

It is noted by the Rev. A. Margöschis * that "the Hindus observe a special day at the commencement of the palmyra season (in Tinnevelly), when the jaggery season begins. Bishop Caldwell adopted the custom, and a solemn service in church was held, when one set

* "Christianity and Caste," 1893.

of all the implements used in the occupation of palmyra-climbing was brought to the church, and presented at the altar. Only the day was changed from that observed by the Hindus. The perils of the palmyra-climber are great, and there are many fatal accidents by falling from trees forty to sixty feet high, so that a religious service of the kind was particularly acceptable and peculiarly appropriate to our people."

The story is told by Bishop Caldwell of a Shānar (toddy-drawer) who was sitting upon a leaf-stalk at the top of a palmyra palm in a high wind, when the stalk gave way, and he came down to the ground safely and quietly sitting on the leaf, which served the purpose of a natural parachute.

The festival of Ayudha Pūja (worship of tools or implements) is observed by all Hindu castes during the last three days of the Dasara or Navarathri in the month of Purattasi (September - October). It is a universal holiday for all Hindu workmen. Even the Brāhman takes part in this pūja. His tools, however, being books, it is called Saraswati pūja, or worship to the goddess or god of learning, who is either Saraswati or Hayagriva. Reading books and repetition of Vēdas must be done, and, for the purpose of worship, all the books in a house are piled up in a heap. Non-Brāhmans clean the various implements used by them in their daily work, and worship them. The Kammālans (artisans) clean their hammers, pincers, anvil, blowpipe, etc. ; the Chettis (merchants) clean their scales and weights, and the box into which they put their money. The racket-marker at the Madras Club decorates the entrance to the scoring-box in which his rackets are kept, with a festoon of mango leaves. The weaving and agricultural classes will be seen to be busy with their looms and agricultural implements. Fishermen pile up their nets for worship. Even the bandywala (cart-driver) paints red and white stripes on the wheels and axles. I have myself been profusely garlanded when present as a guest at the elaborate tool-worshipping ceremony at the Madras School of Arts, where pūja was done to a bust of the late Bishop Gell set up on an improvised altar, with a cast of Saraswati above, and various members of the Hindu Pantheon around.

At the festival held by the Koyis of the Godāvari district in propitiation of a goddess called Pida, very frequently offerings promised long before are sacrificed, and eaten by the pujāri. It is not at all uncommon for a Koyi to promise to offer a seven-horned male (*i.e.* a cock) as a bribe to be let alone, a two-horned male (*i.e.* a goat) being set apart by more wealthy or more fervent suppliants.* When smallpox or other epidemic disease breaks out in a Gadaba village in Vizagapatam, a little go-cart on wheels is constructed. In this a clay image, or anything else holy, is placed, and it is taken to a distant spot, and left there. It is also the custom, when cholera or smallpox is epidemic in the same district, to make a little car, "on which are placed a grain of saffron-stained † rice for every soul in the village, and numerous offerings such as little swings, pots, knives, ploughs, and the like, and the blood of certain sacrificial victims, and this is then dragged with due ceremony to the boundary of the village. By this means the malignant essence of the deity who brings smallpox or cholera is transferred across the boundary. The neighbouring villagers naturally hasten to move the car on with similar ceremony, and

* Rev. J. Cain, *Madras Christian Coll. Mag.*, 1887-8, v. 358.

† In Southern India, turmeric (*Curcuma*) is commonly called saffron (*Crocus*).

it is thus dragged through a whole series of villages, and eventually left by the roadside in some lonely spot." *

Marching on one occasion, towards Hampi in the Bellary district, where an outbreak of cholera had recently occurred, I came across two wooden gods on wheels by the roadside, to whom had been offered baskets of fruit, vegetables, earthen pots, bead necklets, and bangles, which were piled up in front of them. It is recorded † by Bishop Whitehead that, when an epidemic breaks out in a certain village in the Telugu country,

"the headman of the village gets a new earthenware pot, besmears it with turmeric and kunkuma (red powder), and puts inside it some clay bracelets, necklaces, and earrings, three pieces of charcoal, three pieces of turmeric, three pieces of incense, a piece of dried cocoanut, a woman's cloth, and two annas worth of coppers—a strange collection of miscellaneous charms and offerings. The pot is then hung up on a tree near the image of the village deity, as a pledge that, if the epidemic disappears, the people will celebrate a festival."

It is further recorded ‡ by Bishop Whitehead that, during the festival of Māriamma at Kannanur in the Trichinopoly district, "many people who have made vows bring sheep, goats, fowls, pigeons, parrots, cows, and calves, to the temple, and leave them in the compound alive. At the end of the festival, these animals are all sold to a contractor. Two years ago, they fetched Rs. 400—a good haul for the temple."

Between the Madras museum and the Government

* "Gazetteer of the Vizagapatam District," 1907, i. 75.

† *Madras Museum Bull.*, 1907, v., No. 3, 134.

‡ *Ibid.*, 171.

maternity hospital, a small municipal boundary stone has been set up by the side of the road. To this stone supernatural powers are attributed, and it is alleged that in a banyan tree in a private garden close by a Mūni lives, who presides over the welfare of the patients in the hospital, and must be propitiated if the pregnant woman is to get over her confinement without complications. Women vow that they will, if all goes well, give a cocoanut, betel, or flowers when they leave. Discharged patients can be seen daily, going to the stone and making offerings. On the day of their discharge, their friends bring camphor and other articles, and the whole family goes to the stone, where the camphor is burnt, a cocoanut broken, and perhaps some turmeric or flowers placed on it. The new-born child is placed on the bare ground in front of the stone, and the mother, kneeling down, bows before it. The foreheads of both mother and child are marked with the soots from the burning camphor. If her friends do not bring the requisite articles, the woman goes home, and returns with them to do pūja to the stone, or it is celebrated at a temple or her house. The offerings are removed by those who present them, or by passers-by on the road.

The Kudubi cutch (catechu) makers of South Canara, before the commencement of operations, select an *Areca Catechu* tree, and place a sword, an axe, and a cocoanut on the ground near it. They prostrate themselves before the tree, with hands uplifted, burn incense, and break cocoanuts. The success of the operations is believed to depend on the good-will of a deity named Siddēdēvaru. Before they commence work, the Kudubis make a vow that, if they are successful, they will offer a fowl.

"A palmyra tree in the jungle near Ramnād with seven distinct trunks, each bearing a goodly head of fan-shaped leaves is," General Burton writes,* "attributed to the action of a deity, and stones smeared with oil and vermilion, broken cocoanuts, and fowl's feathers lying about, testify that pūja and sacrifice were performed here."

On the Rangasvāmi peak on the Nīlgiris are two rude walled enclosures sacred to the god Ranga and his consort, within which are deposited various offerings, chiefly iron lamps and the notched sticks used as weighing-machines. The hereditary priest is an Irula (jungle tribesman).† Certain caves are regarded by the Muduvars of the Travancore hills as shrines, wherein spear-heads, tridents, and copper coins are placed, partly to mark them as holy places, and partly as offerings to bring good luck.

Prehistoric stone cells, found in the bed of a river, are believed to be the thunderbolts of Vishnu, and are stacked as offerings by the Malaiālis of the Shevaroy hills in their shrines dedicated to Vignēswara the elephant god, who averts evil, or in little niches cut in rocks.

Of a remarkable form of demon worship in Tinnevelly, Bishop Caldwell wrote that ‡ "an European was till recently worshipped as a demon. From the rude verses which were sung in connection with his worship, it would appear that he was an English officer, who was mortally wounded at the taking of the Travancore lines in 1809, and was buried about twenty-five miles from the scene of the battle in a sandy waste, where, a few years ago, his worship was established by the Shānāns of the neighbourhood. His worship consisted in the offering to his manes of spirituous liquors and cheroots."

A similar form of worship, or propitiation of demons,

* "An Indian Olio," 79-80.

† "Gazetteer of the Nilgiris," 1908, i. 340.

‡ "The Tinnevelly Shānars," 1849.

is recorded* by Bishop Whitehead from Malabar. He was told that "the spirits of the old Portuguese soldiers and traders are still propitiated on the coast with offerings of toddy and cheroots. The spirits are called Kāppiri (probably Kaffirs or foreigners). This superstition is dying out, but is said to be common among the fishermen of the French settlement of Mai (Mahé)."

On one occasion, a man who had been presented with two annas as the fee for lending his body to me for measurement, offered it, with flowers and a cocoanut, at the shrine of the village goddess, and dedicated to her another coin of his own as a peace-offering, and to get rid of the pollution caused by my money.

* *Madras Dioc. Mag.*, March, 1903.

VI

CHARMS

MANTRAMS, or consecrated formulæ, are supposed to be very powerful, and by their aid even gods can be brought under control. They are, *inter alia*, believed to be efficacious in curing disease, in protecting children against devils, and women against miscarriage, in promoting development of the breasts, in bringing offspring to barren women, in warding off misfortune consequent on marriage with a girl who has an unlucky mark, in keeping wild pigs from the fields, and warding off cattle disease. For the last purpose, the magical formula is carved on a stone pillar, which is set up in the village. They are divided into four classes, viz., mantrasara, or the real essence of magic; yantrasara, or the science of cabalistic figures; prayogasara, or the method of using these for the attainment of any object; tantrasara, or the science of symbolical acts with or without words.

Mantrasara includes all mantrams, with their efficacy for good and evil, and the methods of learning and reciting them with the aid of a guru (spiritual preceptor). They are said to be effective only when the individual who resorts to them is pure in mind and body. This can be attained by the recitation of ajapagayithri (216,000 inhalations and exhalations in twenty-four hours). These have to be divided among the deities Ganēsa, Brahma, Vishnu, Rudra, Jīvathma, Paramathma, and the guru, in the proportion of 600, 6000, 6000, 6000, 1000, 1000, 1000. A man can only become learned in mantrams (mantravādi) by the regular performance of the recognised ceremonial, by proper recital of the mantrams, by burning the sacred fire, and by taking food. A Lambādi has been seen repeating mantrams over his patients, and touching their heads at the same time with a book, which was a small edition of the Telugu translation of St John's gospel. Neither the physician nor the patient could read, and had no idea of the contents of the book.* It is noted by the Abbé Dubois,† that one of the principal reasons why so little confidence is placed in European doctors by Hindus is that, when administering their remedies, they recite neither mantrams nor prayers.

Yantrasara includes all cabalistic figures, the method of drawing and using them, and the objects to be attained by them. They are usually drawn on thin plates of gold, silver, copper, or lead. The efficacy of the figures, when drawn on gold, will, it is said, last for a century, while those drawn on the less precious metals will only be effective for six months or a year. Leaden plates are used when the yantrams are to be buried underground. The figures should possess the symbols of life, the eyes, tongue, eight cardinal points of the compass, and the five elements.

Prayogasara includes attraction or summoning by enchantment, driving out evil spirits, stupefaction, tempting or bringing a deity or evil spirits under control, and enticement for love, destruction, and the separation of friends.

The following are examples of cases in which a

* Rev. J. Cain, "Ind. Ant.," 1879, viii. 219.

† "Hindu Manners, Customs, and Ceremonies,' translation by H. K. Beauchamp, 1897, i. 143.

European, who, having been trained by a guru, was well versed in the theory and practice of native magic, was called in to administer to Natives, who were under the spell of devils. In the first case, a Telugu girl, about seventeen years old, had been for some time possessed by her sister's husband, under whose influence she used to eat abnormal quantities of food, tear off her clothes, and use indecent language in a voice other than her own. When the European arrived in her room, the devil, speaking through the girl, threatened to kill her, or the European, or the individual who put it into her. Under the spell of a suitable mantram, the devil departed, and its return was prevented by the wearing of a yantram. The other case was that of a boy, who was possessed by a devil. He was found, on the occasion of the visit of the European, lying down in the courtyard of his house, clad in an ample loin-cloth, and with a high temperature. Suddenly, through some invisible agency, a corner of his loin-cloth caught fire, which was stamped out. It then caught fire in another place, and eventually was riddled with burnt holes. This was the way in which the devil manifested its influence, and sometimes the boy got burnt. A mantram was recited, with the result that the burning ceased, and the fever abated. An impromptu yantram was made out of vibhūti (sacred ashes), and tied round the boy's neck. A religious mendicant came along a short time afterwards, and treated the boy for some ordinary sickness not connected with the devil, but the medicine did him no good. Finding the yantram round his neck, the mendicant asserted that it was the cause of his failure, and ordered its removal. This the boy's relations refused to permit. But the holy man ripped it off. Whereon the boy instantly fell down comatose. In recording these two cases, I have reproduced my notes made on the occasion of an interview with the European.

Reference has been made (p. 180) to mantrams carved on stone pillars. The story of a stone slab at Rāyalcheruvu in the Anantapur district, known as the yantram rāyi or magic stone, is narrated by Mr Francis.*

"The charm consists of eighty-one squares, nine each way, within a border of tridents. Each square contains one or more Telugu letters, but these will not combine into any intelligible words. At the bottom of the stone are cut a lingam and two pairs of foot-prints. Some twelve years ago, it is said, the village suffered severely from cholera for three years in succession, and a Telugu mason, a foreigner who was in the village at the time, cut this charm on the stone to stop the disease. It was set up with much ceremony. The mason went round the village at night without a stitch of clothing on him, and with the entrails of a sheep hanging round his neck. Many cocoanuts were offered to the stone, and many sheep slain before it. The mason tossed a lamb in the air, caught it as it fell, tore its throat open with his teeth, and then bounded forward, and spat out the blood. More sheep and cocoanuts were offered, and then the slab was set up. The mason naturally demanded a substantial return for the benefit he had conferred on the inhabitants. When cholera now breaks out, the villagers subscribe together, and do *pūja* (worship) to the stone in accordance with directions left by him."

Of similar stones in the South Arcot district, Mr Francis writes as follows †:—

"In several villages in the west of the district are magical slabs, which are supposed to cure cholera and cattle disease. On them, surrounded by a border of trisulas

* "Gazetteer of the Anantapur District," 1905, i. 198.

† "Gazetteer of the South Arcot District," 1906, i. 93.

(the trident of Siva) are cut a series of little squares, in each of which is some Tamil letter. The villagers usually explain their existence by saying that, some forty years ago, an ascetic, whom they call the sangili (chain) sanyāsi from his predilection for wearing red-hot chains round his neck, came there when cholera and cattle disease were rife, and (for a consideration) put up these slabs to ward off his ills. He left directions that, when either disease reappeared, 108 pots of water were to be poured over the slab, 108 bilva (*Ægle Marmelos*) leaves tied to it and so on, and that men and animals were then to walk through the water which had been poured over it."

Mr Francis writes further* that "in many places, stone slabs may be seen set up in the outskirts of the villages, on what are said to be the old boundaries. These are thought to be able to ward off sickness, and other harm which threatens to enter the place, and are revered accordingly. Some are quite blank, others have letters cut on them, while others again bear the rude outline of a deity, and are accordingly given such names as Pidāri or Ellai Amman (the goddess of the boundary). To these last, periodical worship is often performed, but, in the case of the others, the attentions of the villagers are confined to an annual ceremony, whereat cocoanuts are broken, camphor is burnt, and a light is placed on the stone."

It was noted by Lieutenant R. F. Burton † that, in some hamlets, the Kotas of the Nīlgiris have set up curiously carved stones, which they consider sacred, and attribute to them the power of curing diseases, if the member affected is rubbed against them. At cross-roads in Bellary, odd geometric patterns may sometimes

* "Gazetteer of the South Arcot District," 1906, i. 92-3.

† "Goa and the Blue Mountains," 1851, 339.

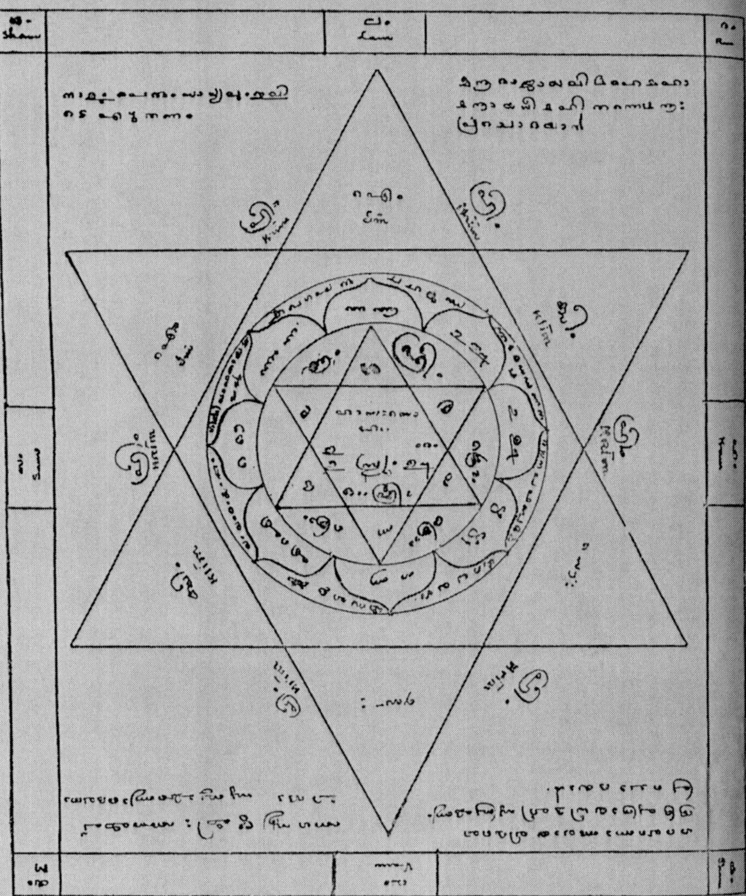

SUBRAMANIYA YANTRAM, MALABAR.

To face p. 185.

be noticed. These are put there at night by people suffering from disease, in the hope that the affliction will pass to the person who first treads on the charm.*

As examples of yantrams, the following, selected from a very large repertoire, may be cited :—

Ganapathi yantram should be drawn on metal, and worship performed. It is then enclosed in a metal cylinder, and tied by a thread round the neck of females, or the waist or arm of men. It will cure disease, conquer an enemy, or entice any one. If the sacred fire is kept up while the formula is being repeated, and dry cocoanut, plantain fruits, money, ghī (clarified butter), and sweet bread put into it, the owner will be blessed with wealth and prosperity.

Bhadrakāli yantram. The figure is drawn on the floor with flour or rice, turmeric, charcoal powder, and leaves of the castor-oil plant. If the deity is worshipped at night, it will lead to the acquisition of knowledge, strength, freedom from disease and impending calamities, wealth, and prosperity. If pūja (worship) is celebrated by a mantravādi for twelve days with the face turned towards the south, it will produce the death of an enemy.

Sudarsana yantram, when drawn on a sheet of metal, and enclosed in a cylinder worn round the neck or on the arm, will relieve those who are ill or possessed by devils. If it is drawn on butter spread on a plantain leaf, pūja performed, and the butter given to a barren woman, there will be no danger to herself or her future issue.

Suthakadosham yantram. Children under one year of age are supposed to be affected, if they are seen by a woman on the fourth day of menstruation with wet clothes and empty stomach after bathing. She may not even

* "Gazetteer of the Bellary District,' 1904, i. 60.

see her own baby or husband till she has changed her clothes, and taken food. To avert the evil, a waist-band, made of the bark of the arka plant (*Calotropis gigantea*), is worn.

Sarabha yantram will cure persons suffering from epilepsy or intermittent fever.

Subramaniya yantram, if regularly worshipped, will expel devils from those attacked by them, and from houses.

Hanumān yantram will protect those who are out on dark nights, and produce bodily strength and wisdom. If drawn on a sheet of gold, and pūja is performed to it every Saturday, it will bring prosperity, and help pregnant women during their confinement.

Pakshi yantram, if drawn on a sheet of lead, and kept in several places round a house, will keep snakes away.

Vatugabhairava yantram cures disease in those who are under eighteen years old, and drives out all kinds of evil spirits. If ashes are smeared on the face, and the mantram is uttered sixteen times, it will be very effective.

Varati yantram is very useful to any one who wishes to kill an enemy. He should sit in a retired spot at night, with his face turned towards the south, and repeat the mantram a thousand times for twenty days.

Prathingiri yantram is drawn on a sheet of lead, and buried at a spot over which a person, whose death is desired, will pass. It is then placed on the floor, on which the sacred fire is kindled. The mantram should be repeated eight hundred times for seven nights.

Chāmundi and Raktha Chāmundi yantrams are used for causing the death of enemies. The mantram should be written on a sheet of lead, and pūja, with the sacrifice of toddy and mutton, performed.

Asvārūda yantram enables a person wearing it to cover

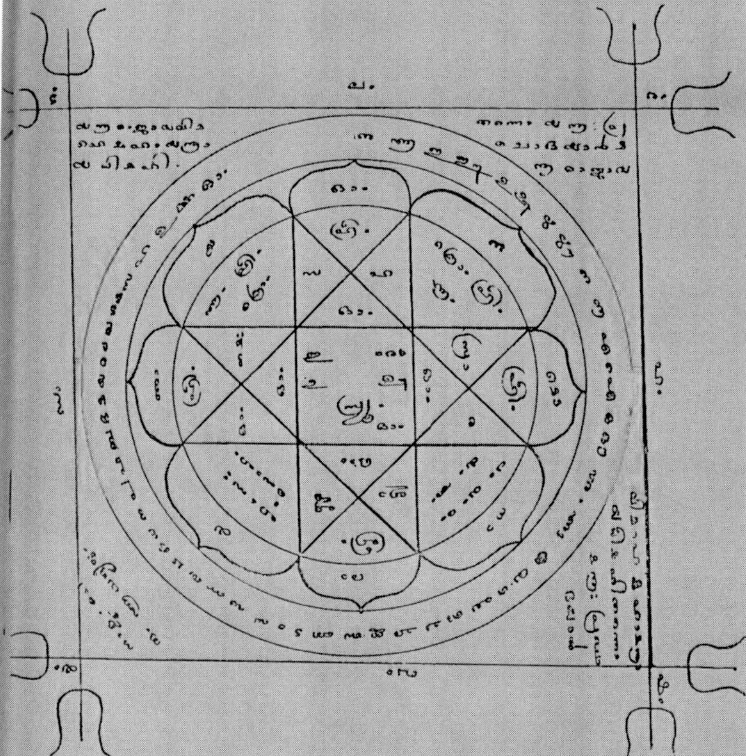

HANUMĀN YANTRAM, MALABAR.

To face p. 186.

long distances on horseback, and he can make the most refractory horse amenable by tying it round its neck.*

An inhabitant of Malabar presented Mr Fawcett with a yantram against the evil eye, which, if whispered over a piece of string, and tied round any part of the body affected, would work an instantaneous cure. A Cheruman at Calicut, who was wearing on his loin-string a copper cylinder containing a brass strip with mantrams, sold it to me for a rupee with the assurance that it would protect me from devils.

To produce an ulcer, which will cause the death of an enemy in ninety days, a mantram is written on a piece of cadjan (palm leaf), enclosed in an egg with a small quantity of earth on which he has urinated, and buried in an ant-hill. A fowl is killed, and its blood and some toddy are poured over the egg. To cure fever, the formula is written with the finger in water contained in a basin, and the appropriate words are repeated while the water is being drunk.

By some Muhammadans, on festival days, the names of holy persons, together with their sayings, are written on mango or palmyra leaves in ink made of charred rice. When the ink is dry, the leaves are washed in water, which is drunk. This is supposed to cure people of many obstinate diseases. A European official was informed by a Native magistrate in the Vizagapatam district that, when he wanted to tear up some old abkāri (liquor) licenses, a man implored him not to do so, as they had brought him life for a year, and were therefore worshipped. So the medicine was water, in which an old license had been dipped.

It is recorded† by Mr Logan that "in 1877, a poor Māppilla (Muhammadan) women residing in one of the Laccadive islands was put upon her trial for witchcraft

* F. Fawcett, *Madras Museum Bull.*, 1901, iii., No. 3, 307.

† "Malabar," 1887, i. 175.

for importing into the island a betel leaf with a certain cabalistic and magical inscription on it; but it fortunately turned out for her that she had merely pounded it up, and rubbed it over her daughter's body to cure her of fits. Ibn Batuta (the Arab traveller who visited South India in the fourteenth century) wrote of a Malayāli king who was converted to Islām by the leaf of 'the tree of testimony,' a tree of which it was related to him that it does not generally drop its leaves, but at the season of autumn in every year one of them changes its colour, first to yellow, then to red, and that upon this is written 'There is no God but God: Muhammad is the Prophet of God,' and that this leaf alone falls. The falling of the leaf was an annual event, and the leaf itself was efficacious in curing diseases. Nowadays the belief among the Muhammadans still subsists, that the leaves of a certain tree growing on Mount Deli (in Malabar) possess similar virtues."

Metal bowls, engraved both on the outside and inside with texts from the Qurān, are taken or sent by Muhammadans to Mecca, where they are placed at the head of the tomb of the Prophet, and blessed. They are highly valued, and used in cases of sickness for the administration of medicine or nourishment.

It is on record that, at the battle of Seringapatam in 1799, an officer took from off the right arm of the dead body of Tipu Sultān a talisman, which contained sewed up in pieces of fine flowered silk a charm made of a brittle metallic substance of the colour of silver, and some manuscripts in magic Arabic and Persian characters. A notorious Māppilla dacoit, who was shot by the police a few years ago, and whom his co-religionists tried to make a saint, was at the time of his death wearing five copper and silver charm cylinders round his waist.

It is noted by Mr Logan* that "when affliction comes, the animal affected is served with grass, fruit, etc., on which charms have been whispered, or is bathed in charmed water, or has a talisman in the shape of a palm leaf inscribed with charms rolled up and tied round its neck."

The tooth or claw of a tiger, worn on the neck or round the loins, is considered effective against evil influences. A tiger's whiskers are held to be a most potent poison when chopped up; so, when a tiger is killed, the whiskers are immediately singed off.† They are represented in stuffed heads by the delicate bristles of the porcupine. When a Savara of Ganjam is killed by a tiger, the Kudang goes through a performance on the following Sunday to prevent a similar fate overtaking others. Two pigs are killed outside the village, and every man, woman, and child is made to walk over the ground whereon the pig's blood is spilled, and the Kudang gives to each individual some kind of tiger medicine as a charm.‡

In Malabar the tusks of a wild boar are, in cases of protracted labour, pressed over the abdomen of the woman from above downwards.

The hair of the bear is enclosed in a casket or cylinder, and tied to the girdle round the loins of male children, and in strings round the neck of female children, as a remedy against fever, and to prevent involuntary discharge of urine during sleep.§

One of the occupations of the Kuruvikkārans (bird-catchers and beggars) is the manufacture and sale of

* "Malabar," 1887, i. 175.

† M. J. Walhouse, "Ind. Ant.," 1876, v. 23.

‡ F. Fawcett, *Journ. Anthrop. Soc., Bombay*, i. 260.

§ "Manual of the Kurnool District," 1886, 116.

spurious jackal horns, known as narikompu. To catch the jackals they make an enclosure of a net, inside which a man seats himself armed with a big stick. He then proceeds to execute a perfect imitation of the jackal's cry, on hearing which the jackals come running to see what is the matter, and are beaten down. Sometimes the entire jackal's head is sold, skin and all. The process of manufacture of the horn is as follows. After the brain has been removed, the skin is stripped off a limited area of the skull, and the bone at the place of junction of the sagittal and lambdoid sutures above the occipital foramen is filed away, so that only a point, like a bony outgrowth, is left. The skin is then brought back, and pressed over the little horn which pierces it. The horn is also said to be made out of the molar tooth of a dog or jackal, introduced through a small hole in a piece of jackal's skin, round which a little blood or turmeric paste is smeared to make it look more natural. In most cases only the horn, with a small piece of skull and skin, is sold. Sometimes, instead of the skin from the part where the horn is made, a piece of skin is taken from the snout, where the long black hairs are. The horn then appears surrounded by long black bushy hairs. The Kuruvikkārans explain that, when they see a jackal with such long hairs on the top of its head, they know that it possesses a horn. A horn-vendor, whom I interviewed, assured me that the possessor of a horn is a small jackal, which comes out of its hiding-place on full-moon nights to drink the dew. According to another version, the horn is only possessed by the leader of a pack of jackals. A nomad Dommara, whom I saw at Coimbatore, carried a bag containing a miscellaneous assortment of rubbish used in his capacity as medicine-man and snake-charmer, which included a collection of spurious jackal horns. To prove the genuineness thereof, he showed me not only the horn, but also the feet with nails complete, as evidence that the horns were not made from the nails. Being charged with manufacturing the horns, he swore, by placing his hand on the head of a child who accompanied him, that he was not deceiving me. The largest of the horns in his bag, he gravely assured me, was from a jackal which he dug out of its hole on the last new-moon night. The Sinhalese and Tamils regard the horn as a talisman, and believe that its fortunate possessor can command the realisation of every wish. Those who have jewels to conceal rest in perfect security if, along with them, they can deposit a narikompu.* The ayah (nurse) of a friend who possessed such a talisman, remarked : "Master going into any law-court, sure to win the case." Two horns, which I possessed, were stolen from my study table, to bring luck to some Tamil member of my establishment.

The nasal bone of a jackal or fox, enclosed in a receptacle, is believed to ward off many evils. The nose of a hyæna is also held in great estimation as a charm. When a hyæna is killed, the end of the nose is cut off and dried, and is supposed to be a sovereign charm in cases of difficult labour, indigestion, and boils, if applied to the nostrils of the patient.†

In Malabar, silver finger-rings with a piece of bristle from the tail of an elephant set in them, are worn as a charm.

In the Vizagapatam district, a most efficacious charm, supposed to render a man invulnerable to every ill, consists of a small piece of black wool, given to every one who takes a black sheep for the priest of a temple on the Bopelli ghāt. Another much valued charm in this

* Tennent, "Ceylon," 1860, i. 145.

† "Manual of the Cuddapah District," 1875, 292.

district is called chemru mausa, which is described as being a small musk-rat only an inch and a half long, very scarce, and only found on rocky hills. It is worn in a gold or silver receptacle on the arm, and is supposed to render a man invulnerable against sword cuts and musket shots. In like manner, a mixture of gingelly (*Sesamum*) oil, the red dye which women use, and other ingredients, put into a small piece of hollow bamboo, and worn on the arm, are believed to protect a man against being shot with a bow or musket.

Many of the Kādir infants on the Ānaimalai hills have tied round the neck a charm, which takes the form of a dried tortoise foot; the tooth of a crocodile mimicking a phallus, and supposed to ward off attacks from a mythical water elephant which lives in the mountain streams, or wooden imitations of tiger's claws.

The joints taken from the tail of the black scorpion are believed to ward off illness, if children wear them on their waist-thread.*

Of charms worn by the Nambūtiri Brāhmans in Malabar, the following are recorded by Mr F. Fawcett †:—

Ring, in which an ānavarāhan coin is set. This is a very lucky ring. Spurious imitations are often set in rings, but it is the genuine one which brings good luck.

Gold case fastened to a string round the waist, and containing a figure written on a silver plate. The man had worn it for three years, having put it on because he used to feel hot during the cold season, and attributed his condition to the influence of an evil spirit.

Two cylinders, one of gold, the other of silver. In each were some chakrams (Travancore silver coins) and a gold leaf, on which a charm was inscribed. One of

* *Madras Mail*, 26th January, 1906.

† *Madras Museum Bull.*, 1900, iii., No. 1, 41.

the charms was prepared by a Māppilla, the other by a Nambūtiri.

In connection with the wearing of charms by the Nāyars of Malabar, Mr Fawcett writes * as follows:—

"One individual wore two rings made of an amalgamation of gold and copper, called tambāk on the ring-finger of the right hand for good luck. Tambāk rings are lucky rings. It is a good thing to wash the face with the hand, on which is a tambāk ring. Another wore two rings of the pattern called trilōham on the ring-finger of each hand. Each of these was made during an eclipse. An Akattu Charna Nāyar wore an amulet, to keep off the spirit of a Brāhman who died by drowning."

As examples of charms worn by Bēdar men in the Canarese country, the following may be cited:—

String tied round right arm with metal box attached to it, to drive away devils. String round ankle for the same purpose.

Necklet of coral and ivory beads worn as a vow to the goddess Huligamma.

Necklets of ivory beads, and a gold disc with the Vishnupād (feet of Vishnu) engraved on it, purchased from a religious mendicant to bring good luck.

In an account of the Mandulas (medicine-men) of the Telugu country, Bishop Whitehead records † that a baby three days old had an anklet made of its mother's hair tied round the right ankle, to keep off the evil eye. The mother, too, had round her ankle a similar anklet, which she put on before her confinement. One of the men was also wearing an anklet of hair, as he had recently been bitten by a snake.

A metal charm-cylinder is sometimes attached to the

* *Madras Museum Bull.*, 1901, iii., No. 3, 195-6.

† *Madras Dioc. Mag.*, July, 1905.

sacred thread, which is worn by Dēvāngas (a weaving caste), who claim to be Dēvānga Brāhmans.

I have seen the child of a Kuruba (Canarese agriculturist) priest wearing a necklet with a copper ornament engraved with cabalistic devices, a silver plate bearing a figure of Hanumān (the monkey god), as all his other children had died, and a piece of pierced pottery from the burial-ground, to ward off whooping-cough. The Rev. S. Nicholson informs me that, if a Māla (Telugu Pariah) child grinds its teeth in its sleep, a piece of a broken pot is brought from a graveyard, and, after being smoked with incense, tied round the child's neck with a piece of string rubbed with turmeric, or with a piece of gut. In the Tamil country, the bark of a tree on which any one has hanged himself, a cord with twenty-one knots, and the earth from a child's grave, are hung round the neck, or tied to the waist-string as talismans.

A Kota woman at Kotagiri on the Nīlgiris, was wearing a glass necklet, with a charm pendant from it, consisting of the root of some tree rolled up in a ball of cloth. She put it on when her baby was quite young, to protect it against devils. The baby had a similar charm on its neck. By some jungle Chenchus pieces of stick strung on a thread, or seeds of *Givotia rottleriformis* are worn, to ward off various forms of pain.

Small flat plates of copper, called takudu, are frequently worn by Tamil Paraiyan children. One side is divided into sixteen squares in which what look like the Telugu numerals nine, ten, eleven and twelve, are engraved. On the other side a circle is drawn, which is divided into eight segments, in each of which a Telugu letter is inscribed. This charm is supposed to protect the wearer from harm coming from any of the eight cardinal points of the Indian compass. Charms, in the form of metal cylinders, are worn for the same purpose by adults and children, and procured from some exorcist.*

By some Mēdaras of the Telugu country, a figure of Hanumān (the monkey god) is engraved on a thin plate of gold with cabalistic letters inscribed on it, and worn on the neck. On eclipse days, a piece of root of the arka plant (*Calotropis gigantea*) is worn on the neck of females, and on the waist or arm of males.

In a note regarding moon-shaped amulets against the evil eye described by Professor Tylor,† Mr Walhouse mentions that crescents, made of thin plates of metal, sometimes gold, are worn by children on the west coast, suspended upon the breast with the point upwards. Neck ornaments in the form of a crescent are commonly worn by Muhammadan children.

Concerning the use of coins as charms, Mr V. Devasahayam writes as follows ‡ :—

"Seeing a woman with several old coins strung on the tāli (marriage badge) string round the neck, I offered to buy them of her for a good price, but got only a torrent of abuse, since she, in her ignorance and superstition, supposed that Lutchmi, the goddess of fortune, would forsake her if she parted with the coins. In Tranquebar there lives a head mason, who always carries in his betel-nut bag a copper coin bearing the inscription of Konēri Rāyan, one of the later Pāndyans or early Nāyakars. The man would on no account part with this coin, for he believes that his success in business has improved since he came into possession of it, and that it will continue as long as he carries it with him. He says that he shall bequeath it to his family at his death, to hold in veneration almost amounting to worship. For

* Rev. A. C. Clayton, *Madras Museum Bull.*, 1906, v., No. 2, 86.

† *Journ. Anthrop. Inst.*, 1890, xix., 56.

‡ *Madras Christian Coll. Mag.*, January, 1907, vi. No. 7.

dog bite, some Natives tie an old copper coin with a bandage over the wound, and wear it till it has healed. Others rub the coin against a copper vessel, using a few drops of the juice of the datura plant in order to form a paste, and apply the paste to the wound. Whooping-cough is believed to be caused by the displeasure of Bhairava, the dog-god, and the whooping is regarded as a sort of barking, under possession by the god. To appease his anger, an old coin is hammered into a flat round disc, a rude figure of a dog engraved on it, and suspended as a charm to the sick child's waist. In the treatment of skin disease, dyspepsia, and leprosy, old copper coins are ground to dust, heated till the dust is like ashes, and administered medicinally. Soon after a Sonaga woman is delivered of a child, she is made to swallow a small old copper coin together with some water. Natives believe that, during delivery, the whole system is so irritated that strong counter-irritants must be administered to prevent tetanus."

Mercury cups, said to be made of an amalgam of mercury and tin, are stated to possess the property of allowing mercury, when poured in, to ooze through them, and pass out. Milk preserved in such a cup for a few hours is said to turn into hard curd. Milk kept over night in one of these cups, or an amulet made from the cup materials, are believed to exercise a most potent influence over the male fertilising element. Such an amulet, applied to the neck of a chorister, is said to have increased his vocal powers three or four times. Piles, and other bodily ailments, are believed to be cured by wearing rings, in the composition of which mercury is one of the ingredients.

In a case which was tried before a magistrate in Travancore, the accused, in order to win his case, had concealed in his under-cloth some yantrams, which had been prepared for him by a sorcerer. The plaintiff, having got scent of this, gave information, and the charms were handed over to the magistrate. It is recorded in the Vigada Thūthan that, when a woman who gets tired of her husband sues him for maintenance, she wears charm bundles (manthira kattu), so that his evidence may be confused and incoherent. Such charms are said to be concealed in the hair of the head or in the headdress, and generally to consist of a lime fruit, which has been charmed by magical spells in a graveyard, after the sorcerer has performed certain ceremonies to guard him against devils catching him during the incantations. It is said that, in former times, if the chastity of a Tamil Paraiyan bride was suspected, she had to establish her virtue by picking some cakes out of boiling oil, and then husking some rice with her bare hand. Her hair, nails, and clothes were examined, to see that she had no charm concealed about her.*

A friend once dismissed a servant for cheating and lying. A short time afterwards, he found nailed to a teapoy a paper scroll containing a jasmine flower tied up with coloured threads. On the scroll were inscribed in Tamil the mystic syllable, "Om," and "Nāma Sīva R. U. Masthān Sāhibu avergal pādame thunai" (I seek for help at the feet of Masthān sāhib). Masthān is a Muhammad saint. The servant of a European police officer, who had been caught out in all sorts of malpractices, tried to win back the good-will of his master by means of a charm, for which he paid fifteen rupees, placed under his master's pillow.

It is recorded by Marco Polo † that South Indian

* Rev. A. C. Clayton, *Madras Museum Bull.*, 1906, v., No. 2, 66.

† "The Book of Ser Marco Polo, the Venetian," translation, 3rd ed., 1903, ii. 332.

pearl divers * call in the services of an Abraiman (Brāhman ?) to charm the sharks. "And their charm holds good for that day only; for at night they dissolve the charm, so that the fishes can work mischief at their will." The prospects of a pearl fishery, when success seems certain, may be abruptly ruined by accidents from sharks, of which the divers have a superstitious, but not altogether unreasonable, dread. Before the fishery of 1889, at which I was present, the divers of Kilakarai on the Madura coast, as a preliminary to starting for the scene thereof, performed a ceremony, at which prayers were offered for protection against the attacks of sharks.

"The only precaution," Tennent writes,† "to which the Ceylon diver devotedly resorts is the mystic ceremony of the shark-charmer, whose power is believed to be hereditary. Nor is it supposed that the value of his incantations is at all dependent upon the religious faith professed by the operator, for the present head of the family happens to be a Roman Catholic. At the time of our visit, this mysterious functionary was ill, and unable to attend; but he sent an accredited substitute, who assured me that, although he was himself ignorant of the grand and mystic secret, the fact of his presence, as a representative of the higher authority, would be recognised and respected by the sharks."

At the Tuticorin fishery in 1890, a scare was produced by a diver being bitten by a shark, but subsided as soon as a "wise woman" was employed. Her powers do not, however, seem to have been great, for more cases of shark-bite occurred, and the fishery had to be abandoned at a time when favourable breezes, clear water, plenty of boats, and oysters selling at a good price, indicated a successful financial result.

* The pearl fisheries are conducted from Tuticorin in the Tinnevelly district.

† "Ceylon," 1860, ii. 564-5.

VII

HUMAN SACRIFICE

"THE best known case," Mr Frazer writes,* "of human sacrifices systematically offered to ensure good crops, is supplied by the Khonds or Kandhs, a Dravidian race in Bengal and Madras. Our knowledge of them is derived from the accounts written by British officers, who, forty or fifty years ago, were engaged in putting them down. The sacrifices were offered to the earth goddess, Tari Pennu or Bera Pennu, and were believed to ensure good crops, and immunity from all diseases and accidents. In particular, they were considered necessary in the cultivation of turmeric, the Khonds arguing that the turmeric could not have a deep red colour without the shedding of blood. The victim, a Meriah, was acceptable to the goddess only if he had been purchased, or had been born a victim, that is, the son of a victim father, or had been devoted as a child by his father or guardian."

In 1837, Mr Russell, in a report on the districts entrusted to his control, wrote as follows †:—

"The ceremonies attending the barbarous rite (Kondh human sacrifice) vary in different parts of the country. In the Māliahs of Goomsur, the sacrifice is offered annually to Thadha Pennoo, under the effigy of a bird intended to

* "The Golden Bough," 1900, ii. 241 *et seq.* Bibliography of human sacrifice among the Kondhs, *see* Thurston, "Castes and Tribes of Southern India," 1909, iii. 412-5.

† "Selections from the Records of the Government of India," No. v., Suppression of human sacrifice and infanticide, 1854. The subject of Meriah sacrifice is also dealt with by F. E. Penny, in her novel entitled "Sacrifice," 1910.

represent a peacock, with the view of propitiating the deity to grant favourable seasons and crops. The ceremony is performed at the expense of, and in rotation, by certain mootahs (districts) composing a community, and connected together from local circumstances. Besides these periodical sacrifices, others are made by single mootahs, and even by individuals, to avert any threatening calamity from sickness, murrain, or other causes. Grown men are the most esteemed (as victims), because the most costly. Children are purchased, and reared for years with the family of the person who ultimately devotes them to a cruel death, when circumstances are supposed to demand a sacrifice at his hands. They seem to be treated with kindness, and, if young, are kept under no constraint; but, when old enough to be sensible of the fate that awaits them, they are placed in fetters, and guarded. Most of those who were rescued had been sold by their parents or nearest relations, a practice which, from all we could learn, is very common. Persons of riper age are kidnapped by wretches who trade in human flesh. The victim must always be purchased. Criminals, or prisoners captured in war, are not considered fitting subjects. The price is paid indifferently in brass utensils, cattle, or coin. The zanee (or priest), who may be of any caste, officiates at the sacrifice, but he performs the poojah (offering of flowers, incense, etc.) to the idol through the medium of the Toomba, who must be a Khond child under seven years of age. This child is fed and clothed at the public expense, eats with no other person, and is subjected to no act deemed impure. For a month prior to the sacrifice, there is much feasting and intoxication, and dancing round the Meriah, who is adorned with garlands, etc., and, on the day before the performance of the barbarous rite, is stupefied with toddy, and made to sit, or, if necessary, is bound at the bottom of a post bearing the effigy above described. The assembled multitude then dance around to music, and, addressing the earth, say 'Oh! God, we offer the sacrifice to you. Give us good crops, seasons, and health.' After which they address the victim. 'We bought you with a price, and did not seize you. Now we sacrifice you according to custom, and no sin rests with us.' On the following day, the victim being again intoxicated, and anointed with oil, each individual present touches the anointed part, and wipes the oil on his own head. All then proceed in procession around the village and its boundaries, preceded by music, bearing the victim and a pole, to the top of which is attached a tuft of peacock's feathers. On returning to the post, which is always placed near the village deity called Zakaree Pennoo, and represented by three stones, near which the brass effigy in the shape of the peacock is buried, they kill a pig in sacrifice, and, having allowed the blood to flow into a pit prepared for the purpose, the victim who, if it has been found possible, has been previously made senseless from intoxication, is seized and thrown in, and his face pressed down until he is suffocated in the bloody mire amid the noise of instruments. The Zanee then cuts a piece of the flesh from the body, and buries it with ceremony near the effigy and village idol, as an offering to the earth. All the rest afterwards go through the same form, and carry the bloody prize to their villages, where the same rites are performed, part being interred near the village idol, and little bits on the boundaries. The head and face remain untouched, and the bones, when bare, are buried with them in the pit. After this horrid ceremony has been completed, a buffalo calf is brought in front of the post, and, his forefeet having been cut off, is left there till the following day. Women, dressed in male attire, and armed as men, then drink, dance, and sing round the spot, the calf is killed and eaten, and the Zanee is dismissed with a present of rice, and a hog or calf."

In the same year, Mr Arbuthnot, Collector of Vizagapatam, reported as follows:—

"Of the hill tribe Codooloo (Kondh), there are said to be two distinct classes, the Cotia Codooloo and Jathapoo

Codooloo. The former class is that which is in the habit of offering human sacrifices to the god called Jenkery, with a view to secure good crops. This ceremony is generally performed on the Sunday preceding or following the Pongal feast. The victim is seldom carried by force, but procured by purchase, and there is a fixed price for each person, which consists of forty articles such as a bullock, a male buffalo, a cow, a goat, a piece of cloth, a silk cloth, a brass pot, a large plate, a bunch of plantains, etc. The man who is destined for the sacrifice is immediately carried before the god, and a small quantity of rice coloured with saffron (turmeric) is put upon his head. The influence of this is said to prevent his attempting to escape, even though set at liberty. It would appear, however, that, from the moment of his seizure till he is sacrificed, he is kept in a continued state of stupefaction or intoxication. He is allowed to wander about the village, to eat and drink anything he may take a fancy to, and even to have connection with any of the women whom he may meet. On the morning set apart for the sacrifice, he is carried before the idol in a state of intoxication. One of the villagers officiates as priest, who cuts a small hole in the stomach of the victim, and with the blood that flows from the wound the idol is besmeared. Then the crowds from the neighbouring villages rush forward, and he is literally cut into pieces. Each person who is so fortunate as to procure it carries away a morsel of the flesh, and presents it to the idol of his own village."

Concerning a method of Kondh sacrifice, which is illustrated by the wooden post preserved in the Madras Museum, Colonel Campbell records* that "one of the most common ways of offering the sacrifice in Chinna Kimedi is to the effigy of an elephant (hatti mundo or elephant's head) rudely carved in wood, fixed on the top

* "Personal Narrative of Service among the Wild Tribes of Khondistan," 1864.

MERIAH SACRIFICE POST.
(*Halli mundo.*)

To face p. 202.

of a stout post, on which it is made to revolve. After the performance of the usual ceremonies, the intended victim is fastened to the proboscis of the elephant, and, amidst the shouts and yells of the excited multitude of Khonds, is rapidly whirled round, when, at a given signal by the officiating Zanee or priest, the crowd rush in, seize the Meriah, and with their knives cut the flesh off the shrieking wretch so long as life remains. He is then cut down, the skeleton burnt, and the horrid orgies are over. In several villages I counted as many as fourteen effigies of elephants, which had been used in former sacrifices. These I caused to be overthrown by the baggage elephants attached to my camp in the presence of the assembled Khonds, to show them that these venerated objects had no power against the living animal, and to remove all vestiges of their bloody superstition."

It is noted by Risley * that, while the crowd hacked the body of the victim, they chanted a ghastly hymn, an extract from which illustrates very clearly the theory of sympathetic magic underlying the ritual :—

> "As the tears stream from thine eyes,
> So may the rain pour down in August;
> As the mucus trickles from thy nostrils,
> So may it drizzle at intervals;
> As thy blood gushes forth,
> So may the vegetation sprout;
> As thy gore falls in drops,
> So may the grains of rice form."

In another report, Colonel Campbell describes how the miserable victim is dragged along the fields, surrounded by a crowd of half intoxicated Kondhs who, shouting and screaming, rush upon him, and with their knives cut the flesh piecemeal from the bones, avoiding the head and

* "The People of India," 1908, 62.

bowels, till the living skeleton, dying from loss of blood, is relieved from torture, when its remains are burnt, and the ashes mixed with the new grain to preserve it from insects. Yet again, he describes a sacrifice which was peculiar to the Kondhs of Jeypore.

"It is," he says, "always succeeded by the sacrifice of three human beings, two to the sun in the east and west of the village, and one in the centre, with the usual barbarities of the Meriah. A stout wooden post about six feet long is firmly fixed in the ground, at the foot of it a narrow grave is dug, and to the top of the post the victim is firmly fastened by the long hair of his head. Four assistants hold his outstretched arms and legs, the body being suspended horizontally over the grave, with the face toward the earth. The officiating Junna or priest, standing on the right side, repeats the following invocation, at intervals hacking with his sacrificing knife the back part of the shrieking victim's neck. 'Oh! mighty Manicksoro, this is your festal day. To the Khonds the offering is Meriah, to the kings Junna. On account of this sacrifice, you have given to kings kingdoms, guns, and swords. The sacrifice we now offer you must eat, and we pray that our battle-axes may be converted into swords, our bows and arrows into gunpowder and balls; and, if we have any quarrels with other tribes, give us the victory. Preserve us from the tyranny of kings and their officers.' Then, addressing the victim, 'That we may enjoy prosperity, we offer you as a sacrifice to our god Manicksoro, who will immediately eat you, so be not grieved at our slaying you. Your parents were aware, when we purchased you from them for sixty rupees, that we did so with intent to sacrifice you. There is, therefore, no sin on our heads, but on your parents. After you are dead, we shall perform your obsequies.' The victim is then decapitated, the body thrown into the grave, and the head left suspended from the post till devoured by wild beasts. The knife remains fastened to the post till the three sacrifices have been performed, when it is removed with much ceremony."

The Kondhs of Bara Mootah promised to relinquish the Meriah rite on condition, *inter alia*, that they should be at liberty to sacrifice buffaloes, monkeys, goats, etc., to their deities, with all the solemnities observed on occasions of human sacrifice; and that they should further be at liberty, upon all occasions, to denounce to their gods the Government, and some of its servants in particular, as the cause of their having relinquished the great rite. The last recorded Meriah sacrifice in the Ganjam Māliahs occurred in 1852, and there are still Kondhs alive, who were present at it. The veteran members of a party of Kondhs, who were brought to Madras for the purpose of performing their dances before the Prince and Princess of Wales in 1906, became widely excited when they came across the relic of their barbarous custom at the museum. Twenty-five descendants of persons who were rescued by Government officers, returned themselves as Meriah at the census, 1901.

It is noted by Mr W. Francis that* "goats and buffaloes nowadays take the place of human meriah victims, but the belief in the superior efficacy of the latter dies hard, and every now and again revives. When the Rampa rebellion of 1879-80 spread in this district, several cases of human sacrifice occurred in the disturbed tracts. In 1880, two persons were convicted of attempting a meriah sacrifice near Ambadāla in Bissamkatak. In 1883, a man (a beggar and a stranger) was found at daybreak murdered in one of the temples in Jeypore in circumstances which pointed to his having been slain as a meriah; and, as late as 1886, a formal enquiry

* "Gazetteer of the Vizagapatam District," 1907, i. 202.

showed that there were ample grounds for the suspicion that the kidnapping of victims still went on in Bastar."

Even so recently as 1902, a European magistrate in Ganjam received a petition, asking for permission to perform a human sacrifice, which was intended to give a rich colour to the turmeric crop.

The flowers with which the sheep and goats which take the place of human beings are decorated are still known as meriah pushpa in Jeypore.*

In an account † of a substituted sacrifice, which was carried out by the Kondhs in the Ganjam Māliahs in 1894, it is stated that, "the Janni gave the buffalo a tap on the head with a small axe. An indescribable scene followed. The Khonds in a body fell on the animal, and, in an amazingly short time, literally tore the living victim to shreds with their knives, leaving nothing but the head, bones, and stomach. Death must mercifully have been almost instantaneous. Every particle of flesh and skin had been stripped off during the few minutes they fought and struggled over the buffalo, eagerly grasping for every atom of flesh. As soon as a man had secured a piece thereof, he rushed away with the gory mass, as fast as he could, to his fields, to bury it therein according to ancient custom, before the sun had set. As some of them had to do good distances to effect this, it was imperative that they should run very fast. A curious scene now took place. As the men ran, all the women flung after them clods of earth, some of them taking very good effect. The sacred grove was cleared of people, save a few that guarded the remnants left of the buffalo, which were taken, and burnt with ceremony at the foot of the stake."

* "Gazetteer of the Vizagapatam District," 1907, i. 262-3.

† *Madras Weekly Mail*, 6th June, 1894.

The buffalo sacrifice is not unaccompanied by risk, as the animal, before dying, sometimes kills one or more of its tormentors. This was the case near Balliguda in 1899, when a buffalo killed the sacrificer. In the previous year, the desire of a village to intercept the bearer of the flesh from a neighbouring village led to a fight, in which two men were killed.

Like the Kondhs, the Koyis of the Godāvari district believe in the efficacy of a sacrifice, to ensure good crops. In this connection, the Rev. J. Cain writes * that "the Koyi goddess Māmili or Lēle must be propitiated early in the year, or else the crops will undoubtedly fail; and she is said to be very partial to human victims. There is strong reason to think that two men were murdered this year (1876) near a village not far from Dummagudem as offerings to this dēvata, and there is no reason to doubt that every year strangers are quietly put out of the way in the Bastar country, to ensure the favour of the bloodthirsty goddess."

Mr Cain writes further † that a langur monkey is now substituted for the human victim under the name of erukomma potu or male with small breasts, in the hope of persuading the goddess that she is receiving a human sacrifice.

On the site of the old fort at Rāmagiri in the Vizagapatam district, a victim was formerly sacrificed every third year.

"The poor wretch was forced into a hole in the ground, three feet deep and eighteen inches square, at the bottom of which the goddess was supposed to dwell, his throat was cut, and the blood allowed to flow into the hole, and afterwards his head was struck off and placed on

* "Ind. Ant.," 1876, v. 359.

† *Madras Christian Coll. Mag.*, 1887-88, v. 357.

his lap, and the mutilated body covered with earth and a mound of stones until the time for the next sacrifice came round, when the bones were taken out and thrown away. At Malkanagiri, periodical sacrifices occurred at the four gates of the fort, and the Rāni had a victim slain as a thank-offering for her recovery from an illness." *

The nomad Koravas are said to have formerly performed human sacrifices, one effect of which was to increase the fertility of the soil. The following account of such a sacrifice was given to Mr C. Hayavadana Rao by an old inhabitant of the village of Asūr near Walajabad in the Chingleput district. A big gang of Koravas settled at the meeting point of three villages of Asūr, Mēlputtūr, and Avalūr, on an elevated spot commanding the surrounding country. They had with them their pack-bullocks, each headman of the gang owning about two hundred head. The cow-dung which accumulated daily attracted a good many of the villagers, on one of whom the headman fixed as their intended victim. They made themselves intimate with him, plied him with drink and tobacco, and gave him the monopoly of the cow-dung. Thus a week or ten days passed away, and the Koravas then fixed a day for the sacrifice. They invited the victim to visit them at dusk, and witness a great festival in honour of their caste goddess. At the appointed hour, the man went to the settlement, and was induced to drink freely. Meanwhile, a pit, large enough for a man to stand upright in, had been prepared. At about midnight, the victim was seized, and forced to stand in the pit, which was filled in up to his neck. This done, the women and children of the gang made off with their belongings. As soon as the last of them had quitted the settlement, the

* "Gazetteer of the Vizagapatam District," 1907, i. 202.

headmen brought a large quantity of fresh cow-dung, and placed a ball of it on the head of the victim. The ball served as a support for an earthen lamp, which was lighted. The man was by this time nearly dead, and the cattle were made to pass over his head. The headmen then made off, and, by daybreak, the whole gang had disappeared. The sacrificed man was found by the villagers, who have, since that time, scrupulously avoided the Koravas. The victim is said to have turned into a Munisvara, and for a long time troubled those who happened to go near the spot at noon or midnight. The Koravas are said to have performed the sacrifice, so as to insure their cattle against death from disease. The ground, on which they encamped, and on which they offered the human sacrifice, is stated to have been barren prior thereto, and, as the result thereof, to have become very fertile.

A similar form of human sacrifice was practised in former days by the nomad Lambādis, concerning which the Abbé Dubois writes as follows * :—

"When they wish to perform this horrible act, it is said, they secretly carry off the first person they meet. Having conducted the victim to some lonely spot, they dig a hole, in which they bury him up to the neck. While he is still alive, they make a sort of lamp of dough made of flour, which they place on his head. This they fill with oil, and light four wicks in it. Having done this, the men and women join hands, and, forming a circle, dance round their victim, singing and making a great noise, till he expires."

It is recorded by the Rev. J. Cain † that the Lambādis

* "Hindu Manners, Customs, and Ceremonies," translation by H. K. Beauchamp, 1897, i. 70-1.

† "Ind. Ant.," 1879, viii. 219.

confessed that, in former days, it was the custom among them, before starting out on a journey, to procure a little child, and bury it in the ground up to the shoulders, and then drive their loaded bullocks over the unfortunate victim. In proportion to their thoroughly trampling the child to death, so their belief in a successful journey increased. I am informed by the Rev. G. N. Thomssen that, at the present day, the Lambādis sacrifice a goat or chicken, in case of removal from one part of the jungle to another, when sickness has come. They hope to escape death by leaving one camping ground for another. Half-way between the old and new grounds, the animal selected is buried alive, the head being allowed to be above ground. Then all the cattle are driven over the buried creature, and the whole camp walk over the buried victim.

In the course of an interview with Colonel Marshall on the subject of infanticide * among the Todas of the Nīlgiri hills, an aged man of the tribe remarked that † "those tell lies who say that we laid the child down before the opening of the buffalo-pen, so that it might be run over and killed by the animals. We never did such things, and it is all nonsense that we drowned it in buffaloes' milk. Boys were never killed—only girls; not those who were sickly and deformed—that would be a sin; but, when we had one girl, or in some families two girls, those that followed were killed. An old woman used to take the child immediately after it was born, and close its nostrils, ears, and mouth with a cloth. It would shortly droop its head and go to sleep. We then buried it in the ground."

The old man's remark about the cattle-pen refers to the Malagasy custom of placing a new-born child at the

* Infanticide, *see* Thurston, "Ethnographic Notes in Southern India," 1907, 502-9.

† Marshall, "A Phrenologist amongst the Todas," 1873, 195.

entrance to a cattle-pen, and then driving the cattle over it, to see whether they would trample on it or not.*

It is recorded by Bishop Whitehead,† in a note on offerings and sacrifices in the Telugu country, that "sometimes, when there is a cattle disease, a pig is buried up to its neck at the boundary of the village, a heap of boiled rice is deposited near the spot, and then all the cattle of the village are driven over the head of the unhappy pig. . . . When I was on tour in the Kurnool district, an old man described to me the account he had received from his 'forefathers' of the ceremonies observed when founding a new village. An auspicious site is selected on an auspicious day, and then, in the centre of the site, is dug a large hole, in which are placed different kinds of grains, small pieces of the five metals, and a large stone called boddu-rayée (navel-stone), standing about three and a half feet above the ground, very like the ordinary boundary stones seen in the fields. Then, at the entrance of the village, in the centre of the main street, where most of the cattle pass in and out on their way to and from the fields, they dig another hole, and bury a pig alive."

It is suggested by Bishop Whitehead that the custom of thus burying a pig may be connected with the worship of an agricultural goddess, or a survival of a former custom of infanticide or human sacrifice, such as prevailed among the Lambādis.

It has been suggested that certain rites performed by the Pānan and Malayan exorcists of Malabar are survivals, or imitations of human sacrifice. Thus, in the Ucchavēli ceremony of the Pānans for driving out devils, there is a mock burial of the principal performer, who is placed in

* Ellis, "History of Madagascar."

† "The Village Deities of Southern India," *Madras Museum Bull.*, 1907, v. 3, 137, 186.

a pit. This is covered with planks, on the top of which a sacrifice (hōmam) is performed with a fire kindled with jak (*Artocarpus integrifolia*) branches.*

The disguise of Ucchavēli is also assumed by the Malayans for the propitiation of the demon, when a human sacrifice is considered necessary. The Malayan who is to take the part puts on a cap made of strips of cocoanut leaf, and strips of the same leaves tied to a bent bamboo stick round his waist. His face and chest are daubed with yellow paint, and designs are drawn thereon in red or black. Strings are tied tightly round the left arm near the elbow and wrist, and the swollen area is pierced with a knife. The blood spouts out, and the performer waves the arm, so that his face is covered with blood. In the ceremony for propitiating the demon Nenaveli (bloody sacrifice), the Malayan smears the upper part of the body and face with a paste made of rice-flour reddened with turmeric powder and chunam (lime), to indicate a sacrifice. Before the paste dries, parched paddy (unhusked rice) grains, representing smallpox pustules, are sprinkled over it. Strips of young cocoanut leaves, strung together so as to form a petticoat, are tied round the waist, a ball of sacred ashes (vibhūthi) is fixed on the tip of the nose, and two strips of palm leaf are placed in the mouth to represent fangs. If it is thought that a human sacrifice is necessary to propitiate the devil, the man representing Nenaveli puts round his neck a kind of framework made of plantain leaf sheaths ; and, after he has danced with it on, it is removed, and placed on the ground in front of him. A number of lighted wicks are stuck in the middle of the framework, which is sprinkled with the blood of a fowl, and then beaten and crushed. Sometimes this is not regarded as sufficient, and the performer is made

* "Gazetteer of Malabar," 1908, i. 132.

to lie in a pit, which is covered over by a plank, and a fire kindled. A Malayan, who acted the part of Nenaveli before me, danced and gesticulated wildly, while a small boy, concealed behind him, sang songs in praises of the demon, to the accompaniment of a drum. At the end of the performance, he feigned extreme exhaustion, and laid on the ground in a state of apparent collapse, while he was drenched with water brought in pots from a neighbouring well.

A very similar rite has been recorded by Mr Lewis Rice as being carried out by the Coorgs, when a particular curse, which can only be removed by an extraordinary sacrifice, rests on a house, stable, or field. Concerning this sacrifice, Mr Rice writes as follows * :—

"The Kaniya (religious mendicant) † sends for some of his fraternity, the Panikas or Bannus, and they set to work. A pit is dug in the middle room of the house or in the yard, or in the stable, or in the field, as the occasion may require. Into this one of the magicians descends. He sits down in Hindu fashion, muttering mantras. Pieces of wood are laid across the pit, and covered with earth a foot or two deep. Upon this platform a fire of jackwood is kindled, into which butter, sugar, different kinds of grain, etc., are thrown. This sacrifice continues all night, the Panika sacrificer above, and his immured colleague below, repeating their incantations all the while. In the morning the pit is opened, and the man returns to the light of day. These sacrifices are called maranada bali, or death atonements. Instead of a human being, a cock is sometimes shut up in the pit, and killed afterwards."

Evidence is produced by Mr Rice ‡ that, in former days, human sacrifices were offered in Coorg, to secure

* "Mysore and Coorg Manual," 1878, iii. 265.

† The Kaniyans of the west coast are exorcisers.

‡ "Mysore and Coorg Manual," 1878, iii. 264-5.

the favour of the Grāma Dēvatas (village goddesses) Mariamma, Durga, and Bhadra Kali.

"In Kirinadu and Koniucheri Grāmas," he writes, "once every three years, in December and June, a human sacrifice used to be brought to Bhadra Kali, and, during the offering by the Panikas, the people exclaimed 'Al Amma' (a man, Oh mother), but once a devotee shouted 'Al all Amma, Adu' (not a man, oh mother, a goat), and since that time a he-goat without blemish has been sacrificed. Similarly, in Bellur, once a year, by turns from each house, a man was sacrificed by cutting off his head at the temple; but, when the turn came to a certain home, the devoted victim made his escape to the jungle. The villagers, after an unsuccessful search, returned to the temple, and said to the pūjāri (priest) 'Kalak Adu,' which has a double meaning, viz., Kalake next year, adu he will give, or adu a goat, and thenceforth only scapegoats were offered."

Human sacrifice is considered efficacious in appeasing the earth spirit, and in warding off devils during the construction of a new railway or big bridge. To the influence of such evil spirits the death of several workmen by accident in a cutting on the railway, which was under construction at Cannanore in Malabar, was attributed. A legend is current at Anantapur that, on one occasion, the embankment of the big tank breached. Ganga, the goddess of water, entered the body of a woman, and explained through her that, if some one was thrown into the breach, she would cause no further damage. Accordingly, one Musalamma was thrown in, and buried within it. The spot is marked by several margosa (*Melia Azadirachta*) trees, and sheep, fowls, etc., are still occasionally offered to the girl who was thus sacrificed. When a tank bund (embankment) was under construction in Mysore, there was a panic among the workmen, owing to a rumour that three virgins were going to be sacrificed. When a mantapam or shrine was consecrated, a human sacrifice was formerly considered necessary, but a cocoanut is now sometimes used as a substitute. At Kalasapād in the Cuddapah district, a missionary told Bishop Whitehead that, when a new ward was opened at the mission dispensary in 1906, none would enter it, because the people believed that the first to enter would be offered as a sacrifice. Their fears were allayed by a religious service. During the building of a tower at the Madras Museum, just before the big granite blocks were placed in position, the coolies contented themselves with the sacrifice of a goat. On the completion of a new building, some castes on the west coast sacrifice a fowl or sheep, to drive away the devils, which are supposed to haunt it.

In a field outside a village in South Canara, Mr Walhouse noticed a large square marked in lines with whitewash on the ground, with magic symbols in the corners, and the outline of a human figure rudely drawn in the middle. Flowers and boiled rice had been laid on leaves round the figure. He was informed that a house was to be built on the site marked out, and the figure was intended to represent the earth spirit supposed to be dwelling in the ground (or a human sacrifice?). Without this ceremony being performed before the earth was dug up, it was believed that there would be no luck about the house.*

Belief in the efficacy of human sacrifice as a means of discovering hidden treasure is widespread. It is recorded by Mr Walhouse† that "one of the native notions respecting pāndu kuli, or kistvaens, is that men of old constructed them for the purpose of hiding treasure.

* "Ind. Ant.," 1881, x. 366.

† *Ibid.*, 1876, v. 22.

Hence it is that antiquarians find so many have been ransacked. It is also believed that spells were placed over them as a guard, the strongest being to bury a man alive in the cairn, and bid his ghost protect the deposit against any but the proprietor. The ghost would conceal the treasure from all strangers, or only be compelled to disclose it by a human sacrifice being offered."

Many beliefs exist with regard to the purpose for which the large prehistoric burial jars, such as are found in various parts of Southern India, were manufactured. In Travancore, some believe that they were made to contain the remains of virgins sacrificed by the Rājas on the boundaries of their estates, to protect them.* According to another idea, the jars were made for the purpose of burying alive in them old women who refused to die.

In a note on the Velamas of the Godāvari district, Mr F. R. Hemingway writes that they admit that they always arrange for a Māla (Telugu Pariah) couple to marry, before they have a marriage in their own houses, and that they provide the necessary funds for the Māla marriage. They explain the custom by a story to the effect that a Māla once allowed a Velama to sacrifice him in order to obtain a hidden treasure, and they say that this custom is observed out of gratitude for the discovery of the treasure which resulted. The Rev. J. Cain gives a similar custom among the Velamas of Bhadrāchalam in the Godāvari district, only in this case it is a Palli (fisherman) who has to be married. Some years ago, a Native of the west coast, believing that treasure was hidden on his property, took council with an astrologer, who recommended the performance of a human sacrifice,

* "Ind. Ant.," 1878, vii. 177.

which happily was averted. On one occasion, a little Brāhman girl is said to have been decoyed when on her way to school, and murdered in the god's room at a temple in Vellore, in which treasure was supposed to be concealed.

In 1901, a Native of the Bellary district was tried for the murder of his child, in the belief that hidden treasure would thereby be revealed to him. The man, whose story I heard from himself in the lock-up, had apparently implicit faith that the god would bring the child to life again. The case, as recorded in the judgment of the Sessions Judge, was as follows:—

"The prisoner has made two long statements to the Magistrate, in each of which he explains why he killed the child. From these statements it appears that he had been worshipping at the temple of Kona Irappa for six or seven years, and that, on one or more occasions, the god appeared to him, and said: 'I am much pleased with your worship. There is wealth under me. To whom else should it be given but you?' The god asked the prisoner to sacrifice sheep and buffaloes, and also said: 'Give your son's head. You know that a head should be given to the god who confers a boon. I shall raise up your son, and give you the wealth which is under me.' At that time, the prisoner had only one son—the deceased boy was not then born. The prisoner said to the god: 'I have only one son. How can I give him?' The god replied: 'A son will be born. Do not fear me. I shall revive the son, and give you wealth.' Within one year, the deceased boy was born. This increased the prisoner's faith in the god, and it is apparent from his own statement that he has for some time past been contemplating human sacrifice. He was advised not to sacrifice the son, and for a time was satisfied with sacrificing a buffalo and goats, but, as a result, did not succeed in getting the wealth that he was anxious to secure. The prisoner says he dug up some portion of the temple, but the temple people did not let him dig further. The boy was killed on a Sunday, because the prisoner says that the god informed him that the human sacrifice should be on the child's birthday, which was a Sunday. The prisoner mentions in his statement how he took the child to the temple on the Sunday morning, and cut him with a sword. Having done so, he proceeded to worship, saying: 'I offered a head to the bestower of boons. Give boons, resuscitate my son, and show me wealth.' While the prisoner was worshipping the god, and waiting for the god to revive his son, the Reddi (headman) and the police came to the temple, and interrupted the worship. The prisoner believes that thereby the god was prevented from reviving the son. . . . The facts seem to be clear. The man's mind is sound in every respect but as regards this religious delusion. On that point, it is unsound."

A bad feature of the case, which was reckoned against the prisoner, was that he deferred the sacrifice until a second son was born, so that, in any case, he was not left without male issue. It was laid down by Manu that a man is perfect when he consists of three—himself, his wife, and his son. In the Rig Vēda it is laid down that, when a father sees the face of a living son, he pays a debt in him, and gains immortality. In Sanskrit works, Pūtra, or son, is defined as one who delivers a parent from a hell called put, into which those who have no son fall. Hence the anxiety of Hindus to marry, and beget male offspring.

A few years ago, in the Mysore Province, two men were charged with the kidnapping and murder of a female infant, and one was sentenced to transportation for life. The theory of the prosecution was that the child was killed, in order that it might be offered as a sacrifice with the object of securing hidden treasure, which was believed to be buried near the scene of the murder. A witness gave evidence to the effect that the second accused was the pūjāri (priest) of a Gangamma temple. He used to tell people that there was hidden treasure, and that, if a human sacrifice were offered, the treasure might be acquired. He used to make pūja, and tie yantrams (charms). He also made special pūjas, and exorcised devils. Another witness testified that her mother had buried some treasure during her lifetime, and she asked the pūjāri to discover it. He came to her house, made an earthen image, and did pūja to it. He dug the ground in three places, but no treasure was found. In dealing with the evidence in the Court of Appeal, the Judges stated that "it is well known that ignorant persons have various superstitions about the discovery of hidden treasure, and the facts that the second accused either shared such superstitious beliefs, or traded on the credulity of his neighbours by his pretensions of special occult power, and that a Sanyāsi (religious mendicant) had some four years ago given out that treasure might be discovered by means of a human sacrifice, cannot justify any inference that the second accused would have acted on the last suggestion, especially when the witnesses cannot even say that the second accused heard the Sanyāsi's suggestion."

The temple was searched, and the following articles were found:—three roots of the banyan tree having suralay (coil), a suralay of the banyan tree, round which two roots were entwined, a piece of banyan root, and a wheel (alada chakra) made of banyan root. Besides, there were a copper armlet, copper thyati (charm cylinder), nine copper plates, on which letters were engraved, a copper mokka mattoo (copper plate bearing figures of deities), a piece of thread coloured red, white and black, for tying yantrams, a tin case containing kappu (a black substance), a ball of human hair, and a pen-knife. There was also a dealwood box containing books and papers relating to bhūta vidya (black art).

A man was accused in 1907, in the Kurnool district, of stabbing a supposed wizard in the darkest hours of a new-moon night. In the course of his judgment, the Judge stated that "what may be taken as the facts of the case are very curious. The accused and his elder brother saw an 'iguana' (lizard) run from the foot of a hill. This is supposed to be one of the signs of buried treasure. They killed the animal (and ate it eventually), and dug, and found, where it had slept, treasure in the shape of a pot full of old-time pagodas (gold coins). Now a goddess (called here Shatti, *i.e.*, Sakti) is supposed to guard such buried treasure, and the finder ought to sacrifice a cock to the goddess before receiving the treasure. The brother of the accused neglected to do so, and came to the deceased, who was supposed to be a warlock, though his wife represents him to be merely a worshipper of Vīra Brahma, and a distributor of holy water (thirtham) and holy ashes to people possessed with devils. The deceased gave holy water to Pedda Pichivadu to avert ill-luck, but the man suddenly died from running a thorn into his foot, and his leg swelling in consequence. About the same time, the accused's younger brother got palsy in his head, and the deceased failed to cure him, though he made the attempt."

At Girigehalli in the Anantapur district, there is a temple, concerning which the story goes that the stomach of the goddess was once opened by an avaricious individual, who expected to find treasure within it. The goddess appeared to him in a dream, and said that he should suffer like pain to that which he had inflicted upon her, and he shortly afterwards died of some internal complaint.*

In the Cuddapah district, many of the inhabitants are said † to believe that there is much treasure hidden from the troublous days of the eighteenth century, but they have a superstitious dread against looking for it, since the successful finder would be smitten by the guardian demon with a sudden and painful death.

The Pānos (hill weavers) of Ganjam are said, on more than one occasion, to have rifled the grave of a European, in the belief that buried treasure would be found.

Many years ago, a woman was supposed to be possessed with a devil, and an exorcist was consulted, who declared that a human sacrifice was necessary. A victim was selected, and made very drunk. His head was cut off, and the blood, mixed with rice, was offered to the idol. The body was then hacked so as to deceive the police, and thrown into a pond.‡

At a village near Berhampur in Ganjam, Mr S. P. Rice tells us, § a number of villagers went out together. By and bye, according to a preconcerted plan, one of the party suggested a drink. The intended victim was drugged, and taken along to the statue of the goddess, or shrine containing what did duty for the statue. He was then thrown down with his face on the ground in an attitude suggesting supplication, and, while he was still in a state of stupor, his head was chopped off with an axe.

It is narrated by Chevers || that, in 1840, a religious mendicant, on his way back from Rāmēsvaram, located himself in a village near Ramnād, and gave himself out

* "Gazetteer of the Anantapur District," 1905, i. 179.

† "Manual of the Cuddapah District," 1875, 284.

‡ Lieutenant-General F. F. Burton, "An Indian Olio," 307.

§ "Occasional Essays on Native South Indian Life," 1901, 72-3.

|| "Manual of Medical Jurisprudence in India," 1870.

to be gifted with the power of working miracles. One evening, the chucklers (leather-workers) of the village, observing crows and vultures hovering near a group of trees, and suspecting that there was carrion for them to feast upon, were tempted to visit the spot, where they found a corpse, mangled most fearfully, and with the left hand and right leg cut off. Many nails were driven into the head, a garland was placed round the neck, and the forehead smeared with sandal paste. It was rumoured that a certain person was ailing, and that the holy man decreed that nothing short of a human sacrifice could save him, and that the victim should bear his name. The holy man disappeared, but was captured shortly afterwards.

A copper-plate grant, acquired a few years ago at Tirupati, and believed to be a forgery, records that a temple car was made for the goddess Kālikadēvi of Conjeeveram by certain Panchālans (members of the artisan classes). While it was being taken to the temple, a magician stopped it by means of incantations. The help of another magician was sought, and he cut off the head of his pregnant daughter, suspended it to the car, and performed certain rites. The car then moved, and the woman, whose head was cut off, was brought back to life. A somewhat similar legend is recorded in another copper-plate grant discovered in 1910 in the North Arcot district, which is also believed to be a forgery. It is there stated that the five castes of artisans made a bell-metal car for the Kāmākshiamman temple at Conjeeveram. Members of these five castes, belonging to the left-hand faction, commenced to drag it, but Seniyasingapuli, belonging to the right-hand faction, by means of magical powers, raised a thousand evil spirits against each wheel, and arrested its progress. A woman, named Mangammal, offered to sacrifice her son, and the artisans accordingly purchased the boy, saying that they would give her a head equal to that of a new-born child. Eventually, Mangammal herself laid down before the car. Her head was cut off, and hung at the top of the car. Her abdomen was torn open, and the fœtus removed therefrom, and dedicated to the evil spirit. The headless trunk was buried in the path of the wheels.

VIII

MAGIC AND HUMAN LIFE

SOME of the cases here brought together serve as an illustration of the difficulty which frequently arises in arriving at a decision as to how far the taking of human life is justified as being carried out in accordance with a genuine superstitious belief, and when the act renders the perpetrator thereof liable to punishment under the Indian Penal Code.

Five persons were charged a few years ago at the Coimbatore sessions with the murder of a young woman. The theory put forward by the prosecution was that two of the accused practised sorcery, and were under the delusion that, if they could obtain the fœtus from the uterus of a woman who was carrying her first child, they would be able to work some wonderful spells with it. With this object, they entered into a conspiracy with the three other accused to murder a young married woman, aged about seventeen, who was seven months advanced in pregnancy, and brutally murdered her, cutting open the uterus, removing the fœtus contained therein, and stealing her jewels. The five accused persons (three men and two women) were all of different castes. Two of the men had been jointly practising sorcery for some years. It was proved that, about two years before, they had performed an incantation near a river with some raw beef, doing pūja (worship) near the water's edge in a state of nature. Evidence was produced to prove that two of the accused decamped after the murder with a suspicious bundle, a few days before an eclipse of the moon, to Tiruchengōdu where there is a celebrated temple. It was suggested that the bundle contained the uterus, and was taken to Tiruchengōdu for the purpose of performing magical rites. When the quarters in which two of the accused lived were searched, three palm-leaf books were found containing mantrams regarding the pilli suniyam, a process of incantation by means of which sorcerers are supposed to be able to kill people. The record of the case states that "there can be little doubt that the first and fourth accused were taken into the conspiracy in order to decoy the deceased. The inducement offered to them was most probably immense wealth by the working of charms by the second and third accused with the aid of the fœtus. The medical evidence showed that the dead woman was pregnant, and that, after her throat had been cut, the uterus was taken out."

In 1829, several Natives of Malabar were charged with having proceeded, in company with a Paraiyan magician, to the house of a pregnant woman, who was beaten and otherwise ill-treated, and with having taken the fœtus out of her uterus, and introduced in lieu thereof the skin of a calf and an earthen pot. The prisoners confessed before the police, but were acquitted mainly on the ground that the earthen pot was of a size which rendered it impossible to credit its introduction during life. The Paraiyas of Malabar and Cochin are celebrated for their magical powers, and the practice of odi.

"There are," Mr Govinda Nambiar writes,* "certain specialists among mantravādis (dealers in magical spells),

* *Indian Review*, May, 1900.

who are known as Odiyans. Conviction is deep-rooted that they have the power of destroying whomever they please, and that, by means of a powerful bewitching matter called pilla thilum (oil extracted from the body of an infant), they are enabled to transform themselves into any shape or form, or even to vanish into air, as their fancy may suggest. When an Odiyan is hired to cause the death of a man, he waits during the night at the gate of his intended victim's house, usually in the form of a bullock. If, however, the person is inside the house, the Odiyan assumes the shape of a cat, enters the house, and induces him to come out. He is subsequently knocked down and strangled. The Odiyan is also credited with the power, by means of certain medicines, of inducing sleeping persons to open the doors, and come out of their houses as somnambulists do. Pregnant women are sometimes induced to come out of their houses in this way, and they are murdered, and the fœtus extracted from them. Murder of both sexes by Odiyans was a crime of frequent occurrence before the British occupation of the country."

In a case which was tried at the Malabar Sessions a few years ago, several witnesses for the prosecution deposed that a certain individual was killed by odi. One man gave the following account of the process. Shoot the victim in the nape of the neck with a blunt arrow, and bring him down. Proceed to beat him systematically all over the body with two sticks (resembling a policeman's truncheon, and called odivaddi), laying him on his back and applying the sticks to his chest, and up and down the sides, breaking all the ribs and other bones. Then raise the person, and kicks his sides. After this, force him to take an oath that he will never divulge the names of his torturer. All the witnesses agreed about the blunt arrow, and some bore testimony to the sticks.

A detailed account of the odi cult, from which the

following information was obtained, is given by Mr Anantha Krishna Iyer.* The disciple is taught how to procure pilla thilum (fœtus oil) from the six or seven months fœtus of a young woman in her first pregnancy. He (the Paraiyan magician) sets out at midnight from his hut to the house of the woman he has selected, round which he walks several times, shaking a cocoanut containing gurasi (a compound of water, lime, and turmeric), and muttering some mantrams to invoke the aid of his deity. He also draws a yantram (cabalistic figure) on the earth, taking special care to observe the omens as he starts. Should they be unfavourable, he puts it off for a more favourable opportunity. By the potency of his cult, the woman is made to come out. Even if the door of the room in which she might sleep be under lock and key, she would knock her head against it until she found her way out. She thus comes out, and yields herself to the influence of the magician, who leads her to a retired spot either in the compound (grounds), or elsewhere in the neighbourhood, strips her naked, and tells her to lie flat. She does so, and a chora kindi (gourd, *Lagenaria*) is placed close to the uterus. The fœtus comes out in a moment. A few leaves of some plant are applied, and the uterus contracts. Sometimes the womb is filled with rubbish, and the woman instantly dies. Care is taken that the fœtus does not touch the ground, lest the purpose be defeated, and the efficacy of the medicine completely lost. It is cut into pieces, dried, and afterwards exposed to the smoke above a fireplace. It is then placed in a vessel provided with a hole or two, below which there is another vessel. The two together are placed in a larger vessel filled with water, and heated over a bright fire. The heat must be so intense as to affect the fœtus, from which a

* "The Cochin Tribes and Castes," Madras, 1909, i. 77-81.

kind of liquid drops, and collects in the second vessel in an hour and a half. The magician then takes a human skull, and reduces it to a fine powder. This is mixed with a portion of the liquid. A mark is made on the forehead with this mixture, and the oil is rubbed on certain parts of the body, and he drinks some cow-dung water. He then thinks that he can assume the figure of any animal he likes, and successfully achieves the object in view, which is generally to murder or maim a person. A magic oil, called angola thilum, is extracted from the angola tree (*Alangium Lamarckii*), which bears a very large number of fruits. One of these is believed to be capable of descending and returning to its position on dark nights. Its possession can be secured by demons, or by an expert watching at the foot of the tree. When it has been secured, the extraction of the oil involves the same operations as those for extracting the pilla thilum, and they must be carried out within seven hours. The odi cult is said to have been practised by the Paraiyas some twenty years ago to a very large extent in the rural parts of the northern division of the Cochin State, and in the tāluks of Palghāt and Valuvanād, and even now it has not quite died out. Cases of extracting the fœtus, and of putting persons to death by odi, are not now heard of owing to the fear of government officials, landlords, and others.

Of the odi cult as practised by the Pānan magicians of the Cochin State, the following account is given by Mr Anantha Krishna Iyer.*

"A Pānan, who is an adept in the black art, dresses in an unwashed cloth, and performs pūja to his deity, after which he goes in search of a kotuveli plant (*Plumbago zeylanica*). When he has found it, he goes round it three times every day, and continues to do so for ninety days,

* "The Cochin Tribes and Castes," Madras, i. 176-7.

prostrating himself every day before it, and on the last night, which must be a new moon night, at midnight, he performs pūja to the plant, burning camphor and frankincense, and, after going round it three times, prostrates himself before it. He then thrusts three small candles on it, and advances twenty paces in front of it. With his mouth closed, he plucks the root, and buries it in the ashes on the cremation ground, after which he pours the water of seven green cocoanuts on it. He then goes round it twenty-one times, uttering all the while certain mantrams. This being over, he plunges himself in water, and stands erect until it extends to his mouth. He takes a mouthful of water which he empties on the spot, and takes the plant with the root which he believes to possess peculiar virtues. When it is taken to the closed door of a house, it has the power to entice a pregnant woman, and cause her to come out, when the fœtus is removed. It is all secretly done at midnight. The head, hands, and legs are cut off, and the trunk is taken to a dark-coloured rock, on which it is cut into nine pieces, which are burned until they are blackened. At this stage one piece boils, and it is placed in a new earthen pot, to which is added the water of nine green cocoanuts. The pot is removed to the burial ground, where the Pānan performs a pūja in honour of his favourite deity. He fixes two poles deep in the earth, at a distance of thirty feet from each other. The two poles are connected by a strong wire, from which is suspended the pot to be heated and boiled. Seven fireplaces are made beneath the wire, over the middle of which is the pot. The branches of bamboo, katalati (*Achyranthes aspera*), conga (*Bauhinia variegata*), cocoanut palm, jack tree (*Artocarpus integrifolia*), and pavatta (*Pavetta indica*), are used in forming a bright fire. The mixture in the pot soon boils and becomes oily, at which stage it is passed through a fine cloth. The oil is preserved, and a mark made with it on the forehead enables the possessor to realise anything which is thought of. The sorcerer must be in a state of vow for twenty-one days, and live on a diet of chama kanji (gruel). The deity whose aid is necessary is also propitiated by offerings."

In 1908, the following case, relating to the birth of a monster, was tried before the Sessions Judge of South Canara. A young Gauda girl became pregnant by her brother-in-law. After three days' labour, the child was born. The accused, who was the mother of the girl, was the midwife. Finding the delivery very difficult, she sent for a person to come and help her. The child was, as they thought, still-born. On its head was a red protuberance like a ball; round each of its forearms were two or three red bands; the eyes and ears were fixed very high in the head; and the eyes, nose, and mouth were abnormally large. The mother was carried out of the outhouse, lest the devil child should do her harm, or kill her. The accused summoned a Muhammadan, who was in the yard. He came in, and she showed him the child, and asked him to call the neighbours, to decide what to do. The child, she said, was a devil child, and must be cut and killed, lest it should devour the mother. While they were looking at the child, it began to move and roll its eyes about, and turn on the ground. It is a belief of the villagers that such a devil child, when brought in contact with the air, rapidly grows, and causes great trouble, usually killing the mother, and sometimes killing all the inmates of the house. The accused told the Muhammadan to cover the child with a vessel, which he did. Then there was a sound from inside the vessel, either of the child moving, or making a sound with its mouth. The accused then put her hand under the vessel, dragged the child half-way out, and, while the Muhammadan pressed the edge of the vessel on the abdomen of the child, took a knife, and cut the body in half. When the body was cut in two, there was no blood, but a mossy-green or black liquid oozed out. The accused got two areca leaves, and put one piece of the child on one, and one on the other, and told the Muhammadan to get a spade, and bury them. So they went to the jungle close to the house, and the Muhammadan dug two holes, one on one hillock, and one on another. In these holes, the two pieces of the child were buried. The object of this was to prevent the two pieces joining together again, in which case the united devil child would have come out of the grave, and gone to kill the mother.

Years ago, it was not unusual for people to come long distances for the purpose of engaging Paniyans of the Wynād (in Malabar) to help them in carrying out some more than usually desperate robbery or murder. Their mode of procedure, when engaged in an enterprise of this sort, is evidenced by two cases, which had in them a strong element of savagery. On both these occasions, the thatched homesteads were surrounded at dead of night by gangs of Paniyans carrying large bundles of rice straw. After carefully piling up the straw on all sides of the building marked for destruction, torches were at a given signal applied, and those of the inmates who attempted to escape were knocked on the head with clubs, and thrust into the fiery furnace. In 1904, some Paniyans were employed by a Māppilla (Muhammadan) to murder his mistress, who was pregnant, and threatened that she would noise abroad his responsibility for her condition. He brooded over the matter, and one day, meeting a Paniyan, promised him ten rupees if he would kill the woman. The Paniyan agreed to commit the crime, and went with his brothers to a place on a hill, where the Māppilla and the woman were in the habit of gratifying their passions. Thither the man and woman followed the Paniyans, of whom one ran out, and struck the victim on the head with a chopper. She was then gagged with a cloth, carried some distance, and killed.

In 1834, the inhabitants of several villages in Malabar attacked a village of Paraiyans on the alleged ground that deaths of people and cattle, and the protracted labour of a woman in childbed, had been caused by the practice of sorcery by the Paraiyans. They were beaten inhumanely with their hands tied behind their backs, so that several died. The villagers were driven, bound, into a river, immersed under water so as nearly to produce suffocation, and their own children were forced to rub sand into their wounds. Their settlement was then razed to the ground, and they were driven into banishment.

The Kādirs of the Ānaimalais are believers in witchcraft, and attribute diseases to the working thereof. They are expert exorcists, and trade in mantravādam or magic. It is recorded by Mr Logan * that "the family of famous trackers, whose services in the jungles were retained for H.R.H. the Prince of Wales's (afterwards King Edward VII.) projected sporting tour in the Ānamalai mountains, dropped off most mysteriously one by one, stricken down by an unseen hand, and all of them expressing beforehand their conviction that they were under a certain individual's spell, and were doomed to certain death at an early date. They were probably poisoned, but how it was managed remains a mystery, although the family was under the protection of a European gentleman, who would at once have brought to light any ostensible foul play."

The Badagas of the Nīlgiris live in dread of the jungle Kurumbas, who constantly come under reference in their folk-stories. The Kurumba is the necromancer of the hills,

* "Malabar," 1887, i. 174.

and believed to be possessed of the power of outraging women, removing their livers, and so causing their death, while the wound heals by magic, so that no trace of the operation is left. The Badaga's dread of the Kurumba is said to be so great, that a simple threat of vengeance has proved fatal. The Badaga or Toda requires the services of the Kurumba, when he fancies that any member of his family is possessed by a devil. The Kurumba does his best to remove the malady by means of mantrams (magical formulæ). If he fails, and if any suspicion is aroused in the mind of the Badaga or Toda that he is allowing the devil to play his pranks instead of loosing his hold on the supposed victim, woe betide him. Writing in 1832, Harkness states* that "a very few years before, a Burgher (Badaga) had been hanged by the sentence of the provincial court for the murder of a Kurumba. The act of the former was not without what was considered great provocation. Disease had attacked the inhabitants of the hamlet, a murrain their cattle. The former had carried off a great part of the family of the murderer, and he himself had but narrowly escaped its effects. No one in the neighbourhood doubted that the Kurumba in question had, by his necromancy, caused all this misfortune, and, after several fruitless attempts, a party of them succeeded in surrounding him in open day, and effecting their purpose."

In 1835, no less than fifty-eight Kurumbas were murdered, and a smaller number in 1875 and 1882. In 1891, the inmates of a single Kurumba hut were said to have been murdered, and the hut burnt to ashes, because one of the family had been treating a sick Badaga child, and failed to cure it. The district judge, however, disbelieved

* "Description of a Singular Aboriginal Race inhabiting the summit of the Neilgherry Hills," 1832, 83-4.

the evidence, and all who were charged were acquitted. Again, in 1900, a whole family of Kurumbas was murdered, of which the head, who had a reputation as a medicine man, was believed to have brought disease and death into a Badaga village. The sympathies of the whole countryside were so strongly with the murderers that detection was made very difficult, and the persons charged were acquitted.*

"It is," Mr Grigg writes,† "a curious fact that neither Kota, Irula, or Badaga, will slay a Kurumba, until a Toda has struck the first blow, but, as soon as his sanctity has been violated by a blow, they hasten to complete the murderous work, which the sacred hand of the Toda has begun."

Some years ago, a Toda was found dead in a sitting posture on the top of a hill near a Badaga village, in which a party of Todas had gone to collect the tribute due to them. The body was cremated, and a report made to the police that the man had been murdered. On enquiry, it was ascertained that the dead man was supposed to have bewitched a little Badaga girl, who died in consequence, and the presumption was that he had been murdered by the Badagas out of spite.

In 1906, two men were found guilty of killing a man by shooting him with a gun in South Canara. It is recorded in the judgment that "the accused have a brother, who has been ill for a long time. They thought deceased, who was an astrologer and mantravādi, had bewitched him. They had spent fifty or sixty rupees on deceased for his treatment, but it did no good, and accused came to believe that deceased not only would not cure their brother himself, but would not allow

* "Madras Police Administration Report," 1900.

† "Manual of the Niligiri District," 1880, 212.

other doctors to do so. Also, a certain theft having occurred some months ago, deceased professed by his magic arts to have discovered that accused and others were the thieves. In consequence of these things, accused had expressed various threats against deceased. One witness, who is a mantravādi in a small way, was consulted by one of the accused to find some counter-treatment for deceased's bewitchment. Accused said that deceased refused to cure their brother, and would not let others do so, unless they gave him certain gold coins called Rāma Tanka, said to be in their possession. They desired this possession, so would not satisfy deceased. So their brother was dying by inches under deceased's malign influence. This witness professed to have discovered that accused's brother was being worried by one black devil and two malignant spirits of the dead. It is clear from the evidence that accused, who are ignorant men of a low type, really believed that deceased was by his magic wilfully and slowly killing their brother. They believed that the only way to save their brother's life was to kill the magician."

During an epidemic of smallpox in the Jeypore hill tracts, a man lost his wife and child. A local subscription had been organised for a sorcerer, on the understanding that he was to stay the course of the epidemic. The bereaved man charged him with being a fraud, and, in the course of a quarrel, split his skull open with a tangi (axe).

In 1906, a Kōmati woman died of cholera in a village in Ganjam. Her son sought the assistance of certain men of the "Reddika" caste in obtaining wood for the pyre, carrying the corpse to the burning-ground, and cremating it. The son set fire to the pyre, and withdrew, leaving the Reddikas on the spot. Among them was one, who is said to have learnt sorcery from a Bairāgi (religious mendicant), and to have been generally feared and hated in the village.

To him the spread of cholera by letting loose the goddess of the cremation-ground, called Mashani Chendi, was attributed. Arrack (liquor) was passed round among those who were attending to the burning corpse, and they got more or less drunk. Two of them killed the sorcerer by severe blows on the neck with wood-choppers. His corpse was then placed on the burning pyre of the Kōmati woman, and cremated. The men who delivered the death blows were sentenced to transportation for life, as their intoxicated state and superstitious feeling were held to plead in mitigation of the punishment.

In 1904 a case illustrating the prevailing belief in witchcraft occurred in the Vizagapatam hill tracts. The youngest of three brothers died of fever, and, when the body was cremated, the fire failed to consume the upper portion. The brothers concluded that death must have been caused by the witchcraft of a certain Kondh. They accordingly attacked him, and killed him. After death, the brothers cut the body in half and dragged the upper half of it to their own village, where they attempted to nail it up on the spot where their deceased brother's body failed to burn. They were arrested on the spot, with the fragment of the Kondh's corpse. They were sentenced to death.*

In the North Arcot district, a few years ago, a reputed magician, while collecting the pieces of a burning corpse, to be used for the purposes of sorcery, was seized and murdered, and his body cast on the burning pyre. From the recovery of duplicate bones, it was proved that two bodies were burnt, and the murder was detected. Two persons were sentenced to transportation for life.†

* "Madras Police Administration Report," 1904.

† *Ibid.*, 1905-6.

JUMADI BHUTHA, SOUTH CANARA.

To face p. 237.

IX

MAGIC AND MAGICIANS

It has been stated * that sorcerers usually unite together to form a society, which may attain great influence among backward races. In Southern India there are certain castes which are summed up in the "Madras Census Report," 1901, as "exorcists and devil-dancers," whose most important avocation is the practice of magic. Such, for example, are the Nalkes, Paravas, and Pompadas of South Canara, who are called in whenever a bhūtha (demon) is to be propitiated, and the Pānans and Malayans of Malabar, whose magical rites are described by me in detail elsewhere.†

Concerning sorcery on the west coast, the Travancore Census Commissioner, 1901, writes as follows :—

"The forms of sorcery familiar to the people of Malabar are of three kinds :—(1) kaivisham, or poisoning food by incantations; (2) the employment of Kuttichāttan, a mysteriously-working mischievous imp; (3) setting up spirits to haunt men and their houses, and cause illness of all kinds. The most mischievous imp in Malabar demonology is an annoying quip-loving little spirit, as black as night, and about the size of a well-nourished twelve-year-old boy. Some people say that they have seen

* A. C. Haddon, "Magic and Fetishism" (Religions, ancient and modern), 1906, 51.

† *See* the articles devoted to these castes in my "Castes and Tribes of Southern India," 1909.

him *vis-à-vis*, having a forelock. There are Nambūtiris (Brāhmans) in Malabar to whom these are so many missiles, which they may throw at anybody they choose. They are, like Shakespeare's Ariel, little active bodies, and most willing slaves of the master under whom they happen to be placed. Their victims suffer from unbearable agony. Their clothes take fire; their food turns to ordure; their beverages become urine; stones fall in showers on all sides of them, but curiously not on them; and their bed becomes a bed of thorns. With all this annoying mischief, Kuttichāttan or Boy Satan does no serious harm. He oppresses and harasses, but never injures. A celebrated Brāhman of Changanacheri is said to own more than a hundred of these Chāttans. Household articles and jewelry of value may be left in the premises of homes guarded by Chāttan, and no thief dares to lay his hand on them. The invisible sentry keeps diligent watch over his master's property, and has unchecked powers of movement in any medium. As remuneration for all these services, the Chāttan demands nothing but food, but that in a large measure. If starved, the Chāttans would not hesitate to remind the master of their power, but, if ordinarily cared for, they would be his most willing drudges. As a safeguard against the infinite power secured for the master by Kuttichāttan, it is laid down that malign acts committed through his instrumentality recoil on the prompter, who dies either childless or after frightful physical and mental agony. Another method of oppressing humanity, believed to be in the power of sorcerers, is to make men and women possessed with spirits. Here, too, women are more subject to their evil influence than men. Delayed puberty, permanent sterility, and still-births, are not uncommon ills of a devil-possessed woman. Sometimes the spirits sought to be exorcised refuse to leave the victim, unless the sorcerer promises them a habitation in his own compound (grounds), and arranges for daily offerings being given. This is agreed to as a matter of unavoidable necessity, and money and lands are conferred upon the mantravādi Nambūtiri to enable him to fulfil his promise."

Reference has been made (p. 238) to the falling of stones round those attacked by Chāttans. Hysteria, epilepsy, and other disorders, are, in Malabar, ascribed to possession by devils, who can also cause cattle disease, accidents, and misfortunes of any kind. Throwing stones on houses, and setting fire to the thatch, are supposed to be their ordinary recreations. The mere mention of the name of a certain Nambūtiri family is said to be enough to drive them away.* A few years ago, an old Brāhman woman, in the Bellary district, complained to the police that a Sūdra woman living in her neighbourhood, and formerly employed by her as sweeper, had been throwing stones into her house for some nights. The woman admitted that she had done so, because she was advised by a Lingāyat priest that the remedy for intermittent fever, from which she was suffering, was to throw stones at an old woman, and extract some blood from her body on a new or full-moon day.

Some demons are believed to have human mistresses and concubines, and it is narrated † that a Chetti (merchant) in the Tamil country purchased a Malabar demon from a magician for ninety rupees. But hardly a day had passed before the undutiful spirit fell in love with its new owner's wife, and succeeded in its nefarious purpose.

Quite recently a woman, in order to win the affection of her husband, gave him a love-charm composed of dhatura in chutney. The dose proved fatal, and she was sentenced to two years' rigorous imprisonment.‡ A

* B. Govinda Nambiar, *Indian Review*, May, 1900.

† M. J. Walhouse, "Ind. Ant.," 1876, v. 22.

‡ "Report of the Chemical Examiner, Madras," 1908, 5.

love-philtre, said to be composed of the charred remains of a mouse and spider, was once sent to the chemical examiner to Government for analysis in a suspected case of poisoning. In connection with the dugong (*Halicore dugong*), which is caught in the Gulf of Manaar, Dr Annandale writes as follows * :—

"The presence of large glands in connection with the eye afford some justification for the Malay's belief that the dugong weeps when captured. They regard the tears of the īkan dugong (dugong fish) as a powerful love-charm. Muhammadan fishermen of the Gulf of Manaar appeared to be ignorant of this usage, but told me that a 'doctor' once went out with them to collect the tears of a dugong, should they capture one."

Native physicians in the Tamil country are said to prepare an unguent, into the composition of which the eye of the slender Loris (*Loris gracilis*), the brain of the dead offspring of a primipara, and the catamenial blood of a young virgin, enter, as an effective preparation in necromancy. The eye of the Loris is also used for making a preparation, which is believed to enable the possessor to kidnap and seduce women. The tail of a chamæleon, secured on a Sunday, is also believed to be an excellent love-charm.

A young married student at a college in Madras attributed his illness to the administration by his wife of a love-philtre containing the brains of a baby which had been exhumed after burial. Among the Tamil Paraiyans and some other classes, a first-born child, if it is a male, is buried near or even within the house, so that its corpse may not be carried away by a sorcerer, to be used in magical rites.† If a first-born child dies,

* *Journ. and Proc. Asiat. Soc., Bengal*, 1905, i. No. 9.

† Rev. A. C. Clayton, *Madras Museum Bull.*, 1906, v., No. 2, 82.

a finger is sometimes cut off, lest a sorcerer should dig up the body, and extract an essence (karuvu) from the brain, wherewith to harm his enemies.* The Rev. J. Castets informs me that he once saw a man being initiated into the mysteries of the magician's art. The apparatus included the top of the skull of a first-born male child inscribed with Tamil characters.

A station-house police officer informed Mr S. G. Roberts that first-born children, dying in infancy, are buried near the house, lest their heads should be used in sorcery, a sort of ink or decoction (mai) being distilled from them. This ink is used for killing people at a distance, or for winning a woman's love, or the confidence of those from whom some favour is required. In the last two cases, the ink is smeared over the eyebrows. It is believed that, if an infant's head is used for this purpose, the mother will never have a living child. When Mr Roberts was at Salem, he had to try a case of this practice, and the Public Prosecutor informed him that it is believed that, if a hole is made in the top of the head of the infant when it is buried, it cannot be effectively used in sorcery. In the Trichinopoly district, the police brought to Mr Roberts' notice a sorcerer's outfit, which had been seized. There were the most frightful Tamil curses invoking devils, written backwards in "looking-glass characters" on an olai (strip of palm leaf), and a looking-glass to read them by. Spells written backwards are said to be very potent. There was also a small round tin, containing a black treacly paste with a sort of shine on it, which was said to have been obtained from the head of a dead child. There is a Tamil proverb "Kuzhi pillai, madi pillai," meaning grave child, lap child, in reference to a belief that, the

* *Cf.* odi cult, 228-9.

quicker a first-born child is buried, the quicker is the next child conceived.

The following form of sorcery in Malabar is described by Mr Walhouse.*

"Let a sorcerer obtain the corpse of a maiden, and on a Saturday night place it at the foot of a bhuta-haunted tree on an altar, and repeat a hundred times: Om! Hrim! Hrom! O goddess of Malayāla who possessest us in a moment! Come! Come! The corpse will then be inspired by a demon, and rise up; and, if the demon be appeased with flesh and arrack (liquor), it will answer all questions put to it."

A human bone from a burial-ground, over which powerful mantrams have been recited, if thrown into an enemy's house, will cause his ruin. Ashes from the burial-ground on which an ass has been rolling on a Saturday or Sunday, if thrown into the house of an enemy, are said to produce severe illness, if the house is not vacated.

From Malabar, a correspondent writes as follows:—

"I came across a funny thing in an embankment in a rice-field. The tender part of a young cocoanut branch had been cut into three strips, and the strips fastened one into the other in the form of a triangle. At the apex a reed was stuck, and along the base and sides small flowers, so that the thing looked like a ship in full sail. My inspector informed me, with many blushes, that it contained a devil, which the sorcerer of a neighbouring village had cut out of a young girl. Mrs Bishop, in her book on Korea, mentions that the Koreans do exactly the same thing, but, in Korea, the devil's prison is laid by the wayside, and is carefully stepped over by every passer-by, whereas the one I saw was carefully avoided by my peons (orderlies) and others."

In the Godāvari district, Mr H. Tyler came across the

* "Ind. Ant," 1876, v. 22.

burning funeral pyre of a Koyi girl, who had died of syphilis. Across a neighbouring path leading to the Koyi village was a basket fish-trap containing grass, and on each side thorny twigs, which were intended to catch the malign spirit of the dead girl, and prevent it from entering the village. The twigs and trap containing the spirit were to be burnt on the following day. By the Dōmbs of Vizagapatam, the souls of the dead are believed to roam about, so as to cause all possible harm to mankind, and also to protect them against the attacks of witches. A place is prepared for the Dūma in the door-hinge, or a fishing-net, wherein he lives, is placed over the door. The witches must count all the knots of the net, before they can enter the house.*

At cross-roads in the Bellary district, geometric patterns are sometimes made at night by people suffering from disease, in the belief that the affliction will pass to the person who first treads on the charm.†

"At cross-roads in the South Arcot district may be sometimes seen pieces of broken pot, saffron (turmeric), etc. These are traces of the following method of getting rid of an obstinate disease. A new pot is washed clean, and filled with a number of objects (the prescription differs in different localities), such as turmeric, coloured grains of rice, chillies, cotton-seed, and so forth, and sometimes a light made of a few threads dipped in a little dish of oil, and taken at dead of night to the cross-roads, and broken there. The disease will then disappear. In some places it is believed that it passes to the first person who sees the débris of the ceremony the next morning, and the performer has to be careful to carry it out unknown to his neighbours, or the consequences are unpleasant for him." ‡

* Gloyer, Jeypore, Breklum, 1901.

† "Gazetteer of the Bellary District," 1904, i. 60.

‡ "Gazetteer of the South Arcot District," 1906, i. 93.

Some Valaiyans, Paraiyans, and Kallans, on the occasion of a death in the family, place a pot filled with dung or water, a broomstick, and a firebrand, at some place where three roads meet, or in front of the house, to prevent the ghost from returning.* When a Paraiyan man dies, camphor is burnt, not at the house, but at the junction of three lanes.

In the Godāvari district, a sorcerer known as the Ejjugadu (male physician) is believed, out of spite or in return for payment, to kill another by invoking the gods. He goes to a green tree, and there spreads muggu or chunam (lime) powder, and places an effigy of the intended victim thereon. He also places a bow and arrow there, recites certain spells, and calls on the gods. The victim is said to die in a couple of days. But, if he understands that the Ejjugadu has thus invoked the gods, he may inform another Ejjugadu, who will carry out similar operations under another tree. His bow and arrow will go to those of the first Ejjugadu, and the two bows and arrows will fight as long as the spell remains. The man will then be safe.

Writing concerning the nomad Yerukalas, Mr F. Fawcett says † that "the warlock takes the possessed one by night to the outskirts of the village, and makes a figure on the ground with powdered rice, powders of various colours, and powdered charcoal. Balls of the powders, half cocoanut shells, betel, four-anna pieces, and oil lamps, are placed on the hands, legs, and abdomen. A little heap of boiled rice is placed near the feet, and curds and vegetables are set on the top of it, with limes placed here and there. The subject of the incantation sits near the head, while the magician mutters mantrams. A he-goat is then

* "Gazetteer of the Tanjore District," 1906, i. 76.

† *Journ. Anthrop. Soc., Bombay*, ii. 1890, 282-5.

sacrificed. Its head is placed near the foot of the figure, and benzoin and camphor are waved. A little grain is scattered about the figure to appease the evil spirits. Some arrack is poured into a cup, which is placed on the body of the figure, and the bottle which contained it is left on the head. The limes are cut in two, and two cocoanuts are broken. The patient then walks by the left side of the figure to its legs, takes one step to the right towards the head, and one step to the left towards the feet, and walks straight home without looking back."

In Malabar, Mr Govinda Nambiar writes,* "when a village doctor attending a sick person finds that the malady is unknown to him, or will not yield to his remedies, he calls in the astrologer, and subsequently the exorcist, to expel the demon or demons which have possessed the sick man. If the devils will not yield to ordinary remedies administered by his disciples, the mantravādi himself comes, and a devil dance is appointed to be held on a certain day. Thereat various figures of mystic device are traced on the ground, and in their midst a huge and frightful form representing the demon. Sometimes an effigy is constructed out of cooked and coloured rice. The patient is seated near the head of the figure, and opposite sits the magician adorned with bundles of sticks tied over the joints of his body, tails, and skins of animals, etc. Verses are chanted, and sometimes cocks are sacrificed, and the blood is sprinkled on the demon's effigy. Amidst the beating of drums and blowing of pipes, the magician enters upon his diabolical dance, and, in the midst of his paroxysm, may even bite live cocks, and suck with ferocity the hot blood."

When a Malayan exorcist is engaged in propitiating a demon, a fowl is sometimes waved before him, and

* *Indian Review*, May, 1900.

decapitated. He puts the neck in his mouth, and sucks the blood. By the Tiyans of Malabar a number of evil spirits are supposed to devote their attention to a pregnant woman, and to suck the blood of the child *in utero*, and of the mother. In the process of expelling them, the woman lies on the ground and kicks. A cock is thrust into her hand, and she bites it, and drinks its blood.

It is noted by Mr L. K. Anantha Krishna Iyer that by the Thanda Pulayans of the west coast "a ceremony called urasikotukkuka is performed with the object of getting rid of a devil, with which a person is possessed. At a place far distant from the hut, a leaf, on which the blood of a fowl has been made to fall, is spread on the ground. On a smaller leaf, chunam and turmeric are placed. The person who first sets eyes on these becomes possessed by the devil, and sets free the individual who was previously under its influence. The Thanda Pulayans also practise maranakriyas, or sacrifices to demons, to bring about the death of an enemy. Sometimes affliction is supposed to be brought about by the enmity of those who have got incantations written on a palm leaf, and buried in the ground near a house by the side of a well. A sorcerer is called in to counteract the evil charm, which he digs up and destroys."

In a note on the Paraiyas of Travancore,* the Rev. S. Mateer writes that Sūdras and Shānars † frequently employ the Paraiya devil-dancers and sorcerers to search for and dig out magical charms buried in the earth by enemies, and counteract their enchantments.

A form of sorcery in Malabar called marana (destruc-

* *Journ. Royal Asiat. Soc.*, 1884, xvi. 185-6.

† For a detailed account of demonolatry among the Shānans, I would refer the reader to the Rev. R. (afterwards Bishop) Caldwell's now scarce "Tinnevelly Shānans," 1849.

tion) is said by Mr Fawcett * to be carried out in the following manner :—

"A figure representing the enemy to be destroyed is drawn on a small plate of metal (gold by preference), and to it some mystic diagrams are added. It is then addressed with a statement that bodily injury, or the death of the person, shall take place at a certain time. This little sheet is wrapped up in another metal sheet or leaf (of gold if possible), and buried in some place which the person to be injured or destroyed is in the habit of passing. Should he pass over the place, it is supposed that the charm will take effect at the time named."

One favourite tantra of the South Indian sorcerer is said † to consist of "what is popularly known in Tamil as pavai, that is to say, a doll made of some plastic substance, such as clay or wheat-flour. A crude representation of the intended victim is obtained by moulding a quantity of the material, and a nail or pin is driven into it at a spot corresponding to the limb or organ that is intended to be affected.‡ For instance, if there is to be paralysis of the right arm, the pin is stuck into the right arm of the image; if madness is to result, it is driven into the head, and so on, appropriate mantras being chanted over the image, which is buried at midnight in a neighbouring cremation ground. So long as the pavai is underground, the victim will grow from bad to worse, and may finally succumb, if steps are not taken in time. Sometimes, instead of a doll being used, the corpse of a child recently buried is dug out of the ground, and re-interred after being similarly treated. The only remedy consists in another sorcerer being called in for the purpose of digging out the pavai. Various are the

* *Madras Museum Bull.*, 1900, iii., No. 1, 51.

† *Madras Mail*, 18th November, 1905.

‡ An example of so-called homœopathic magic. *See* Haddon, "Magic and Fetishism" (Religions ancient and modern), 1906, 19-22.

methods he adopts for discovering the place where the doll is buried, one of them being very similiar to what is known as crystal-gazing. A small quantity of a specially prepared thick black fluid is placed on the palm of a third person, and the magician professes to find out every circumstance connected with the case of his client's mental or physical condition by attentively looking at it. The place of the doll's burial is spotted with remarkable precision, the nail or pin extracted, and the patient is restored to his normal condition as by a miracle."

The following form of sorcery resorted to in Malabar in compassing the discomfiture of an enemy is recorded by Mr Walhouse.*

"Make an image of wax in the form of your enemy; take it in your right hand at night, and hold your chain of beads in your left hand. Then burn the image with due rites, and it shall slay your enemy in a fortnight. Or a figure representing an enemy, with his name and date of his birth inscribed on it, is carved out of *Strychnos Nux-vomica* wood. A mantram is recited, a fowl offered up, and the figure buried in glowing rice-husk embers. Or, again, some earth from a spot where an enemy has urinated, saliva expectorated by him, and a small tuft of hair, are placed inside a tender cocoanut, and enclosed in a piece of *Strychnos Nux-vomica.* The cocoanut is pierced with twenty-one nails and buried, and a fowl sacrificed."

A police inspector, when visiting a village a few years ago, was told by one of the villagers that a man was going to bury two wax dolls, in order to cause his death. The inspector accordingly went to the house of the suspected enemy, where he found the two dolls, and some books on witchcraft.

The Native servant of a friend in Madras found buried

* "Ind. Ant." 1876, v. 22.

FIGURE WASHED ASHORE AT CALICUT.

To face p. 249.

in a corner of his master's garden the image of a human figure, which had been deposited there by an enemy who wished to injure him. The figure was made of flour, mixed with "walking foot earth," *i.e.*, earth from the ground, which the servant had walked over. Nails, fourteen in number, had been driven into the head, neck, and each shoulder, elbow, wrist, hip, knee, and ankle. Buried with the figure were fourteen eggs, limes, and balls of camphor, and a scrap of paper bearing the age of the servant, and the names of his father and mother. A Muhammadan fortune-teller advised the servant to burn the image, so at midnight he made an offering of a sheep, camphor, betel nuts, and cocoanuts, and performed the cremation ceremony.

In 1903, a life-size nude female human figure with feet everted and directed backwards, carved out of the soft wood of *Alstonia scholaris*, was washed ashore at Calicut in Malabar. Long nails had been driven in all over the head, body, and limbs, and a large square hole cut out above the navel. Inscriptions in Arabic characters were scrawled over it. By a coincidence, the corpse of a man was washed ashore close to the figure. Possibly it represented the figure of a woman who was possessed by an evil spirit, which was attached to it by a nail between the legs before it was cast into the sea, and was made on the Laccadive islands,* some of the residents on which are notorious necromancers. It has been suggested † that the figure may represent some notorious witch; that the nails were driven into it, and the mutilation made in order to injure her, and the spells added to destroy her magical powers; finally, that the image was cast into the sea as a means of getting rid of the

* Laccadiveans come to the Malabar coast in sailing-boats.

† *Nature*, 18th October, 1906.

sorceress. There is a tradition that the goddess Bhagavati, who is worshipped at Kodungallur in Malabar, was rescued by a fisherman when she was shut up in a jar, and thrown into the sea by a great magician. The Lingadars of the Kistna district are said* to have made a specialty of bottling evil spirits, and casting the bottles away in some place where no one is likely to come across them, and liberate them.

A few years ago, another wooden representation of a human being was washed ashore at Calicut. The figure is 11 inches in height. The arms are bent on the chest, and the palms of the hands are placed together as in the act of saluting. A square cavity, closed by a wooden lid, has been cut out of the abdomen, and contains apparently tobacco, ganja (Indian hemp), and hair. An iron bar has been driven from the back of the head through the body, and terminates in the abdominal cavity. A sharp cutting instrument has been driven into the chest and back in twelve places.

A life-size female figure, rudely scratched on a plank of wood, with Arabic inscriptions scrawled on it, and riddled with nails, was washed ashore on the beach at Tellicherry in Malabar. In the same district, a friend once picked up on the shore at Cannanore a wooden figure about 6 inches high, riddled with nails. His wife's ayah implored him to get rid of it, as it would bring nothing but misfortune. He accordingly made a present of it to a recently married friend, whose subsequent career was characterised by a long series of strokes of bad luck, which his wife attributed entirely to the possession of the dreadful image.

Sometimes, in Malabar, "a mantram is written on the stem of the kaitha plant, on which is also drawn a figure

* *Madras Mail*, 18th November, 1905.

representing the person to be injured. A hole is bored to represent the navel. The mantram is repeated, and at each repetition a certain thorn (kāramullu) is stuck into the limbs of the figure. The name of the person, and of the star under which he was born, are written on a piece of cadjan, which is stuck into the navel. The thorns are removed, and replaced twenty-one times. Two magic circles are drawn below the nipples of the figure. The stem is then hung up in the smoke of the kitchen. A pot of toddy, and some other accessories, are procured, and with them the warlock performs certain rites. He then moves three steps backwards, and shouts aloud thrice, fixing in the thorns again, and thinking all the while of the particular mischief with which he will afflict the person to be injured. When all this has been done, the person whose figure has been drawn on the stem, and pricked with thorns, feels pain."*

The following variant of the above rite has been described †:—

"A block of lead is moulded into the effigy of a man about a span in length. The stomach is opened, and the name and star of the intended victim are inscribed along with a charm on a lead plate, and placed therein. The effigy is laid recumbent on a plantain leaf, on which a little water mixed with sandal has first been sprinkled, and the smoke of an extinguished wick is passed thrice over it. Then nine little square pieces of plantain leaf (or leaves of *Strychnos Nux-vomica*) are placed round the effigy, and in each square some rice-flour, and chouflower petals. Beside the effigy are shells holding toddy and arrack (liquor), a burning lamp, and several little wicks. One of the wicks is lighted, and the flame passed thrice over the collection. Nine wicks are lighted,

* F. Fawcett, *Madras Museum Bull.*, 1901, iii., No. 3, 317.

† *Madras Mail*, 19th November, 1897.

and put on the nine squares. The charm inscribed on the lead plate is at this stage repeated fervently in an undertone no less than twenty-one times. This preamble, or one closely resembling it, is generally the beginning of the mantravādi's programme. The rest of it is guided by the special circumstances of each case. Let us suppose that the wizard, having a victim in view, wishes the latter to be afflicted with burning pains and insufferable heat all over his body. The following is the ceremony he would perform. Thinking of the victim, he drives a thorn of *Canthium parviflorum* into the effigy, and then, folding up the collection detailed above in the plantain leaf, he proceeds to a tank or pool, and immerses himself up to the neck. He places the bundle on the surface of the water—he tells you it will float despite the lead—and, calling for a cock, cuts off its head, permitting the blood and the head to fall on the bundle. He presses the bundle down into the water, and submerges himself at the same time. Coming to the surface, he goes ashore, whistling thrice, and being very careful not to look behind him. Within twenty-one days, the charm will take effect. In order to induce a boil or tumour to appear in a victim's foot, the mantravādi inscribes a certain charm on a sheet of lead, and stuffs the plate into a frog's mouth, repeats another charm, and blows into the batrachian's mouth, which is then stitched up, after which the creature is bound with twenty-one coils of string. The frog is next set down on a plantain leaf, the ritual already described with the squares, toddy, etc., is performed, the frog is wrapped up together with the various substances in the leaf, and buried at some spot where two or more roads meet, and which the victim is likely to pass. Should he cross the fateful spot, he will suddenly become conscious of a feeling in his foot, as though a thorn had pricked him. From that moment dates the beginning of a week of intense agony. His foot swells, fever sets in, he has pains all over his body, and for seven days existence is intolerable. The cherukaladi is another form of odi mantram, and the manner in which it is performed is extremely interesting. The wizard takes three balls of rice, blackens one, reddens another, and passes through the third a young yetah fish (*Bagarius yarrellii*), after having put down its throat seven green chillies, seven grains of raw rice, and as many of pepper. In the carapace of a crab some toddy, and in the valve of a particular kind of mussel, some arrack is placed. The sorcerer conveys all these things to a hill built by termites (white-ants). The crown of the hill is knocked off, and the substances are thrown in. Walking round the mound thrice, the magician recites a charm, and comes away without looking over his shoulder.* Within a very short time, similar effects are produced as those resulting from the previously described form of sorcery."

A grāndha (palm-leaf book), describing how an enemy may be struck down, gives the following details. The head of a fowl with dark-coloured flesh is cut off. The head is then split open, and a piece of cadjan (palm-leaf), on which are written the name of the person to be injured, and the name of the star under which he was born, is stuck in the split head, which is then sewn up and the tongue stitched to the beak. The head is then inserted into a certain fruit, which is tied up with a withe of a creeper, and deposited under the enemy's gateway.

In Malabar, a wooden figure is sometimes made, and a tuft of a woman's hair tied on its head. It is fixed to a tree, and nails are driven into the neck and breast, to inflict hurt on an enemy. Sometimes a live frog or lizard is buried within a cocoanut shell, after nails have been stuck into its eyes and stomach. The deaths of

* In like manner, the chief mourner at the funeral among many castes, after breaking a water-pot at the graveside, retires without looking back.

the animal and the person are supposed to take place simultaneously.* When a Tamil woman of the Parivāram caste who commits adultery outside the caste is punished with excommunication, a mud image representing her is made, two thorns are poked into its eyes, and it is thrown away outside the village.† At Bangalore in the Mysore province, a monthly festival is held in honour of Gurumurthi Swāmi, at which women disturbed by the spirits of drowned persons become possessed. The sufferer is dragged by the hair of the head to a tree, to which a lock of the hair is nailed. She flings herself about in a frenzy, and throws herself on the ground, leaving the lock of hair torn out by the roots fastened to the tree by the nail. Eventually the spirit goes up the tree, and the woman recovers.‡ In the Madura district, women possessed by devils may be seen at the great temple at Madura every Navarātri, waiting for release.

"There are many professional exorcists, who are often the pūjāris (priests) at the shrine of the local goddess. At dead of night they question the evil spirit, and ask him who he is, why he has come there, and what he wants to induce him to go away. He answers through the mouth of the woman, who works herself up into a frenzy, and throws herself about wildly. If he will not answer, the woman is whipped with the rattan which the exorcist carries, or with a bunch of margosa (*Melia Azadirachta*) twigs. When he replies, his requests for offerings of certain kinds are complied with. When he is satisfied, and agrees to leave, a stone is placed on the woman's head, and she is let go, and dashes off into darkness. The place at which the stone drops to the ground is

* F. Fawcett, *Madras Museum Bull.*, 1900, iii., No. 1, 51.

† "Gazetteer of the Madura District," 1906, i. 103.

‡ F. Fawcett, *Journ. Anthrop. Soc.*, Bombay, i. 533-5.

supposed to be the place where the evil spirit is content to remain, and, to keep him there, a lock of the woman's hair is nailed with an iron nail to the nearest tree." *

Sometimes a sorcerer makes an evil spirit take a vow that it will not trouble any one in the future, and, in return, offers to it the blood of fowls, a goat, etc. He then orders the spirit to climb a tree, and drives three large iron nails into the trunk thereof. As iron is disliked by evil spirits, the result is to confine the spirit in the tree, for it cannot descend beyond the nails. In the Telugu country, when a person is supposed to be possessed by a devil, it is often the practice to take him to some special tree, which is believed to be a favourite residence of demons, and drive a nail into the trunk. If the devil has any proper feeling, he thereupon leaves the man or woman, and takes up his abode in the tree. This ceremony is performed with certain religious rites, and involves considerable expenditure. Sometimes, devil drivers are called in, who "seat the woman in a fog of resin smoke, and work upon or beat her until she declares the supposed desires of the devil in the way of sacrifice; and, when these have been complied with, one of her hairs is put in a bottle, formally shown to the village goddess, and buried in the jungle, while iron nails are driven into the threshold of the woman's house to prevent the devil's return." †

At the first menstrual ceremonies of a Pulaya girl in the Cochin State, she stands on the morning of the seventh day before some Parayas, who play on their flute and drum, to cast out the demons, if any, from her body. If she is possessed by them, she leaps with frantic

* "Gazetteer of the Madura District," 1906, i. 87.
† "Gazetteer of the Vizagapatam District," 1907, i. 73.

movements. In this case, the demon is transferred to a tree by driving a nail into the trunk, after offerings have been made.* When an Oddē (Telugu navvy) girl reaches puberty, she is confined in a special hut, in which a piece of iron, and other things, are placed, to keep off evil spirits. In some castes, when a woman is in labour, an iron sickle is kept on the cot for a similar purpose. After delivery, she keeps iron in some form, *e.g.*, a small crowbar, knife, or nails, in the room, and takes it about with her when she goes out. At a Nāyar funeral in Malabar, the chief mourner holds in his hand, or tucks into his waist-cloth, a piece of iron, generally a long key.† At a marriage among the Mūsu Kammas in the Telugu country, an iron ring is tied to the milk-post. For curing sprains, it is said to be a common practice to keep near the patient a sickle, an iron measure, or any article of iron which is at hand. A ceremony, called Dwāra Pratishta, is performed by Lingāyats when the door-frame of a new house is set up, and an iron nail is driven into the frame, to prevent devils or evil spirits from entering the house. A former Rāja of Vizianagram would not allow the employment of iron in the construction of buildings in his territory, because it would inevitably be followed by smallpox or other epidemic.‡

A few years ago, a Native servant was charged with beating with a cane a woman who was suffering from malarial fever after her confinement, in order to drive out a devil, which was said to be the spirit of a woman who was drowned some time previously. The woman died three days after the beating, and various abrasions were found on the head and body. The sub-magistrate held

* L. K. Anantha Krishna Iyer, "The Cochin Tribes and Castes," 1909, i. 99.

† F. Fawcett, *Madras Museum Bull.*, 1901, iii., No. 3, 247.

‡ M. J. Walhouse, "Ind. Ant." 1881, x. 364.

that the hurt was part of the ceremony, to which the husband and mother of the woman, and the woman herself, gave their consent. But, as the hurt was needlessly severe, the servant was fined twenty-five rupees, or in default five weeks' rigorous imprisonment.

The practice of extracting or knocking out some of the teeth of a magician is widespread throughout Southern India. In connection therewith Mr R. Morris writes to me as follows:—

"A sorcerer's spells depend for their efficacy upon the distinctness with which they are pronounced. The words uttered by a man, some or all of whose front teeth are damaged, are not so clear and distinct as those of a man whose teeth are intact. Consequently, if a sorcerer's front teeth are smashed, he is ruined as a sorcerer. And, if the front teeth of his corpse are broken or extracted, his ghost is prevented from bewitching people. It is necessary to mutilate a corpse, in order to prevent the ghost doing what the live man unmutilated could have done. For example, when a man is murdered, he is hamstrung, to prevent the ghost from following in pursuit."

In connection with sorcery among the Oriyas, Mr S. P. Rice tells us * that a girl was suffering from mental disease, and believed to be possessed by a devil. She declared that she was bewitched by a certain man, who had to be cured of his power over her. Accordingly, the friends and relatives of the girl went to this man's house, dragged him out into the road, laid him on his back, and sat on his chest. They then proceeded to extract two of his front teeth with a hammer and pincers. Mr Rice adds that it does not appear how the cure was to work — whether the operators thought that words of cursing or magic, coming through the orifice of the teeth,

* "Occasional Essays on Native South Indian Life," 1901, 70-1.

would be mumbled, and thus lose some of their incisive force, and therefore of their power for evil, or whether it was thought that the devil wanted room to fly out. Attacks upon supposed sorcerers are said to be not uncommon in the Jeypore Agency. In one instance, a wizard's front teeth were pulled out by the local blacksmith, to render him unable to pronounce his spells with the distinctness requisite to real efficiency.* In the Vizagapatam district, where a village was supposed to contain a witch, a Dāsari (religious mendicant) was called upon to examine his books, and name the person. He fixed on some wretched woman, whose front teeth were knocked out, and her mouth filled with filth. She was then beaten with a switch made from the castor-oil plant. A few years ago, a woman in the North Arcot district was suffering from severe pain in the abdomen, and she and her husband were made to believe that she was possessed by a devil, which a Bairāgi (religious mendicant) offered to expel. His treatment went on for some days, and the final operations were conducted by the side of a pond. The Bairāgi repeated mantrams, while the woman was seated opposite him. Suddenly she grew violently excited, and possessed by the deity Muniswara. She pulled the Bairāgi backwards by his hair, and cried out, "Break his teeth." She then opened his mouth by pulling up the upper lip, and her husband took a small stone, and broke some of the incisor teeth. The woman continued to cry out, "He is chanting mantrams; pour water into his mouth, and stop his breathing." A third party brought water, and the woman's husband poured it into the Bairāgi's mouth. A struggle ensued, and the woman called out, "I am losing my life; he is chanting; the mantram is in his throat; he is binding me by his

* "Gazetteer of the Vizagapatam District," 1907, i. 205.

spell; put a stick into his throat." The third party then brought the Bairāgi's curved stick (yōgathandam), which the husband thrust into the Bairāgi's mouth, with the result that he died. The woman was sent to a lunatic asylum, and her husband, as there was no previous intention to cause death, and he was evidently under the influence of blind superstition, received only four and a half months' imprisonment. In a further case which occurred in the North Arcot district, a man was believed to have great power over animals, of which he openly boasted, threatening to destroy all the cattle of one of his neighbours. This man and his friends believed that they could deprive the sorcerer of his power for evil by drawing all his teeth, which they proceeded to do with fatal results. In the Kistna district, a Māla weaver was suspected of practising sorcery by destroying men with devils, and bringing cholera and other diseases. He was met by certain villagers, and asked for tobacco. While he stopped to get the tobacco out, he was seized and thrown on the ground. His hands were tied behind his back, and his legs bound fast with his waist-cloth. One man sat on his legs, another on his waist, and a third held his head down by the kudumi (hair-knot). His mouth was forced open with a pair of large pincers, and a piece of stick was thrust between the teeth to prevent the mouth closing. One of the assistants got a stone as big as a man's fist, and with it struck the sorcerer's upper and lower teeth several times until they were loosened. Then nine teeth were pulled out with the pincers. A quantity of milk-hedge (*Euphorbia*) juice was poured on the bleeding gums, and the unfortunate man was left lying on his back, to free himself from his bonds as best he could.* In the Tamil country, the

* H. J. Stokes, "Ind. Ant.," 1876, v. 355-6.

Vekkil Tottiyans are supposed to be able to control certain evil spirits, and cause them to possess a man. It is believed, however, that they are deprived of their power as soon as they lose one of their teeth.

The Kondhs of Ganjam believe that they can transform themselves into tigers or snakes, half the soul leaving the body and becoming changed into one of these animals, either to kill an enemy, or to satisfy hunger by having a good feed on cattle. During this period they are said to feel dull and listless, and, if a tiger is killed in the forest, they will die at the same time. Mr Fawcett informs me that the Kondhs believe that the soul wanders during sleep. On one occasion, a dispute arose owing to a man discovering that another Kondh, whose spirit used to wander about in the guise of a tiger, ate up his soul, and he fell ill. Like the Kondhs, some Paniyans of Malabar are believed to be gifted with the power of changing themselves into animals. There is a belief that, if they wish to secure a woman whom they lust after, one of the men gifted with the special power goes to the house at night with a hollow bamboo, and goes round it three times. The woman then comes out, and the man, changing himself into a bull or dog, works his wicked will. The woman is said to die in the course of a few days. For assuming the disguise of an animal, the following formulæ are said * to be effective:—

1. Take the head of a dog and burn it, and plant on it a vellakuthi plant. Burn camphor and frankincense, and adore it. Then pluck the root, mix it with the milk of a dog, and the bones of a cat. A mark made with the mixture on the forehead will enable a person to assume the form of any animal he thinks of.

* L. K. Anantha Krishna Iyer, "The Cochin Tribes and Castes," 1909, i. 167.

2. Worship with a lighted wick and incense before a stick of the malankara plant. Then chant the Sakti mantram one hundred and one times. Watch carefully which way the stick inclines. Proceed to the south of the stick, and pluck the whiskers of a live tiger. Make with them a ball of the veerali silk, string it with silk, and enclose it within the ear. Stand on the palms of the hand to attain the disguise of a tiger, and, with the stick in hand, think of a cat, white bull, or any other animal. Then you will appear as such in the eyes of others.

The name Chedipe (prostitute) is applied to sorceresses in the Godāvari district. The Chedipe is believed to ride on a tiger at night over the boundaries of seven villages, and return home at early morn. When she does not like a man, she goes to him bare-bodied at dead of night, the closed doors of the house in which he is sleeping opening before her. She sucks his blood by putting his toe in her mouth. He will then lie like a corpse. Next morning he feels uneasy and intoxicated, as if he had taken ganja, and remains in this condition all day. If he does not take medicine from some one skilled in the treatment of such cases, it is said that he will die. If he is properly treated, he will recover in about ten days. If he makes no effort to get cured, the Chedipe will molest him again, and, becoming gradually emaciated, he will die. When a Chedipe enters a house, all those who are awake will become insensible, those who are seated falling down as if they had taken a soporific drug. Sometimes she drags out the tongue of the intended victim, who will die at once. At other times, slight abrasions will be found on the skin of the victim, and, when the Chedipe puts pieces of stick thereon, they burn as if burnt by fire. Sometimes she will find him behind a bush, and, undressing there, will fall on any passer-by in the jungle, assuming the form of a tiger with one of the legs in human form. When thus disguised, she is called Marulupuli (enchanting tiger). If the man is a brave fellow, and tries to kill the Chedipe with any instrument he may have with him, she will run away; and, if any man belonging to her village detects her mischief, she will assume her real form, and say blandly that she is only digging roots. The above story was obtained by a Native official when he visited a Koyi village, where he was told that a man had been sentenced to several years' imprisonment for being one of a gang who had murdered a Chedipe for being a sorceress.

In the Vizagapatam district, the people believe that a witch, when she wishes to revenge herself on any man, climbs at night to the top of his house, and, making a hole through the roof, drops a thread down till the end of it touches the body of the sleeping man. Then she sucks at the other end, and draws up all the blood out of his body. Witches are said to be able to remove all the bones out of a man's body, or to deposit a fish, ball of hair, or rags in his stomach. The town of Jeypore was once said to be haunted by a ghost. It was described as a woman, who paraded the town at midnight in a state of nudity, and from her mouth proceeded flames of fire. She sucked the blood of any loose cattle she found about, and, in the same way, revenged herself on any man who had insulted her.*

I am informed by Mr G. F. Paddison that, in cases of sickness among the Savaras of Vizagapatam, a buffalo is tied up near the door of the house. Herbs and rice in small platters, and a little brass vessel containing toddy, balls of rice, flowers, and medicine, are brought

* "Gazetteer of the Vizagapatam District," 1907, i. 73.

with a bow and arrow. The arrow is thicker at the basal end than towards the tip. The narrow part goes, when shot, through a hole in front of the bow, which is too small to allow of the passage of the rest of the arrow. A Bēju (wise woman) pours some toddy over the herbs and rice, and daubs the patient over the forehead, breasts, stomach, and back. She croons out a long incantation to the goddess, stopping at intervals to call out "Daru," to attract the attention of the goddess. She then takes the bow and arrow, and shoots twice into the air, and, standing behind the kneeling patient, shoots balls of medicine stuck on the tip of the arrow at her. The construction of the arrow is such that the balls are dislodged from its tip. The patient is thus shot at all over the body, which is bruised by the impact of the medicine balls. Afterwards the Bēju shoots one or two balls at the buffalo, which is taken to a path forming the village boundary, and killed with a tangi (axe). The patient is then daubed with the blood of the buffalo, rice, and toddy, and a feast concludes the ceremonial. Mr Paddison once gave some medicine to the Porojas of Vizagapatam during an epidemic of cholera in a village. They took it eagerly, but, as he was going away, asked whether it would not be a quicker cure to put the witch in the next village, who had brought on the cholera, into jail. In the Koraput tāluk of Vizagapatam, a wizard once had a reputation for possessing the power of transplanting trees, and it was believed that, if a man displeased him, his trees were moved in the night, and planted in some one else's grounds.

It is recorded* by the Rev. J. Cain that the Koyis of the Godāvari district "assert that the death of every one is caused by the machinations of a sorcerer, instigated thereto

* "Ind. Ant.," 1876, v. 358.

by an enemy of the deceased, or of the deceased's friends. So, in former years, inquiry was always made as to the person likely to have been at such enmity with the deceased as to wish for his death; and, having settled upon a suspicious individual, the friends of the deceased used to carry the corpse to the accused, and call upon him to clear himself by undergoing the ordeal of dipping his hands in boiling oil or water.* Within the last two years, I have known of people running away from their village because of their having been accused of having procured by means of a wizard the death of some one with whom they were at enmity about a plot of land."

According to another account,† "some male member of the family of the deceased throws coloured rice over the corpse as it lies on the bed, pronouncing as he does so the names of all the known sorcerers who live in the neighbourhood. It is even now solemnly asserted that, when the name of the wizard responsible for the death is pronounced, the bed gets up, and moves towards the house or village where he resides."

The Rev. J. Cain ‡ once saw a magician at work in the Godāvari district, "discovering the cause of the sickness which had laid prostrate a strong Koyi man. He had in his hand a leaf from an old palmyra leaf book, and, as he walked round and round the patient, he pretended to be reading. Then he took up a small stick, and drew a number of lines on the ground, after which he danced and sang round and round the sick man, who sat looking at him, evidently much impressed with his performance, Suddenly he made a dart at the man, and, stooping down,

* Trial by Ordeal, *see* my "Ethnographic Notes in Southern India," 1907, 407-32.

† "Gazetteer of the Godāvari District," 1907, i. 64.

‡ *Madras Christ. Coll. Mag.*, 1887-8, v. 355.

bit him severely in two or three places in the back. Then, rushing to the front, he produced a few grains, which he said he had found in the man's back, and which were evidently the cause of the sickness."

In another case, a young Koyi was employed to teach a few children in his village, but ere long he was attacked by a strange disease, which no medicine could cure. As a last resource, a magician was called in, who declared the illness to have been brought on by a demoness at the instigation of some enemy, who was envious of the money which the lad had received for teaching. The magician produced a little silver, which he declared to be a sure sign that the sickness was connected with the silver money he was receiving for teaching.

A riot took place, in 1900, at the village of Korravanivasala in the Vizagapatam district, under the following strange circumstances. A Konda Dora (hill cultivator caste) named Korra Mallayya pretended that he was inspired, and gradually gathered round him a camp of four or five thousand people from various places. At first his proceedings were harmless enough, but at last he gave out that he was a reincarnation of one of the five Pāndava brothers, the heroes of the Mahābhārata, who are worshipped by the Konda Doras.* He further announced that his infant son was the god Krishna; that he would drive out the English, and rule the country himself; and that, to effect this, he would arm his followers with bamboos, which would be turned by magic into guns, and would change the weapons of the authorities into water. Bamboos were cut, and rudely fashioned to resemble guns, and, armed with these, the camp was drilled by the Swāmi (god), as Mallayya had come to

* At times of census, the Konda Doras have returned themselves as Pāndava kulam, or Pāndava caste.

be called. The assembly next sent word that they were going to loot Pāchipenta, and, when two constables came to see how matters stood, the fanatics fell upon them, and beat them to death. The local police endeavoured to recover the bodies, but, owing to the threatening attitude of the Swāmi's followers, had to abandon the attempt. The district magistrate then went to the place in person, collected reserve police from various places, and rushed the camp to arrest the Swāmi and the other leaders of the movement. The police were resisted by the mob, and obliged to fire. Eleven of the rioters were killed, others wounded or arrested, and the rest dispersed. Sixty of them were tried for rioting, and three, including the Swāmi, for murdering the constables. Of the latter, the Swāmi died in jail, and the other two were hanged. The Swāmi's son, the god Krishna, also died, and all trouble ended.

A Kāpu (Telugu cultivator) in the Cuddapah district once pretended to have received certain maxims direct from the Supreme Being, and forewarned his neighbours that he would fall into a trance, which actually occurred, and lasted for three days. On his recovery, he stated that his spirit had been during this time in heaven, learning the principles of the Advaita religion from a company of angels. One of his peculiarities was that he went about naked, because, when once engaged in separating two bullocks which were fighting, his cloth tumbled down, after which he never put it on again. This eccentric person is said to have pulled a handful of maggots from the body of a dead dog, to have put them into his mouth, and to have spat them out again as grains of rice. A shrine was built over his grave.*

A few years ago, a Muhammadan fakir undertook to drive away the plague in Bellary. Incantations were

* "Manual of the Cuddapah District," 1875, 290-1.

performed over a black goat, which was sacrificed at a spot where several roads met. A considerable sum of money was collected, and the poor were fed. But the plague was not stayed.

On one occasion, an old woman hearing that her only son was dangerously ill, sought the aid of a magician, who proceeded to utter mantrams, to counteract the evil influences which were at work. While this was being done, an accomplice of the magician turned up, and, declaring that he was a policeman, threatened to charge the two with sorcery if they did not pay him a certain sum of money. The woman paid up, but discovered later on that she had been hoaxed.

Two men were, some years ago, sentenced to rigorous imprisonment under the following circumstances. A lady, who was suffering from illness, asked a man who claimed to be a magician to cure her. He came with his confederate, and told the patient to place nine sovereigns on a clay image. This sum not being forthcoming, a few rupees and a piece of a gold necklace were accepted. These were deposited on the image, and it was placed in a tin box, which was locked up, one of the men retaining the key. On the following day the two men returned, and the rupees and piece of gold were placed on a fresh image. Becoming inspired by the god, one of the men announced that the patient must give a gold bangle off her wrist, if she wished to be cured quickly. The bangle was given up, and placed on the image, which was then converted into a ball containing the various articles within it. The patient was then directed to look at various corners of the room, and repeat a formula. The image was placed in a box, and locked up as before, and the men retired, promising to return next day. This they failed to do, and the lady, becoming suspicious, broke open the box, in which the image was found, but the money and ornaments were missing.

A case relating to the supposed guarding of treasure by an evil spirit came before the Court in the Coimbatore district in 1908. Two Valluvans (Tamil astrologers) were staying in a village, where they were foretelling events. They went to the house of an old woman, and, while telling her fortune, announced that there was a devil in the house guarding treasure, and promised to drive it out, if twenty rupees were given to them. The woman borrowed the money, and presented it to them. In the evening the Valluvans went into the kitchen, and shut the door. Certain ceremonies are said to have been performed, at the conclusion of which the woman and her son entered the room, and, in the light of a flickering torch, were shown a pit, in which there was a copper pot, apparently full of gold sovereigns. One of the astrologers feigned a sudden attack from the devil, and fell down as if unconscious. The other pushed the people of the house outside the door, and again shut it. Eventually the men came out, and announced that the devil was a ferocious one, and would not depart till a wick from an Erode paradēsi was lighted before it, for obtaining which a hundred rupees were required. If the devil was not thus propitiated, it would, they said, kill the people of the house sooner or later. The old woman borrowed the sum required, and her son and the two astrologers went to Karur to take the train to Erode, to meet the paradēsi. At Karur the two men took tickets for different places, and the son, becoming suspicious, informed the police, who arrested them. On them were found some circular pieces of card covered with gold tinsel.

A few years ago, a Zamindar (landowner) in the

Godāvari district engaged a Muhammadan to exorcise a devil which haunted his house. The latter, explaining that the devil was a female and fond of jewelry, induced the Zamindar to leave a large quantity of jewels in a locked receptacle in a certain room, to which only the exorcist, and of course the devil, had access. The latter, it was supposed, would be gratified by the loan of the jewels, and would cease from troubling. The exorcist managed to open the receptacle and steal the jewels, and, such was the faith of his employer, that the offence was not suspected until a police inspector seized Rs. 27,000 worth of jewels in Vizagapatam on suspicion, and they were with difficulty traced to their source.

In a note on wonder-working in India, the Rev. J. Sharrock narrates the following incident.

"A Sanyāsi (ascetic) was ordered with contempt from the house of a rich Zemindar. Thereupon, the former threatened to curse his house by despatching a devil to take possession of it that very night. On one of the doors of the inner courtyard he made a number of magical passes, and then left the house in high dudgeon. As soon as it grew dark, the devil appeared on the door in flickering flames of phosphorus, and almost frightened the Zemindar and the other inmates out of their five senses. Wild with terror, they fled to the Sanyāsi, and begged and entreated him to come and exorcise the devil. Of course he refused, and of course they pressed him with greater and greater presents till he was satisfied. Then he came with kungkuma (a mixture of turmeric, alum, and lime-juice), and rubbed the fiery demon off with the usual recitation of mantras. During the rest of his stay, the Sanyāsi was treated with the most profound respect, while his sishyas (disciples) received the choicest food and fruits that could be obtained."

The following cases are called from the annual reports of the Chemical Examiner to the Government of Madras, in further illustration of the practices of pseudo-magicians.

(*a*) A wizard came to a village, in order to exorcise a devil which possessed a certain woman. He was treated like a prince, and was given the only room in the house, while the family turned out into the hall. He lived there for several days, and then commenced his ceremonies. He drew the figure of a lotus on the floor, made the woman sit down, and commenced to twist her hair with his wand. When she cried out, he sent her out of the room, saying she was unworthy to sit on the lotus figure, but promising nevertheless to exorcise the devil without her being present. He found a half-witted man in the village, drugged him with ganja, brought him to the house, and performed his ceremonies on this man, who, on becoming intoxicated with the drug, began to get boisterous. The wizard tied him up with a rope, because he had become possessed of the devil that had possessed the woman. The man was subsequently traced by his relatives, found in an unconscious state, and taken to hospital. The wizard got rigorous imprisonment.

(*b*) Some jewels were lost, and a mantrakāra (dealer in magical spells) was called in to detect the thief. The magician erected a screen, behind which he lit a lamp, and did other things to impress the crowd with the importance of his mantrams. To the assembly he distributed betel-leaf patties containing a white powder, said to be holy ashes, and the effect of it on the suspected individuals, who formed part of the crowd, is said to have been instantaneous. So magical was the effect of this powder in detecting the thief, that the unfortunate man ultimately vomited blood. When the people remonstrated with the magician for the severity of his magic, he administered to the sufferer an antidote of solution of cow-dung and the juice of some leaf. The holy ashes were found to contain corrosive sublimate, and the magician got eighteen months' rigorous imprisonment.

I may conclude with a reference to an interesting note on the Jesuits of the Madura Mission in the middle of the seventeenth century by the Rev. J. S. Chandler, who writes as follows :—

"Dr Nobili lodged in an incommodious hut, and celebrated mass in another hut. The older he got, the more he added to the austerity of his life. The Pandārams * (non-Brāhman priests) made a new attempt against his life. One fine day they held a council as to the death he should die, and decided on magic. They summoned the most famous magician of the kingdom. Every one knew of it. When the day came, the magician presented himself, followed by a crowd, all alert to witness the vengeance of their gods. He insolently arranged his machines, and then described circles in the air. Dr Nobili regarded him with a composed air. Soon the ceremonies became more noisy. The features of the magician became decomposed, his eyes inflamed, his face contracted like that of one possessed ; he ground his teeth, howled, and struck the ground with his feet, hands, and forehead. Dr Nobili asked what comedy he was pretending to play. Then he recited magical sentences. Dr Nobili begged him to spare his throat. The magician said 'You have laughed, now die,' and threw a black powder into the air, at the same time looking at his victim, to see him fall at his feet, and then . . . skedaddled from the jeers of the crowd. Dr Nobili addressed the crowd, and from that time they regarded him as more than human."

Mr Chandler narrates further that † "a Jōgi (sorcerer

* Some Pandārams are managers of Siva temples.

† "A Madura Missionary, John Eddy Chandler: a Sketch of his Life," Boston.

and exorcist) lost in public opinion by pretending to perform a miracle in imitation of a previous Jōgi, by making a stone bull eat. A quantity of rice and other grains was served to the figure, but the vahānam (vehicle) of Rudra was not hungry. The Jōgi made many grimaces, threatened, and even employed a rattan cane, but the bull remained motionless. Not so the spectators, who overwhelmed the Jōgi with blows, and he was only saved by his friends, conducted to the frontier by soldiers, and forbidden ever again to enter the kingdom."

X

DIVINATION AND FORTUNE-TELLING

It has been said * that "men not only attempt to act directly upon nature, but they usually exhibit a keen desire to be guided as to the best course to take when in doubt, difficulty, or danger, and to be forewarned of the future. The practice of divination is by no means confined to professional magicians, or even to soothsayers, but any one may employ the accessory means."

Of professional diviners in Southern India, perhaps the best example is afforded by the Kaniyans † or Kanisans of Malabar, whose caste name is said to be a Malayālam corruption of the Sanskrit Ganika, meaning astrologer. Duarte Barbosa,‡ at the beginning of the sixteenth century, has a detailed reference to the Kaniyans, of whom he writes that "they learn letters and astronomy, and some of them are great astrologers, and foretell many future things, and form judgements upon the births of men. Kings and great persons send to call them, and come out of their palaces to gardens and pleasure-houses to see

* A. C. Haddon, "Magic and Fetishism" (Religions ancient and modern), 1906, 40.

† For much of the note on Kaniyans I am indebted to Mr N. Subramani Iyer.

‡ "Description of the Coasts of East Africa and Malabar," translation, Hakluyt Society, 1866, 139.

them, and ask them what they desire to know; and these people form judgement upon these things in a few days, and return to those that asked them, but they may not enter the palaces; nor may they approach the king's person on account of being low people. And the king is then alone with him. They are great diviners, and pay great attention to times and places of good and bad luck, which they cause to be observed by those kings and great men, and by the merchants also; and they take care to do their business at the time which these astrologers advise them, and they do the same in their voyages and marriages. And by these means these men gain a great deal."

Buchanan,* three centuries later, notes that the Kaniyans "possess almanacks, by which they inform people as to the proper time for performing ceremonies or sowing their seeds, and the hours which are fortunate or unfortunate for any undertaking. When persons are sick or in trouble, the Cunishun, by performing certain ceremonies in a magical square of 12 places, discovers what spirit is the cause of the evil, and also how it may be appeased."

The Kaniyans are practically the guiding spirits in all the social and domestic concerns in Malabar, and even Christians and Muhammadans resort to them for advice. From the moment of the birth of an infant, which is noted by the Kaniyan for the purpose of casting its horoscope, to the moment of death, the services of the village astrologer are constantly in requisition. He is consulted as to the cause of all calamities, and the cautious answers that he gives satisfy the people. "Putro na putri," which may either mean no son but a daughter, or no daughter but a son, is referred to as the type of

* "Journey through Mysore Canara, and Malabar," 1807, ii. 528.

a Kaniyan's answer, when questioned about the sex of an unborn child.

"It would be difficult," Mr Logan writes,* "to describe a single important occasion in everyday life when the Kanisan is not at hand, foretelling lucky days and hours, casting horoscopes, explaining the cause of calamities, prescribing remedies for untoward events, and physicians (not physic) for sick persons. Seed cannot be sown, or trees planted, unless the Kanisan has been consulted beforehand. He is even asked to consult his shastras to find lucky days and moments for setting out on a journey, commencing an enterprise, giving a loan, executing a deed, or shaving the head. For such important occasions as births, marriages, tonsure, investiture with the sacred thread, and beginning the A, B, C, the Kanisan is, of course, indispensable. His work, in short, mixes him up with the gravest as well as the most trivial of the domestic events of the people, and his influence and position are correspondingly great. The astrologer's finding, as one will assert with all due reverence, is the oracle of God himself, with the justice of which every one ought to be satisfied, and the poorer classes follow his dictates unhesitatingly. The astrologer's most busy time is from January to July, the period of harvest and marriages, but in the other six months of the year he is far from leading an idle life. His most lucrative business lies in casting horoscopes, recording the events of a man's life from birth to death, pointing out dangerous periods of life, and prescribing rules and ceremonies to be observed by individuals for the purpose of propitiating the gods and planets, and so averting the calamities of dangerous times. He also shows favourable junctures for the commencement of undertakings, and the grantham or book, written on palm leaf, sets forth in considerable detail the person's disposition and mental qualities, as affected by the position of the planets in the zodiac at the moment of birth. All this is

* "Malabar," 1887, i. 140-1.

a work of labour, and of time. There are few members of respectable families who are not thus provided, and nobody grudges the five to twenty-five rupees usually paid for a horoscope, according to the position and reputation of the astrologer. Two things are essential to the astrologer, namely, a bag of cowry shells (*Cypræa moneta*), and an almanac. When any one comes to consult him,* he quietly sits down, facing the sun, on a plank seat or mat, murmuring some mantrams or sacred verses, opens his bag of cowries, and pours them on the floor. With his right hand he moves them slowly round and round, solemnly reciting meanwhile a stanza or two in praise of his guru or teacher, and of his deity, invoking their help. He then stops, and explains what he has been doing, at the same time taking a handful of cowries from the heap, and placing them on one side. In front is a diagram drawn with chalk (or soapstone) on the floor, and consisting of twelve compartments (rāsis), one for each month in the year. Before commencing operations with the diagram, he selects three or five of the cowries highest up in the heap, and places them in a line on the right-hand side. [In an account before me, three cowries and two glass bottle-stoppers are mentioned as being placed on this side]. These represent Ganapati (the belly god, the remover of difficulties), the sun, the planet Jupiter, Sarasvati (the goddess of speech), and his own guru or preceptor. To all of these the astrologer gives due obeisance, touching his ears and the ground three times with both hands. The cowries are next arranged in the compartments of the diagram, and are moved about from compartment to compartment by the astrologer, who quotes meanwhile the authority on which he makes the moves. Finally he explains the result, and ends with again worshipping the deified cowries, who were witnessing the operation as spectators."

* The Kaniyan, when wanted in his professional capacity, presents himself with triple ash marks of Siva on his chest, arms, and forehead.

According to another account,* the Kaniyan "pours his cowries on the ground, and, after rolling them in the palm of his right hand, while repeating mantrams, he selects the largest, and places them in a row outside the diagram at its right-hand top corner. They represent the first seven planets, and he does obeisance to them, touching his forehead and the ground three times with both hands. The relative position of the nine planets is then worked out, and illustrated with cowries in the diagram."

The Mulla Kurumbas (jungle tribe) of Malabar are said † to "have a gift of prophecy, some being initiated in the art known as Kotiveykal, literally planting betel vine. The professor, when consulted about any future event, husks a small quantity of rice by hand, places it inside a scooped shell of a dried kuvvalam fruit (*Ægle Marmelos*), and asks one of his men to plant the betel vine. The man understands the meaning, takes out the rice, and spreads it on a plank. The professor invokes the Puthadi deity, makes a calculation, and gives his reply, which is generally found correct."

Concerning a class of people called Velichchapād, who are regarded as oracles in Malabar, Mr F. Fawcett writes as follows ‡ :—

"Far away in rural Malabar, I witnessed the ceremony in which the Velichchapād exhibited his quality. It was in the neighbourhood of a Nāyar house, to which thronged all the neighbours (Nāyar), men and women, boys and girls. The ceremony lasts about an hour. The Nāyar said it was the custom in his family to have it done once

* "Gazetteer of Malabar," 1908, i. 130.

† C. Gopalan Nair, Malabar Series, "Wynad, its People and Traditions," 1911, 70-1.

‡ *Madras Museum Bull.*, 1901, iii., No. 3, 273-4.

a year, but could give no account of how it originated; most probably in a vow, some ancestor having vowed that, if such or such benefit be received, he would for ever after have an annual performance of this ceremony in his house. It involved some expenditure, as the Velichchapād had to be paid, and the neighbours had to be fed. Somewhere about the middle of the little courtyard, the Velichchapād placed a lamp (of the Malabar pattern) having a lighted wick, a kalasam (brass vessel), some flowers, camphor, saffron (turmeric), and other paraphernalia. Bhagavati was the deity invoked, and the business involved offering flowers, and waving a lighted wick round the kalasam. The Velichchapād's movements became quicker, and, suddenly seizing his sword, he ran round the courtyard (against the sun, as sailors say), shouting wildly. He is under the influence of the deity who has been introduced into him, and gives oracular utterances to the deity's commands. What he said I know not, and no one else seemed to know, or care in the least, much interested though they were in the performance. As he ran, every now and then he cut his forehead with the sword, pressing it against the skin and sawing vertically up and down. The blood streamed all over his face. Presently he became wilder, and whizzed round the lamp, bending forward towards the kalasam. Evidently some deity, some spirit was present here, and spoke through the mouth of the Velichchapād. This, I think, undoubtedly represents the belief of all who were present. When he had done whizzing round the kalasam, he soon became a normal being, and stood before my camera. The fee for the self-inflicted laceration is one rupee, some rice, etc. I saw the Velichchapād about three days afterwards, going to perform elsewhere. The wound on his forehead had healed. The careful observer can always identify a Velichchapād by the triangular patch over the forehead, where the hair will not grow, and where the skin is somewhat indurated."

The Kotas of the Nīlgiris worship Māgāli, to whose influence outbreaks of cholera are attributed. When the dread disease breaks out among them, special sacrifices are performed with a view to propitiating the goddess, who is represented by an upright stone in a rude temple near Kotagiri. An annual ceremony takes place there, at which some man becomes possessed, and announces to the people that Māgāli has come. At the seed-sowing ceremony, a Kota priest sometimes becomes inspired, and gives expression to oracular utterances. At a Toda funeral, the men, congregating on the summit of a neighbouring hill, invoked the gods. Four of them, seized, apparently in imitation of the Kota dēvādi (priest), with divine frenzy, began to shiver and gesticulate wildly while running to and fro with closed eyes. They then began to talk in Malayālam, and offer an explanation of an extraordinary phenomenon, which had appeared in the form of a gigantic figure, which disappeared as suddenly as it appeared. The possession by some Todas of a smattering of Malayālam is explained by the fact that, when grazing their buffaloes on the western slopes of the Nīlgiris, they come in contact with Malayālam-speaking people from the neighbouring Malabar country.

For the following note on the Sakuna Pakshi (prophetic bird) mendicant caste, I am indebted to Mr C. Hayavadana Rao. The name of the caste is due to the fact that the members thereof wear on their heads a plume composed of the feathers of the Indian roller (*Coracias indica*) or blue jay of Europeans. This is one of the birds called sakuna pakshi, because they are supposed to possess the power of foretelling events, and on their movements many omens depend. Concerning the roller, Jerdon writes * that

"it is sacred to Siva, who assumed its form, and, at

* "Birds of India," 1877, i. 216-7.

the feast of the Dasserah at Nagpore, one or more used to be liberated by the Rājah, amidst the firing of cannon and musketry, at a grand parade attended by all the officers of the station. Buchanan Hamilton also states that, before the Durga Puja, the Hindus of Calcutta purchase one of these birds, and, at the time when they throw the image of Durga into the river, set it at liberty. It is considered propitious to see it on this day, and those who cannot afford to buy one discharge their matchlocks to put it on the wing."

A Sakuna Pakshi, before starting on a begging expedition, rises early, and has a cold meal. He then puts on the Vaishnava nāmam mark on his forehead, slings on his left shoulder a deer-skin pouch for the reception of the rice and other grain which will be given to him as alms, and takes up his little drum (gilaka or damaraka) made of frog's skin.

Closely allied to the Sakuna Pakshis are the Budubudikēs or Budubudukalas, a class of beggars and fortune-tellers, whose name is derived from the drum (budbuki) which they use when engaged in predicting future events.

"A huge parti-coloured turban, surmounted by a bunch of feathers, a pair of ragged trousers, a loose long coat, which is very often out at elbows, and a capacious wallet, ordinarily constitute the Budubudukala's dress. Occasionally, if he can afford it, he indulges in the luxury of a tiger or cheetah (leopard) skin, which hangs down his back, and contributes to the dignity of his calling. Add to this an odd assortment of clothes suspended on his left arm, and the picture is as grotesque as it can be. He is regarded as able to predict the future of human beings by the flight and notes of birds. His predictions are couched in the chant which he recites. The burden of the chant is always stereotyped, and purports to have been gleaned from the warble of the feathered songsters of the forest. It prognosticates peace, plenty and prosperity to the house, the birth of a son to the fair, lotus-eyed housewife, and worldly advancement to the master, whose virtues are as countless as the stars, and have the power to annihilate his enemies. It also holds out a tempting prospect of coming joy in an unknown shape from an unknown quarter, and concludes with an appeal for a cloth. If the appeal is successful, well and good. If not, the Budubudukala has the patience and perseverance to repeat his visit the next day, and so on until, in sheer disgust, the householder parts with a cloth. The drum, which has been referred to as giving the Budubudukala his name, is not devoid of interest. In appearance it is an instrument of diminutive size, and is shaped like an hour-glass, to the middle of which is attached a string with a knot at the end, which serves as the percutient. Its origin is enveloped in a myth of which the Budubudukala is very proud, for it tells of his divine descent, and invests his vocation with the halo of sanctity. According to the legend, the primitive Budubudukala who first adorned the face of the earth was a belated product of the world's creation. When he was born or rather evolved, the rest of mankind was already in the field, struggling for existence. Practically the whole scheme was complete, and, in the economy of the universe, the Budubudukala found himself one too many. In this quandary, he appealed to his goddess mother Amba Bhavani, who took pity on him, and presented him with her husband the god Parameswara's drum with the blessing 'My son, there is nothing else for you but this. Take it and beg, and you will prosper.' Among beggars, the Budubudukala has constituted himself a superior mendicant, to whom the handful of rice usually doled out is not acceptable. His demand is for clothes of any description, good, bad or indifferent, new or old, torn or whole. For, in the plenitude of his wisdom, he has realised that a cloth is a marketable commodity, which, when exchanged for money, fetches more than the handful of rice. The Budubudukala is continually on the tramp, and regulates his movements according to the seasons of the year. As a rule, he pays his visit to the rural parts after the harvest is gathered, for it is then that the villagers are at their best, and in a position to handsomely remunerate him for his pains. But, in whatever corner of the province he may be, as the Dusserah * approaches, he turns his face towards Vellore in North Arcot, where the annual festival in honour of Amba Bhavani is celebrated." †

The principal tribal deity of the Kuruvikkāran beggars is Kāli or Durga, and each sept possesses a small metal plate with a figure of the goddess engraved on it, which is usually kept in the custody of the headman. It is, however, sometimes pledged, and money-lenders give considerable sums on the security of the idol, as the Kuruvikkārans would on no account fail to redeem it. At the annual festival of the goddess, while some cakes are being cooked in oil, a member of the tribe prays that the goddess will descend on him. Taking some of the cakes out of the boiling oil, he rubs the oil on his head with his palm. He is then questioned by those assembled, to whom he gives oracular replies, after sucking the blood from the cut throat of a goat.

The nomad Koravas or Yerukalas earn a livelihood partly by telling fortunes. The Telugu name Yerukala is said to mean fortune-teller, and, as the women go on their rounds through the streets, they call out "Yeruko, amma, yeruku" *i.e.*, prophecies, mother, prophecies.

Concerning the Pachaikutti (tattooer) or Gadde (soothsayer) section of these people, Mr Paupa Rao Naidu writes ‡ that "the woman proceeds with a basket and a

* The Dusserah or Dasara is also known as Sarasvati pūja or Ayudha pūja (worship of weapons or tools). *See* p. 174.

† *Madras Weekly Mail*, 8th August, 1907.

‡ "History of Railway Thieves," 1904.

KORAVA WOMAN TELLING FORTUNE WITH COWRY SHELLS IN TRAY.

To face p. 283.

winnowing tray to a village, proclaiming their ostensible profession of tattooing and soothsaying, which they do for grain or money. When unfortunate village women, who always lose their children or often fall ill, see these Gadde women moving about, they call them into their houses, make them sit, and, pouring some grain into their baskets, ask them about their past misery and future lot. These women, who are sufficiently trained to speak in suitable language, are clever enough to give out some yarns in equivocal terms, so that the anxious women, who hope for better futurity, understand them in the light uppermost in their own minds. The Korava women will be duly rewarded, and doubly too, for they never fail to study the nature of the house, to see if it offers a fair field for booty for their men." *

It is said that Korava women invoke the village goddesses when they are telling fortunes. They use a winnowing fan and grains of rice in doing this, and prophecy good or evil according to the number of grains on the fan.† They carry a basket, winnow, stick, and a wicker tray in which cowry shells are embedded in a mixture of cow-dung and turmeric. The basket represents the goddess Kolapuriamma, and the cowries Pōlēramma. When telling fortunes, the woman places on the basket the winnow, rice, betel leaves and areca nuts, and the wicker tray. Holding her client's hand over the winnow, and moving it about, she commences to chant, and name all sorts of deities. From time to time, she touches the hand of the person whose fortune is being told with the stick. The Korava women are very clever at extracting information concerning the affairs of a client, before they proceed to tell her fortune. In a note on the initiation of Yerukala

* The Koravas are professional burglars.

† "Madras Census Report," 1901, part i. 164.

girls into the profession of fortune-telling in Vizagapatam, Mr Hayavadana Rao writes that it is carried out on a Sunday succeeding the first puberty ceremony. A caste feast, with plenty of strong drink, is held, but the girl herself fasts. The feast over, she is taken to a spot at a little distance from the settlement, called Yerukonda. This is said to be the name of a place on the trunk road between Vizianagram and Chicacole, to which girls were taken in former days to be initiated. The girl is blindfolded with a cloth. Boiled rice and green gram (grain) are mixed with the blood of a black fowl, black pig, and black goat, which are killed. Of this mixture she must take at least three morsels, and, if she does not vomit, it is taken as a sign that she will become a good fortune-teller. Vomiting would indicate that she would be a false prophetess.

The Irulas of the Tamil country, like the Yerukalas, are professional fortune-tellers. The Yerukala will carry out the work connected with her profession anywhere, at any time, and any number of times in a day. The Irula, on the contrary, remains at his home, and will only tell fortunes close to his hut, or near the hut where his gods are kept. In case of sickness, people of all classes come to consult the Irula fortune-teller, whose occupation is known as Kannimar varnithal. Taking up his drum, he warms it over the fire, or exposes it to the heat of the sun. When it is sufficiently dry to vibrate to his satisfaction, Kannimar is worshipped by breaking a cocoanut, and burning camphor and incense. Closing his eyes, the Irula beats the drum, and shakes his head about, while his wife, who stands near him, sprinkles turmeric water over him. After a few minutes, bells are tied to his right wrist. In about a quarter of an hour he begins to shiver, and breaks out in a profuse perspiration. This is a sure sign that he is inspired by the goddess. The shaking of his body becomes more violent, he breathes rapidly, and hisses like a snake. Gradually he becomes calmer, and addresses those around him as if he were the goddess, saying: "Oh! children, I have come down on my car, which is decorated with mango flowers, margosa, and jasmine. You need fear nothing so long as I exist, and you worship me. This country will be prosperous, and the people will continue to be happy. Ere long my precious car, immersed in the tank (pond) on the hill, will be taken out, and after that the country will become more prosperous," and so on. Questions are generally put to the inspired man, not directly, but through his wife. Occasionally, even when no client has come to consult him, the Irula will take up his drum towards dusk, and chant the praises of Kannimar, sometimes for hours at a stretch, with a crowd of Irulas collected round him.

I gather, from a note by Mr. T. Ranga Rao, that the jungle Yānādis of the Telugu country pose as prophets of human destinies, and pretend to hold intercourse with gods and goddesses, and to intercede between god and man. Every village or circle has one or more soothsayers, who learn their art from experts under a rigid routine. The period of pupilage is a fortnight spent in retreat, on a dietary of milk and fruits. The god or goddess Venkatēswaralu, Subbaroyadu, Malakondroyadu, Ankamma, or Pōlēramma, appears like a shadow, and inspires the pupil, who, directly the period of probation has ceased, burns camphor and frankincense. He then sings in praise of the deity, takes a sea-bath with his master, gives a sumptuous feast, and becomes an independent soothsayer. The story runs that the ardent soothsayers of old wrought miracles by stirring boiling rice with his hand, which was proof against burn or hurt. His modern brother invokes the gods with burning charcoal in his folded hands, to the beat of a drum. People flock in large numbers to learn the truth. The soothsayer arranges the tribal deity Chenchu Dēvudu, and various local gods, in a god-house, which is always kept scrupulously clean, and where worship is regularly carried on. The auspicious days for soothsaying are Friday, Saturday, and Sunday. The chief soothsayer is a male. The applicant presents him with areca nuts, fruit, flowers, and money. The soothsayer bathes, and sits in front of his house smeared with black, white, red, and other colours. His wife, or some other female, kindles a fire, and throws frankincense into it. He beats his drum and sings, while a woman within repeats the chant in a shrill voice. The songs are in praise of the deity, at whose and the soothsayer's feet the applicant prostrates himself, and invokes their aid. The soothsayer feels inspired, and addresses the suppliant thus:—"You have neglected me. You do not worship me. Propitiate me adequately, or ruin is yours." The future is predicted in song, and the rural folk place great faith in the predictions.

As an example of devil worship and divination, the practice thereof by the Tamil Valaiyans and Kallans of Orattanādu in the Tanjore district is described as follows by Mr F. R. Hemingway.*

"Valaiyan houses generally have an odiyan (*Odina Wodier*) tree in the backyard, wherein the devils are believed to live, and, among the Kallans, every street has a tree for their accommodation. They are propitiated at least once a year, the more virulent under the tree itself, and the rest in the house, generally on a Friday or Monday. Kallans attach importance to Friday in Ādi (July and

* "Gazetteer of the Tanjore District," 1906, i. 69.

August), the cattle Pongal day in Tai (January and February), and Kartigai day in the month Kartigai (November and December). A man, with his mouth covered with a cloth to indicate silence and purity, cooks rice in the backyard, and pours it out in front of the tree, mixed with milk and jaggery (crude sugar). Cocoanuts and toddy are also placed there. These are offered to the devils, represented in the form of bricks or mud images placed at the foot of the tree, and camphor is set alight. A sheep is then brought and slaughtered, and the devils are supposed to spring one after another from the tree into one of the bystanders. This man then becomes filled with the divine afflatus, works himself up into a kind of frenzy, becomes the mouthpiece of the spirits, pronounces their satisfaction or the reverse at the offerings, and gives utterance to cryptic phrases, which are held to foretell good or evil fortune to those in answer to whom they are made. When all the devils in turn have spoken and vanished, the man recovers his senses. The devils are worshipped in the same way in the house, except that no blood is shed."

The following example of the conviction of a thief by a diviner is recorded by Mrs Murray-Aynsley.*

"A friend's ayah had her blanket stolen. The native woman rejected the interference of the police, which her mistress proposed, but said she would send for one of her own diviners. He came, caused a fire to be lighted in an earthen vessel, then took a small basket-work grain-sifter used for winnowing rice. Having repeated certain prayers or incantations, the diviner stuck a pair of scissors into the deepest part of this tray, and, having done this, required the two assistants he brought with him each to put a finger beneath the holes in the scissors, and then hold the sifter suspended over the fire. The servants of the house were then all required, each in turn, to take a small quantity of uncooked rice in their

* "Our Tour in Southern India," 1883, 162-3.

hands, and drop it into the flame, between the fork formed by the scissors, the diviner all the time repeating some formula. All went very smoothly till the woman-servant, whom my friend had all along suspected of the theft, performed this ceremony, on which the grain-sifter commenced turning round rapidly. The culprit was convicted, and confessed the theft."

The following method of discovering theft by chewing rice is described by Daniel Johnson.*

"A Brāhmin is sent for, who writes down all the names of the people in the house, who are suspected. Next day he consecrates a piece of ground by covering it with cow-dung and water, over which he says a long prayer. The people then assemble on this spot in a line facing the Brāhmin, who has with him some dry rice, of which he delivers to each person the weight of a four-cornered rupee, or that quantity weighed with the sacred stone called Salagram, which is deposited in a leaf of the pippal or banyan tree. At the time of delivering it, the Brāhmin puts his right hand on each person's head, and repeats a short prayer; and, when finished, he directs them all to chew the rice, which at a given time must be produced on the leaves masticated. The person or persons, whose rice is not thoroughly masticated, or exhibits any blood on it, is considered guilty. The faith they all have of the power of the Brāhmin, and a guilty conscience operating at the same time, suppresses the natural flow of saliva to the mouth, without which the hard particles of the rice bruise and cut the gums, causing them to bleed, which they themselves are sensible of, and in most instances confess the crime."

* "Sketches of Field Sports Followed by the Natives of India," 1822.

XI

SOME AGRICULTURAL CEREMONIES

FOR the following note* on agricultural ceremonies in Malabar, I am indebted to Mr C. Karunakara Menon, who writes as an eye-witness thereof.

"Vishu, the feast of the vernal equinox, is celebrated on the first of the Malabar month Mēdom, between the 10th and 14th of April. To the Tamulians it is the New Year's day, but to the people of Malabar it marks the commencement of the new agricultural year. A Malabar proverb says 'No hot weather after Vishu.' The first thing seen on the morning of Vishu day is considered as an omen for the whole year. Every Malayāli takes care, therefore, to look at an auspicious object. Arrangements are accordingly made to have a kani, which means a sight or spectacle (*see* p. 18). After the first sight, the elders make presents of money to the junior members of the family and the servants. After the distribution of money, the most important function on Vishu morning is the laying of the spade-furrow, as a sign that cultivation operations have commenced. A spade decorated with konna (*Cassia Fistula*) flowers, is brought, and a portion of the yard on the north side smeared with cow-dung, and painted with powdered rice-water. An offering is made on the spot to Ganapathi (the elephant god), and a member of the family, turning to the east, cuts the earth three times. A ceremony on a grander scale is called the Chāl, which literally means

* The note was originally published in *Madras Museum Bull.*, 1906, v., No. 2, 98-105.

a furrow, for an account of which we must begin with the visit of the astrologer (Kanisan) on Vishu eve. Every dēsam (hamlet) in Malabar has its own astrologer, who visits families under his jurisdiction on festive occasions (*see* p. 275). Accordingly, on the eve of the new agricultural year, every Hindu home in the district is visited by the Kanisans of the respective dēsams, who, for a modest present of rice, vegetables, and oils, make a forecast of the season's prospects, which is engrossed on a cadjan (palm leaf). This is called the Vishu phalam, which is obtained by comparing the nativity with the equinox. Special mention is made therein as to the probable rainfall from the position of the planets—highly prized information in a district where there are no irrigation works or large reservoirs for water. But the most important item in the forecast is the day and time at which the first ploughing is to take place. The Chāl is one of the most impressive and solemn of the Malabar agricultural ceremonies, and, in its most orthodox form, is now prevalent only in the Palghāt tāluk. At the auspicious hour shown in the forecast, the master of the house, the cultivation agent, and the Cherumars,* assemble in the barn. A portion of the yard in front of the building is painted with rice-water, and a lighted bell-metal lamp is placed near at hand with some paddy (unhusked rice) and rice, and several cups made of the leaves of the kanniram (*Strychnos Nux-vomica*) — as many cups as there are varieties of seed in the barn. Then, placing implicit faith in his gods and ancestors, the master of the house opens the barn-door, followed by a Cheruman with a new painted basket containing the leaf cups. The master then takes a handful of seed from a seed-basket, and fills one of the cups, and the cultivating agent, head Cheruman, and others who are interested in a good harvest, fill the cups till the seeds are exhausted. The basket, with the cups, is next taken to the decorated portion of the yard.

* The Cherumars are field labourers, who were formerly agrestic slaves, and, like other servile classes, possess special privileges on special occasions.

A new ploughshare is fastened to a new plough, and a pair of cattle are brought onto the scene. Plough, cattle, and basket, are all painted with rice-water. A procession proceeds to the fields, on reaching which the head Cheruman lays down the basket, and makes a mound of earth with the spade. To this a little manure is added, and the master throws a handful of seed into it. The cattle are then yoked, and one turn is ploughed by the head Cheruman. Inside this at least seven furrows are made, and the plough is dropped to the right. An offering is made to Ganapathi, and the master throws some seed into the furrow. Next the head Cheruman calls out, 'May the gods on high, and the deceased ancestors, bless the seed which has been thrown broadcast, and the cattle which are let loose, the mother and children of the house, the master and the slaves. May they also vouchsafe to us a good crop, good sunshine, and a good harvest.' A cocoanut is then cut on the ploughshare, and from the cut portions several deductions are made. If the hinder portion is larger than the front one, it augurs an excellent harvest. If the nut is cut into two equal portions, the harvest will be moderate. If the cut passes through the eyes of the nut, or if no water is left in the cut portions, certain misfortune is foreboded. The cut fragments are then taken with a little water inside them, and a leaf of the tulsi plant* (sacred basil, *Ocimum sanctum*) dropped in. If the leaf turns to the right, a propitious harvest is assured, whereas, if it turns to the left, certain calamity will follow. This ceremonial concluded, there is much shouting, and the names of all the gods are called out in a confused prayer. The party then breaks up, and the unused seeds are divided among the workmen. The actual sowing of the seed takes place towards the middle of May. The local deity who is responsible for good

* The tulsi plant is the most sacred plant of the Hindus, by whom it is grown in pots, or in brick or earthen pillars (brindāvanam) hollowed out at the top, in which earth is deposited. It is watered and worshipped daily.

crops is Cherukunnath Bhagavathi, who is also called Annapūrana, and is worshipped in the Chirakkal tāluk. Before the seed is sown, a small quantity is set apart as an offering to the goddess Annapurna Iswari. By July the crops should be ready for harvesting, and the previous year's stock is running low. Accordingly, several ceremonies are crowded into the month Karkitakam (July-August). When the sun passes from the sign of Gemini to Cancer, *i.e.*, on the last day of Mithuna (June-July), a ceremony called the driving away of Potti (evil spirit) is performed in the evening. The house is cleaned, and the rubbish collected in an old winnowing basket. A woman rubs oil on her head, and, taking the basket, goes three times round the house, while children run after her, calling out, 'Potti, phoo' (run away, evil spirit). On the following morning the good spirit is invoked, and asked to bless every householder, and give a good harvest. Before dawn a handful of veli, a wild yam (*Caladium nymphœiflorum*), and turmeric, together with ten herbs called dasapushpam (ten flowers), such as are worn in the head by Nambūtiri Brāhman ladies after the morning bath, are brought in. They are:—

Thiruthāli (*Ipomœa sepiaria*).
Nilappana (*Curculigo orchioides*).
Karuka (*Cynodon Dactylon*).
Cherupoola (*Ærua lanata*).
Muyalchevi (*Emelia sonchifolia*).
Puvamkurunthala (*Vernonia cinerea*).
Ulinna (*Cardiospermum Halicacabum*).
Mukutti (*Biophytum sensitivum*).
Kannunni (*Eclipta alba*).
Krishnakananthi (*Evolvulus alsinoides*).

"Each of the above is believed to be the special favourite of some deity, *e.g.*, Nilappana of the god of riches, Thiruthāli of the wife of Kāma, the god of love, etc. They are stuck in the front eaves of every house with some cow-dung. Then, before daybreak, Sri Bhagavathi is formally installed, and her symbolical presence is continued daily till the end of the month Karkitakam. A plank, such as is used by Malayālis when they sit at meals, is well washed, and smeared with ashes. On it are placed a mirror, a potful of ointment made of sandal, camphor, musk, and saffron (turmeric), a small round box containing red paint, a goblet full of water, and a grändham (sacred book made of cadjan), usually Dēvi-Mahāthmyam, *i.e.*, song in praise of Bhagavathi. By its side the ten flowers are set. On the first day of Karkitakam, in some places, an attempt is made to convert the malignant Kāli into a benificent deity. From Calicut northward, this ceremonial is celebrated, for the most part by children, on a grand scale. From early morning they may be seen collecting ribs of plantain (banana) leaves, with which they make representations of a ladder, cattle-shed, plough, and yoke. Representations of cattle are made from the leaves of the jak tree (*Artocarpus integrifolia*). These are placed in an old winnowing basket. The materials for a feast are placed in a pot, and the toy agricultural articles and the pot are carried round each house three times, while the children call out 'Kālia, Kālia, monster, monster, receive our offering, and give us plenty of seed and wages, protect our cattle, and support our fences.' The various articles are then placed under a jak tree, on the eastern side of the house if possible. The next important ceremony is called the Nira, or bringing in of the first-fruits. It is celebrated about the middle of Karkitakam. The house is cleaned, and the doors and windows are cleansed with the rough leaves of a tree called pārakam (*Ficus hispida*), and decorated with white rice paint. The walls are white-washed, and the yard is smeared with cow-dung. The ten flowers (dasapushpam) are brought to the gate of the house, together with leaves of the following:—

Athi (*Ficus glomerata*). Ithi (*Ficus infectoria*). Arayāl (*Ficus religiosa*). Pēral (*Ficus bengalensis*).

Illi (tender leaves of bamboo). Nelli (*Phyllanthus Emblica*). Jak (*Artocarpus integrifolia*). Mango (*Mangifera indica*).

"On the morning of the ceremony, the priest of the local temple comes out therefrom, preceded by a man blowing a conch (*Turbinella rapa*) shell.* This is a signal for the whole village, and every household sends out a male member, duly purified by a bath and copiously smeared with sacred ashes, to the fields, to gather some ears of paddy. Sometimes the paddy is brought from the temple, instead of the field. It is not necessary to pluck the paddy from one's own fields. Free permission is given to pluck it from any field in which it may be ripe. When the paddy is brought near the house, the above said leaves are taken out from the gate-house, where they had been kept over night, and the ears of paddy are laid thereon. The bearer is met at the gate by a woman of the house with a lighted lamp. The new paddy is then carried to the house in procession, those assembled crying out 'Fill, fill; increase, increase; fill the house; fill the baskets; fill the stomachs of the children.' In a portion of the verandah, which is decorated with rice paint, a small plank, with a plantain leaf on it, is set. Round this the man who bears the paddy goes three times, and, turning due east, places it on the leaf. On the right is set the lighted lamp. An offering of cocoanuts and sweets is made to Ganapathi, and the leaves and ears of paddy are attached to various parts of the house, the agricultural implements, and even to trees. A sumptuous repast brings the ceremony to a close. At Palghāt, when the new paddy is carried in procession, the people say 'Fill like the Kottāram in Kozhalmannam; fill like the expansive sands of the Perar.' This Kottāram is eight miles west of Palghāt. According to Dr Gundest, the word means a store-house, or place where temple affairs are managed. It is a ruined building with crumbling walls, lined inside with laterite, and outside with slabs of granite. It was the granary of the Maruthūr temple adjoining it, and,

* The sacred conch or chank shell is used as a musical instrument in processions, and during religious services at Hindu temples.

the story goes that the supply in this granary was inexhaustible.

"The next ceremony of importance is called Puthari (meal of new rice). In some places it takes place on Nira day, but, as a rule, it is an independent festival, which takes place during the great national festival Ōnam in August. When the new rice crop has been threshed, a day is fixed for the ceremony. Those who have no land under cultivation simply add some grains of the new rice to their meal. An indispensable curry on this day is made of the leaves of *Cassia Tora*, peas, the fruit of puthari chundanga (*Swertia Chirata*), brinjals (*Solanum Melongena*), and green pumpkins. The first crop is now harvested. There are no special ceremonies connected with the cultivation of the second crop, except the one called Chēttotakam in the month of Thulam (November), which is observed in the Palghāt tāluk. It is an offering made to the gods, when the transplantation is completed, to wipe out the sin the labourers may have committed by unwittingly killing the insects and reptiles concealed in the earth. The god, whose protection is invoked on this occasion, is called Muni. No barn is complete without its own Muni, who is generally represented by a block of granite beneath a tree. He is the protector of cattle and field labourers, and arrack (liquor), toddy, and blood, form necessary ingredients for his worship.

"In well-to-do families, a goat is sacrificed to him, but the poorer classes satisfy him with the blood of a fowl. The officiating priest is generally the cultivation agent, who is a Nāyar, or sometimes a Cheruman. The goat or fowl is brought before the god, and a mixture of turmeric and chunam (lime) sprinkled over it. If the animal shakes, it is a sign that the god is satisfied. If it does not, the difficulty is got over by a very liberal interpretation of the smallest movement of the animal, and a further application of the mixture. The god who ensures sunshine and good weather is Mullan. He is a rural deity, and is set up on the borders and ridges of the rice-fields. Like Muni, he is propitiated by the sacrifice of a fowl. The second crop is harvested in Makaram (end of January), and a festival called Uchāral is observed from the twenty-eighth to the thirtieth in honour of the menstruation of mother earth, which is believed to take place on those days, which are observed as days of abstinence from all work, except hunting. A complete holiday is given to the Cherumans. The first day is called the closing of uchāral. Towards evening some thorns, five or six broomsticks, and ashes, are taken to the room in which the grain is stored. The door is closed, and the thorns and sticks are placed against it, or fixed to it with cow-dung. The ashes are spread before it, and, during that and the following day, no one will open the door. On the second day, cessation from work is scrupulously observed. The house may not be cleaned, and the daily smearing of the floor with cow-dung is avoided. Even gardens may not be watered. On the fourth day the uchāral is opened, and a basketful of dry leaves is taken to the fields, and burnt with a little manure. The Uchāra days are the quarter days of Malabar, and demands for surrender of property may be made only on the day following the festival, when all agricultural leases expire. By the burning of leaves and manure on his estate, the cultivator, it seems to me, proclaims that he remains in possession of the property. In support of this, we have the practice of a new lessee asking the lessor whether any other person has burnt dry leaves in the field. The Uchāral festival is also held at Cherupulcherri, and at Kanayam near Shoranur. Large crowds assemble with representations of cattle in straw, which are taken in procession to the temple of Bhagavathi with beating of drums and the shouting of the crowd."

The fact that the Cherumans, who are agrestic serfs, play a leading part in some of the festivals which have just been described, is significant. In an interesting note on the privileges of the servile classes, Mr M. J. Walhouse writes * that "it is well known that the servile castes in Southern India once held far higher positions, and were indeed masters of the land on the arrival of the Brāhmanical race. Many curious vestiges of their ancient power still survive in the shape of certain privileges, which are jealously cherished, and, their origin being forgotten, are much misunderstood. These privileges are remarkable instances of survivals from an extinct state of society —shadows of long-departed supremacy, bearing witness to a period when the present haughty high-caste races were suppliants before the ancestors of degraded classes, whose touch is now regarded as pollution. In the great festival of Siva at Trivalūr in Tanjore, the headman of the Parēyans is mounted on the elephant with the god, and carries his chauri (yak-tail fly fan). In Madras, at the annual festival of the goddess of the Black Town (now George Town †), when a tāli (marriage badge) is tied round the neck of the idol in the name of the entire community, a Parēyan is chosen to represent the bridegroom. At Mēlkote in Mysore, the chief seat of the followers of Rāmānuja Achārya, and at the Brāhman temple at Bēlur, the Holeyas or Parēyans have the right of entering the temple on three days in the year, specially set apart for them."

The privilege is said to have been conferred on the Holeyas, in return for their helping Rāmānuja to recover the image of Krishna, which was carried off to Delhi by the Muhammadans. Paraiyans are allowed to take part in pulling the cars of the idols in the great festivals at Conjeeveram, Kumbakōnam, and Srīvilliputtūr. Their

* "Ind. Ant," 1873, iii. 191.

† The name Black Town was changed to George Town, to commemorate the visit of H.R.H. the Prince of Wales to Madras in 1906.

touch is not reckoned to defile the ropes used, so that other Hindus will pull with them. It was noted by Mr F. H. Ellis, who was Collector of the Madras district in 1812, that "a custom prevails among the slave castes in Tondeimandalam, especially in the neighbourhood of Madras, which may be considered as a periodical assertion of independence at the close of the Tamil month Auni, with which the revenue year ends, and the cultivation of the ensuing year ought to commence. The whole of the slaves strike work, collect in bodies outside of the villages, and so remain until their masters, by promising to continue their privileges, by solicitations, presents of betel, and other gentle means, induce them to return. The slaves on these occasions, however well treated they may have been, complain of various grievances, real and imaginary, and threaten a general desertion. This threat, however, they never carry into execution, but, after the usual time, everything having been conducted according to māmūl (custom), return quietly to their labours."

Coming to more recent times, it is recorded by Mr Walhouse * that "at particular seasons there is a festival much resembling the classic Saturnalia, in which, for the time, the relation of slaves and masters is inverted, and the former attack the latter with unstinted satire and abuse, and threaten to strike work unless confirmed in their privileges, and humbly solicit to return to labour."

In villages in South Canara there are certain rākshasas (demons), called Kambla Asura, who preside over the fields. To propitiate them, buffalo races,† which are an exciting form of sport, are held, usually in October and November, before the second or sugge crop is sown. It

* *Journ. Anthrop. Inst.*, 1874, iv. 371.

† Buffalo races, *see* my "Castes and Tribes of Southern India," 1909, i. 157-62.

is believed that, if the races are omitted, there will be a failure of the crop. The Koragas (field labourers) sit up through the night before the Kambla day, performing a ceremony called panikkuluni, or sitting under the dew. They sing songs to the accompaniment of a band about their devil Nīcha, and offer toddy and a rice pudding boiled in a large earthen pot, which is broken so that the pudding remains as a solid mass. This pudding is called kandēl addē, or pot pudding. On the morning of the races, the Holeyas (agrestic serfs) scatter manure over the field, in which the races are to take place, and plough it. On the following day, the seedlings are planted. To propitiate various demons, the days following the races are devoted to cock-fighting, in which hundreds of birds may take part.

Important agricultural ceremonies are performed by the Badagas of the Nīlgiris, who carry out most of the cultivation on these hills, at the time of sowing and harvesting the crop. The seed-sowing ceremony takes place in March, and, in some places, a Kurumba (jungle tribesman) plays an important part in it. On an auspicious day—a Tuesday before the crescent moon—a priest of the Devvē temple sets out several hours before dawn with five or seven kinds of grain in a basket and a sickle, accompanied by a Kurumba, and leading a pair of bullocks with a plough. On reaching the field selected, the priest pours the grain into the cloth of the Kurumba, and, yoking the animals to the plough, makes three furrows in the soil. The Kurumba, stopping the bullocks, kneels on the ground between the furrows, facing east. Removing his turban, he places it on the ground, and, closing his ears with his palms, bawls out "Dho, Dho" thrice. He then rises, and scatters the grain thrice on the soil. The priest and Kurumba then return to the village, and the former deposits what remains of the grain in the store-room. A new pot, full of water, is placed in the milk-house, and the priest dips his right hand therein, saying "Nerathubitta" (it is full). This ceremony is an important one, as, until it has been performed, sowing may not commence. It is a day of feasting, and, in addition to rice, *Dolichos Lablab* is cooked.

Another agricultural ceremony of the Badagas is called Devva habba or tenai (*Setaria italica*), and is usually celebrated in June or July, always on a Monday. It is apparently performed in honour of the gods Mahālingaswāmi and Hiriya Udaya, to whom a group of villages will have temples dedicated. The festival is celebrated at one place, whither the Badagas from other villages proceed, to take part in it. About midday, some Badagas and the temple priest go from the temple of Hiriya Udaya to that of Mahālingaswāmi. The procession is usually headed by a Kurumba, who scatters fragments of tūd (*Meliosma pungens*) bark and wood as he goes on his way. The priest takes with him the materials necessary for performing worship, and, after worshipping Mahālingaswāmi, the party return to the Hiriya Udaya temple, where milk and cooked rice are offered to the various gods within the temple precincts. On the following day, all assemble at the temple, and a Kurumba brings a few sheaves of *Setaria italica*, and ties them to a stone set up at the main entrance. After this, worship is done, and the people offer cocoanuts to the god. Later on, all the women of the Madhave sept, who have given birth to a first-born child, come, dressed up in holiday attire, with their babies, to the temple. On this day they wear a special nose ornament called elemukkuththi, which is only worn on one other occasion, at the funeral of a husband.

The women worship Hiriya Udaya, and the priest gives them a small quantity of rice on mīnige (*Argyreia*) leaves. After eating this, they wash their hands with water given to them by the priest, and leave the temple in a line. As soon as the Devvē festival is concluded, the reaping of the crop commences, and a measure or two of grain gathered on the first day is set apart for the Mahālingaswāmi temple.

By the Kotas (artisans and cultivators) of the Nīlgiris, a seed-sowing ceremony is celebrated in the month of Kumbam (February-March) on a Tuesday or Friday. For eight days the officiating priest abstains from meat, and lives on vegetable diet, and may not communicate directly with his wife for fear of pollution, a boy acting as spokesman. On the Sunday before the ceremony, a number of cows are penned in a kraal, and milked by the priest. The milk is preserved, and, if the omens are favourable, is said not to turn sour. If it does, this is attributed to the priest being under pollution from some cause or other. On the day of the ceremony, the priest bathes in a stream, and proceeds, accompanied by a boy, to a field or the forest. After worshipping the gods, he makes a small seed-pan in the ground, and sows therein a small quantity of rāgi (*Eleusine Coracana*). Meanwhile, the Kotas of the village go to the temple, and clean it. Thither the priest and the boy proceed, and the deity is worshipped with offerings of cocoanuts, betel, flowers, etc. Sometimes a Terkāran (priest) becomes inspired, and gives expression to oracular utterances. From the temple all go to the house of the priest, who gives them a small quantity of milk and food. Three months later, on an auspicious day, the reaping of the crop is commenced with a very similar ceremonial.

Writing in 1832, Mr Harkness states * that, during the seed-sowing ceremony, "offerings are made at the temples, and, on the day of the full-moon, after the whole have partaken of a feast, the blacksmith, and the gold and silversmith, constructing separately a forge and furnace within the temple, each makes something in the way of his vocation, the blacksmith a chopper or axe, the silversmith a ring or other kind of ornament."

In connection with the ceremonial observances of the Koyis of the Godāvari district, the Rev. J. Cain writes † that "at present the Koyis around Dummagudem have very few festivals, except one at the harvest of the zonna (*Sorghum vulgare*). Formerly they had one not only for every grain crop, but one when the ippa ‡ (*Bassia*) flowers were ready to be gathered, another when the pumpkins were ripe, at the first tapping of the palm-tree for toddy, etc. Now, at the time the zonna crop is ripe and ready to be cut, they take a fowl into the field, kill it, and sprinkle its blood on any ordinary stone put up for the occasion, after which they are at liberty to partake of the new crop. In many villages they would refuse to eat with any Koi who has neglected this ceremony, to which they give the name Kottalu, which word is evidently derived from the Telugu word kotta (new). Rice-straw cords are hung on trees, to show that the feast has been observed. [In some places, Mr Hemingway tells me, the victim is a sheep, and the first-fruits are offered to the local gods and the ancestors.] Another singular feast occurs soon after the chōlam (zonna) crop has been harvested. Early on the morning of that day, all the men of each village have to turn out into the forest to hunt, and woe betide the

* "A Singular Aboriginal Race of the Nilagiris," 1832, 76.

† "Ind. Ant." 1879, viii. 34.

‡ Liquor is distilled from ippa flowers.

unlucky individual who does not bring home some game, be it only a bird or a mouse. All the women rush after him with cow-dung, mud, or dirt, and pelt him out of their village, and he does not appear again in that village till next morning. The hunter who has been most successful then parades the village with his game, and receives presents of paddy (rice) from every house. Mr Vanstavern, whilst boring for coal at Beddanọlu, was visited by all the Koi women of the village, dressed up in their lord's clothes, and they told him that they had that morning driven their husbands to the forest, to bring home game of some kind or other."

Mr N. E. Marjoribanks once witnessed a grossly indecent pantomime, held in connection with this festival, which is called Bhūdēvi Panduga, or festival of the earth goddess. The performers were women, of whom the drummers and sword-bearers were dressed up as men. In a note on this festival, Mr F. R. Hemingway writes that "when the samalu crop is ripe, the Kois summon the pūjāri on a previously appointed day, and collect from every house in the village a fowl and a handful of grain. The pūjāri has to fast all that night, and bathe early the next morning. After bathing, he kills the fowls gathered the previous evening in the names of the favourite gods, and fastens an ear of samalu to each house, and then a feast follows. In the evening they cook some of the new grain, and kill fresh fowls, which have not to be curried but roasted, and the heart, liver, and lights of which are set apart as the especial food of their ancestral spirits, and eaten by every member of each household in their name. The bean feast is an important one, as, until it is held, no one is allowed to gather any beans. On the second day before the feast, the village pūjāri must eat only bread. The day before, he must fast for the whole twenty-four hours, and, on the day of the feast, he must eat only rice cooked in milk, with the bird offered in sacrifice. All the men of the village accompany the pūjāri to a neighbouring tree, which must be a *Terminalia tomentosa*, and set up a stone, which they thus dedicate to the goddess Kodalamma. Every one is bound to bring for the pūjāri a good hen and a seer of rice, and for himself a cock and half a seer of rice. The pujāri also demands from them two annas as his sacrificing fee."

Seed-drills used by agriculturists in the Bellary district are ornamented with carved representations of the sacred bull Nandi, the monkey-god Hanumān, and the lingam, and decorated with margosa (*Melia Azadirachta*) leaves, to bring good luck.

XII

RAIN-MAKING CEREMONIES

AMONG the Kalyāna Singapu Kondhs of Vizagapatam, a rain-making ceremony called barmarākshasi is performed, which consists in making life-size mud images of women seated on the ground, holding grindstones between their knees, and offering sacrifices to them.*

In times of drought, the Koyis of the Godāvari district hold a festival to Bhīma, one of the Pāndava brothers from whom they claim descent, and, when rain falls, sacrifice a cow or a pig to him. It is said † to be considered very efficacious if the Brāhmans take in procession round the village an image of Varuna (the god of rain) made of mud from the bed of a river or tank. Another method is to pour a thousand pots of water over the lingam in the Siva temple. Mālas (Telugu Pariahs) tie a live frog to a mortar, and put on the top thereof a mud figure representing the deity Gontiyālaṃma. They then take these objects in procession, singing "Mother frog, playing in water, pour rain by pots-full." The villagers of other castes then come and pour water over the Mālas.

The Rev. S. Nicholson informs me that, to produce rain in the Telugu country, two boys capture a frog,

* "Gazetteer of the Vizagapatam District," 1907, i. 73.
† "Gazetteer of the Godāvari District," 1907, i. 47.

and put it into a basket with some nīm (margosa, *Melia Azadirachta*) leaves. They tie the basket to the middle of a stick, which they support on their shoulders. In this manner, they make a circuit of the village, visiting every house, singing the praises of the god of rain. The greater the noise the captive animal makes, the better the omen, and the more gain for the boys, for at every house they receive something in recognition of their endeavours to bring rain upon the village fields.

"In the Bellary district when the rain fails, the Kāpu (Telugu cultivator) females catch a frog, and tie it alive to a new winnowing fan made of bamboo. On this fan, leaving the frog visible, they spread a few margosa leaves, and go singing from door to door, 'Lady frog must have her bath; oh! rain god, give at least a little water for her.' This means that the drought has reached such a stage that there is not even a drop of water for the frogs. When the Kāpu female sings this song, the woman of the house brings a little water in a vessel, pours it over the frog, which is left on the fan outside the door sill, and gives some alms. She is satisfied that such an action will bring down rain in torrents. On the first full-moon day in the month of Bhadrapada (September), the agricultural population in the Bellary district celebrate a festival called Jokumara, to appease the rain-god. The Barike women (said to belong to the Gaurimakkalu section of the Kabbēra caste) go round the village in which they live, with a basket on their heads containing margosa leaves, flowers of various kinds, and sacred ashes. They beg for alms, especially from the cultivating classes, and, in return for the alms bestowed (usually grain or food), they give some of the leaves, flowers, and ashes. The cultivators take these to their fields, prepare cholam (*Sorghum*) kanji or gruel, mix them with it, and sprinkle the kanji over their fields. After this the cultivator proceeds to the potter's kiln in the village, and fetches ashes from it, with which he makes the figure of a human being. This figure is placed in a field, and called Jokumara or rain-god, and is supposed to have the power of bringing down the rain in due season. A second kind of Jokumara worship is called muddam, or the outlining of rude representations of human figures with powdered charcoal. These are made in the early morning, before the bustle of the day commences, on the ground at cross-roads, and along thoroughfares. The Barikes, who draw these figures, are paid a small remuneration in money or kind. The figures represent Jokumara, who will bring down rain, when insulted by people treading on him. Yet another kind of Jokumara worship prevails in the Bellary district. When rain fails, the Kāpu females model a small figure of a naked human being, which they place in a miniature palanquin, and go from door to door, singing indecent songs, and collecting alms. They continue this procession for three or four days, and then abandon the figure in a field adjacent to the village. The Mālas take possession of the abandoned Jokumara, and, in their turn, go about singing indecent songs, and collecting alms for three or four days, and then throw the figure away in some jungle. This form of Jokumara worship is also believed to bring down plenty of rain. In the Bellary district, the agriculturists have a curious superstition about prophesying the state of the coming season. The village of Mailar contains a Siva temple, which is famous throughout the district for an annual festival held there in the month of February. This festival has now dwindled into more or less a cattle fair. But the fame of the temple continues as regards the Karanika, which is a cryptic sentence uttered by the priest, containing a prophecy of the prospects of the agricultural season. The pujāri (priest) of the temple is a Kuruba (cultivating caste). The feast at the temple lasts for ten days. On the last day, the god Siva is represented as returning victorious from the battlefield, after having slain the demon Malla (Mallāsura) with a huge bow. He is met half-way from the field of battle by the goddess. The wooden bow is placed on end before the god. The Kuruba priest climbs up it, as it is held by two assistants, and then gets on their shoulders. In this posture he stands rapt in silence for a few minutes, looking in several directions. He then begins to quake and quiver from head to foot. This is the sign of the spirit of the god Siva possessing him. A solemn silence holds the assembly, for the time of the Karanika has arrived. The shivering Kuruba utters a cryptic sentence, such as 'Thunder struck the sky.' This is at once copied down, and interpreted as a prophecy that there will be much rain in the year to come." *

It is said that, in the year before the Mutiny, the prophecy was "They have risen against the white-ants."

The villagers at Kanuparti in the Guntur district of the Telugu country objected, in 1906, to the removal of certain figures of the sacred bull Nandi and lingams, which were scattered about the fields, on the ground that the rainfall would cease, if these sacred objects were taken away.

To bring down rain, Brāhmans, and those non-Brāhmans who copy their ceremonial rites, have their Varuna japam, or prayers to Varuna, the rain-god. Some of the lower classes, instead of addressing their prayers to Varuna, try to induce a spirit or dēvata named Kodumpāvi (wicked one) to send her paramour Sukra to the affected area. The belief seems to be that Sukra goes away to his concubinage for about six months, and, if he does not then return, drought ensues. The ceremony consists in making a huge figure of Kodumpāvi in clay, which is placed on a cart, and dragged through the streets

* *Madras Mail*, 4th November, 1905.

for seven to ten days. On the last day, the final death ceremonies of the figure are celebrated. It is disfigured, especially in those parts which are usually concealed. Vettiyans (Paraiyan grave-diggers), who have been shaved, accompany the figure, and perform the funeral ceremonies. This procedure is believed to put Kodumpāvi to shame, and to get her to induce Sukra to return, and stay the drought. According to Mr W. Francis,* the figure, which is made of clay or straw, is dragged feet first through the village by the Paraiyans, who accompany it, wailing as though they were at a funeral, and beating drums in funeral time.

I am informed by Mr F. R. Hemingway that, when rain is wanted in the Trichinopoly district, an effigy called Komān (the king) is dragged round the streets, and its funeral performed with great attention to details. Or an effigy of Kodumpāvi is treated with contumely. In some places, the women collect kanji (rice gruel) from door to door, and drink it, or throw it away on a tank bund (embankment), wailing the while as they do at funerals. People of the higher castes repeat prayers to Varuna, and read portions of the Virāta Parvam in the Mahābhārata, in the hope that the land will be as fertile as the country of the Virāts, where the Pāndavas lived. When the tanks and rivers threaten to breach their banks, men stand naked on the bund, and beat drums; and, if too much rain falls, naked men point firebrands at the sky. Their nudity is supposed to shock the powers that bring the rain, and arrest their further progress. According to Mr Francis,† when too much rain falls, the way to stop it is to send the eldest son to stand in it stark naked, with a torch in his hand.

* "Gazetteer of the South Arcot District," 1906, i. 94.

† *Ibid.*

A Native of Coimbatore wrote a few years ago that we have done all things possible to please the gods. We spent about two hundred rupees in performing Varuna japam on a grand scale in a strictly orthodox fashion. For a few days there were cold winds, and some lightning. But, alas, the japam was over, and with that disappeared all signs of getting any showers in the near future. It is noted by Haddon * that, in the Torres Straits, as elsewhere, the impossible is never attempted, and a rain charm would not be made when there was no expectation of rain coming, or during the wrong season.

There is, in some parts of the country, a belief that, if lepers are buried when they die, rain will not visit the locality where their corpses have been deposited. So they disinter the bodies, and throw the remains thereof into the river, or burn them. Some years ago, a man who was supposed to be a leper died, and was buried. His skeleton was disinterred, put into a basket, and hung to a tree with a garland of flowers round its neck. The Superintendent of Police, coming across it, ordered it to be disposed of.

The following quaint superstitions relating to the origin of rain are recorded by Mr Gopal Panikkar.†

"In the regions above the earth, there are supposed to exist large monsters called Kalameghathanmar, to whom is assigned the responsibility of supplying the earth with water. These monsters are under the direction and control of Indra,‡ and are possessed of enormous physical strength. They have two huge horns projecting upwards from the sides of the crown of the head, large flashing eyes, and other remarkable features. All the

* "Magic and Fetishism" (Religions ancient and modern), 1906, 62.

† "Malabar and its Folk," Madras, 2nd ed., 63-4.

‡ Indra presides over the seasons and crops, and is therefore worshipped at times of sowing and reaping.

summer they are engaged in drawing up water from the earth through their mouths, which they spit out to produce rain in the rainy season. A still ruder imagination ascribes rain to the periodical discharge of urine by these monsters. Hence, in some quarters, there exists a peculiar aversion to the use of rain-water for human consumption."

INDEX

ABKĀRI (liquor) license, used as medicine, 187
Adultery, 51, 254
Agricultural ceremonies, 60, 279, 289-304
Aiyanar, 56, 154, 166-7
Alagarswāmi, 169
Alangium Lamarckii, magic oil, 228
Albino crow, 69
Alstonia scholaris, sorcery figure, 249
Amputation of finger, 241
Ancestor, 51, 56, 68, 290, 291, 302, 303
Animal sacrifice, 14, 15, 22, 33, 37, 38, 41, 55, 57, 65, 68, 69, 75, 82, 92, 119, 136, 137, 146, 148, 149, 150, 152, 156, 165, 171, 175, 177, 183, 187, 201, 205-7, 210, 211, 212, 213, 214, 217, 245, 246, 248, 249, 252, 253, 263, 267, 279, 282, 284, 287, 295, 296, 302, 303
Animals, form assumed by human beings, 226, 228, 260-2
Ant, 93, 105, 308
Ant-hill, 36, 129, 132, 133-6, 156, 187, 253
Antelope (black-buck), 82
Araikāsu Nāchiyar, 170
Aranai (lizard) 99
Aravān or Kūttāndar, festival, 152-3
Areca nut, 20-1, 31, 49, 68, 283, 286
—— palm (*Areca Catechu*), 130, 177
Arjuna, 19, 126, 152
Arka (*Calotropis gigantea*), 51-2, 53, 68, 186, 195; marriage, 51
Arrack, 236, 242, 245, 251, 253, 295
—— vendors, superstition, 32
Ashes, ceremonial use, 21, 45, 115, 138, 186, 220, 229, 293, 296; effigies, 44, 307; from burial ground, 242; of meriah victim, 204; omens, 16, 18; sacred, 103, 182, 212, 270-1, 294, 306
Astrologer, 45, 127; Kaniyan, 273-7
Āvaram (*Cassia auriculata*), clothing tied to, 156
Ayilyam festival, 125
Ayudha pūja (worship of tools and implements), 174-5

BĀBŪL (*Acacia arabica*), 153, 155
Badaga, 14, 35, 49, 85, 116, 141, 232-4, 300
Bael or bilva (*Ægle Marmelos*), 33, 184, 277
Bairāgi, 235, 258-9
Bakuda, 81
Balanites Roxburghii, in lying-in chamber, 53
Balija, 118, 159
Bamboo, 113, 114, 148, 192, 212, 229, 260, 265, 293
Bangle insect, 107-8
—— offered to cholera god, 176; to village goddess, 155; worn as vow, 161
Banyan (*Ficus bengalensis*), 177, 219, 288
Barike, 306, 307
Basavi, 47, 142-3
Bathing, ceremonial, 29, 31, 43, 51, 55, 67, 72, 81, 104, 117, 130, 135, 150, 185, 229, 252, 285, 286, 294, 301, 303
Bats, 83
Bauhinia variegata, 118, 229
Bauri or Bāwariya, 41
Bead necklets offered to cholera god, 176
Beads worn as vow, 138
Bear, 78, 189
Bēdar, 68, 136, 142, 171, 193
Bejjo sorcerer, 32
Bēju sorceress, 263
Bells tied on trees, 154
Bēpāri, 74
Bestha, 98, 102
Betel, 20-1, 31, 32, 39, 40, 47, 49, 68, 117, 118, 147, 177, 188, 244, 249, 270, 277, 283, 298, 301
—— insect (vettila poochi), 106-7
Bhadrakāli, 114, 185
Bhagavati, 128, 250, 278, 292, 296
Bhairava, the dog-god, 196
Bhūthas, 162, 242
Bilimagga, 118
Billaikāvus (cat-eaters), 77
Bird excrement, fouling by, 34, 67, 87
—— superstitions, 86-9

Birds, omens, 15, 16, 21, 23, 34, 36, 37, 50, 56, 65-70, 280
Birth, symbolical, from cow, 79-80
Bison, 81-2
Black buffalo, 45; cloth, 31, 112; face painted, 116; fowl, 284; goat, 45, 267, 284; pig, 284; rope, 111; sheep, 52, 191; thread, 220; wool, 191
Blood, human, a cure for fever, 239; offered to idol, 221; sacrificed victim, 201, 202, 207, 221; sprinkling with, 145; sucked by witch, 261, 262
—— of bullock, 80; devil-dancer, 212; fish, 102; monkey, 73
—— of sacrificed animals, 22, 33, 37, 38, 65, 68, 69, 119, 175, 183, 187, 189, 212, 245, 246, 252, 255, 263, 282, 284, 295, 302
Blood-sucker (lizard), 99-100
Boar, wild, 189
Boddu-rāyi (navel-stone), 60, 211
Bones burnt in lying-in chamber, 53; from burial-ground in sorcery, 242; omens, 56, 57; used by toddy-drawers, 76, 82
Bottling evil spirits, 250
Boundary ceremony, 60, 175; dispute, 38; flesh of victim interred, 201; goddess, 37-8, 184; oath, 36; sacrifice, 211, 263
—— stone, birth ceremony, 176-7; reverence, 184; sacrifice, 37
Bow and arrow in magic, 33, 100, 192, 226, 244, 263
—— in rain-making ceremony, 308
Bōya, 22, 50, 135
Brāhman, 15, 17, 22, 26, 27, 28, 31, 43, 45, 50, 51, 52, 58, 59, 66, 67, 68, 79-80, 90, 102, 119, 122, 123, 124, 125, 133, 135, 139, 140, 148, 157, 170, 174, 239, 288, 297
——, Konkani, 172
——, Nambutiri, 85, 192, 193, 239, 292
——, Shivalli, 136
Brāhmani bull, 63; mock marriage, 165-6
—— kite, 65, 86
—— lizard (aranai), 99
Branding of body, 146
Brinjal (*Solanum melongena*), 295
Broom, 16, 40, 115, 244, 296
Budubudukala, 280-2
Buffalo, 45, 76, 81, 202, 263; sacrifice, 22, 38, 137, 148, 201, 205, 206-7, 217
—— races, 114, 298
Bug, 105
Bull, omen, 21
Burial jars, prehistoric, supposed to contain sacrificed virgins, 216
——, mock, 211-3
—— of charm, 181, 186, 187, 229, 246, 252; of fowl with corpse, 69; of placenta, 55; of sorcery figure, 247, 249
Butea frondosa, leaf-cup, 33
Butter, 79, 116, 185, 213. *See* Ghī

CAKES at village festival, 282; in pregnancy ceremony, 54; waved against evil eye, 116-7
Camphor, 50, 115, 117, 177, 184, 229, 244, 245, 249, 260, 278, 284, 285, 287, 293
Canthium parviflorum, thorn, 252
Cassia Fistula, 18, 289
Castor-oil, 97, 105, 116, 185, 258
Cat, 17, 57, 77, 260, 261
Cattle, 44, 60, 62-5, 79, 139-40, 210, 211, 291, 296; sickness, 77, 154, 165, 183, 184, 209
Caves as shrines, 178
Chamæleon, 99, 240
Charcoal, 22, 119, 176, 185, 244, 286, 307
Charm cylinder, 113, 185, 187, 188, 189, 192-5, 219
Charms used by servants of Europeans, 197
Chauri (yak-tail fan), 297
Chedipe sorceress, 261-2
Chenchu, 194
Cheruman, 121, 290, 291, 295, 296
Childbirth, 53, 54, 77, 79, 176-7, 186, 189, 191, 193, 196
Chillies, 22, 115, 116, 119, 243, 253
Cholam (*Sorghum*), 60, 302, 306
Cholera, 36, 83, 98, 119, 148, 166, 175, 176, 183, 184, 236, 259, 263, 279
Chunam, 21, 22, 31, 44, 106, 113, 114, 117, 170, 212, 244, 246, 295
Clay bangles offered to deity, 176; effigies, 148, 247, 308-9; figures, offerings, 14, 162, 166-8
Cobra, 20, 25, 86, 91, 93, 95, 98, 99, 123, 133, 134, 135
Cochlospermum Gossypium (silk-cotton), 36
Cock-fighting, 299
Cocoanut, 18, 33, 39, 50, 55, 78, 83, 96, 97, 105, 117, 119, 122, 124, 125, 130, 131, 135, 136, 139, 146, 150, 160, 176, 177, 178, 183, 184, 185, 212, 215, 227, 229, 242, 244, 245, 248, 249, 253, 284, 287, 291, 294, 300, 301
Coffer-fish (*Ostracion*), 80

Coins, medicine, 196; offerings, 104, 168-71, 176, 178, 179, 244; omen, 46; on magic square, 33; on navel, 55; put in sacred fire, 185; representing deity, 170; tied to marriage cloth, 49; to ward off evil eye, 114; waved round patient, 119; worn as charm, 192, 195-6, as vow, 171
Coloured water (ārati), waving, 117, 118
Comet, 44, 91
Conch, musical instrument, 294; on cow's horns, 111
Concubines kept by demons, 239
Constellations as omens, 55
Coorg, human sacrifice, 213-4
Coral charm, 193
Corpse used in sorcery, 236, 247
Cotton seed, 53, 97, 116, 243
Cow, 17, 58, 59, 79, 80, 88, 111, 150, 156, 176, 202, 301, 305
Cow-dung, 36, 53, 59, 79, 120, 208, 209, 228, 271, 283, 288, 289, 292, 293, 296, 303
Cowry shells in divination and fortune-telling, 276, 277, 283
Crab, 72, 83, 253
Cremation ground, goddess, 236; sorcery ceremony, 229
Crocodile, 100, 192
Cromlech, 14
Cross-roads, 114, 184, 243, 244, 252, 267, 307
Crow, 67-9, 86-7
Crow-pheasant, 87, 111
Curds, 79, 115, 124, 244
Curls as omens, 52-3
Cutch making, vow, 177
Cynodon Dactylon, 45, 292

DACOITY and housebreaking, omens, 21-2, 40, 41-2, 55, 120
Dakni, 49
Dandāsi, 136
Dasara festival, 29, 82, 174, 280, 282
Dāsari, 75-6, 142, 146, 147-8, 258
Date-palm, knots in leaves as vow, 158-9
Datura, love charm, 239
Days, lucky and unlucky, 17, 20, 21-2, 24, 29, 30, 35, 44, 45, 46, 65, 67, 69, 104, 105, 133, 134, 186, 218, 240, 242, 284, 286-7, 299, 300, 301
Death, omens, 15, 19, 20, 31, 54, 57, 62, 65, 66, 67, 69, 70
Debts settled by goddess, 172
Deer, bone and horn, 82; skin, 280
Dēva-dāsi (dancing-girl), 46-7
Dēvānga, 47, 194
Devil dance, 245
Devil-dancer, 114, 212-3, 246
Dharba grass, 52
Dipāvali festival, 135
Dirgāyus, 25
Dog, 25, 53, 57, 58, 196, 260
——, wild, 79
Dolichos Lablab eaten at agricultural festival, 300
Dōmb, 33, 145, 146, 170, 243
Dommara, 94, 98
Donga Dāsari, 41
Donkey, 51, 242
Dreams, lucky and unlucky, 19-20
Drowned persons, spirits, 193, 254, 256
Dugong, 85, 240
Dung beetle, 106
Durga pūja, 280

EARS and tail of dog cut off, 57
Earth, annointing body, 45; against evil eye, 115, 116; balls on corpse, 51; carried by immoral women, 52; effigies, 114, 120, 219, 249, 254, 287, 305; from grave as charm, 194; in boundary dispute, 38; pelting with, 206, 303; rolling in, 145, 146, 150; trodden on against evil eye, 115, by elephant, 83; urine of enemy, 187, 248
——. *See* Ant-hill
—— god, 59
—— goddess, 36, 39, 199, 303
——, menstruation, 296
—— spirit, 214, 215
Earth-eating, 38-9
——-snake, 96, 97
Eclipse, 42-4, 193, 195, 225
Effigy, 244, 250-1; ant earth, 36; ashes, 44, 307; bamboo, 114; brick, 113, 287; charcoal, 307; clay, 148, 247, 308-9; coloured powder, 114, 244; earth, 114, 120, 219, 249, 254, 287, 305; lead, 251-2; rice, 114, 245; straw, 96, 112; wax, 248; wood, 112, 164, 249-50
Eggs, 21, 34, 37, 70, 121, 132, 133, 187, 249
Ejjugadu sorcerer, 244
Elephant, 83, 191, 192, 203, 297
—— post for meriah sacrifice, 202-3
Erythrina indica, milk-post, 49
European casts out devils, 181-2
——, spirit propitiated, 178
Evil eye, 109-20, 187, 193
—— tongue, 120
Excommunication, 52, 68, 110

FASTING, 35, 135, 138, 303
Female, unlucky omen, 21

Ficus hispida, 293
Finger, amputation, 240-1
Fire by friction, 14, 35
——, sacred (hōmam), 51, 185, 186, 212, 213
Fire-walking, offering of hair to deity, 141; omens, 35; priest sits on thorns, 145
First-born child, amputation of finger, 240-1; buried where jackals can devour it, 58; used in magic, 224-5, 277, 240-1
Fish, sacred, 100-1
Fishermen's gods, Ganjam, 164-5
Fishes, superstitions, 100-2
Fishing-net and trap to catch spirit, 243
Flowers, omens, 35, 41-2, 47-8, 56
Fœtus extracted for magic, 223-6, 229
Forefinger unlucky, 30
Fortune-teller, initiation, 284; Irula, 284; Yerukala, 75
Four-legged objects, objection to carrying, 81
Fowl, 36, 70, 98, 105, 150, 154, 171, 246, 295, 304; sacrifice, 15, 37, 41, 55, 68, 69, 88, 120, 133, 137, 148, 149, 152, 156, 175, 176, 177, 178, 187, 210, 214, 245, 248, 252, 253, 255, 284, 296, 302, 303
Fox, 191
Frenzy during divination or possession, 142, 144, 145, 147, 254, 255-6, 278, 279, 284-5, 287
Frog, 252, 253, 280, 305, 306; toad, 100

GADABA, 82, 175
Gamalla, 53, 135
Ganēsa, Ganapathi, or Vigneswara, 75, 103, 130, 156, 178, 180, 185, 276, 289, 291, 294
Ganga, 118, 141, 148, 214
Gangajātra festival, 148
Ganja (Indian hemp), 250, 270
Gaping, omen, 26
Gavara, 142
Gazelle (chinkāra), 82
Geometric patterns to cure disease, 184-5, 243
Ghī, 78, 86, 124, 132, 133, 147, 185. *See* Butter
Gingelly (*Sesamum*), 46, 50, 76, 127, 192
Givotia rottleriformis, charm, 194
Goat, 105, 154, 176, 202; sacrifice, 14, 37, 57, 69, 82, 119, 137, 146, 148, 149, 150, 175, 205, 210, 214, 217, 244-5, 255, 267, 282, 284, 295
Go-cart on wheels as vehicle of god, 175
Gourd (*Lagenaria*) used in sorcery, 227; to ward off evil eye, 114
Grain, omens, 21, 36, 49, 136; in fortune-telling, 283; mixed with meriah ashes, 204; representing goddess, 61; to appease evil spirit, 245
—— crop, omens from cattle, 60
Grāma dēvata (village deities), 14, 22, 27, 145, 151, 283; Amba Bhavani, 281-2; Ankalamma, 22, 65; Ankamma, 285; Chaudēswari, 39; Chenchu Dēvudu, 286; Durgamma, 143, 151; Ellamma, 41, 137; Gangamma, 38, 144, 156, 219; Gurumurthi, 254; Guttalamma, 155; Huligavva, 41; Karuppan, 153; Kodalamma, 36, 304; Kolapuriamma, 283; Kolaramma, 103; Kulanthal Amman, 172-3; Māgāli, 279; Māriamma, 37, 144, 146, 148, 151, 176, 214; Mashani Chendi, 236; Nukalamma, 15; Pīda, 175; Pōleramma, 35, 283, 285; Saptha Kannimar, 166, 284, 285; Sattāndi Amman, 103; Siddēdēvaru, 177; Yerakamma, 75
Grindstone in rain ceremony, 305
Gudigāra, 48, 164
Guest, arrival, omens, 20, 67
Gul bel (*Tinospora cordifolia*), 94
Gun fired off to accelerate childbirth, 54

HADDI, 83, 106
Hair, burning, 53, 115; offered to deity, 137, 138, 140-1; to snakes, 135; shaving, 22, 29, 45, 309; singeing as omen, 35; use in magic, 220, 248, 250, 253-5; worn as charm, 193
Hair-balls vomited by cows, 61
——marks (suli) in horses and cattle, 61-5
Hamstringing of murderer's corpse, 257
Hand, imprint against evil eye, 119-20
Hanged person, bark of tree as charm, 194
Hanumān, 41, 186, 194, 195, 304
Hare, 24, 85
Holeya, 28, 38, 297, 299
Homicide, 199-236; as thank-offering for recovery from illness, 208; for discovering treasure, 215-21; to appease the earth spirit, 214, 215; to cure possession by devil, 221; to ensure good crops, 199-207; to get rid of concubine, 231; to get rid of sorcerer, 232-4, 236; to increase fertility of the soil, 208-9; to insure cattle against disease, 209; to pro-

Homicide—*continued.*
pitiate village deities, 214; to secure fœtus for sorcery, 224-30; to stay epidemic, 235-6
Hoofs burnt in lying-in chamber, 53
Hook-swinging, omens, 71
Horn burnt during eclipse, 44; in lying-in chamber, 53
Horoscope, 80, 274, 275
Horse, 29, 62, 64, 82, 166, 186-7
——, images set up in fields, and at Aiyanar shrines, 166-7
House occupation, omen, 44, 59
House-building, omens, 33, 39-40, 70
Human (meriah) sacrifice, 199-206
—— sacrifice, substituted ceremony, 205-7, 212
Husband's name, pronouncing unlucky, 20
Hyæna, 76, 77, 191

IDAIYAN, 15, 47
"Iguana" (*Varanus*), 16, 71, 100, 132, 220
Image reflected in oil, 45, 55; *cf.* 127, 248
Incense, 14, 53, 102, 118, 130, 176, 177, 194, 200, 229, 260, 261, 284, 285, 286
Indra, 149, 310
Infanticide, Toda, 210
Insect in death ceremony, 106
Insects as omens, 72
Iron against evil eye, 117; at puberty, marriage, death, etc., 69, 256; chains dedicated to deity, 153-4; hung on trees, 156; worn by Saniyāsi, 184; cure for scorpion sting, 105; hooks in back, 140; nails in magic, 148, 222, 247-50, 253-6; omen, 17; swinging on, 145; ordeal, 52, 154; piercing body, 144
Irula, 178, 234, 284
Ivory beads worn as charm, 193

JACKAL, 58, 78, 191; spurious horns, 189-91
Jagganātha temple, Puri, 142
Jaggery, 78, 133, 147, 287
—— season, religious ceremony, 173-4
Jak (*Artocarpus integrifolia*), 46, 212, 213, 229, 293
Janappan, 48, 102
Jasmine, 35, 197, 285
Jōgi, 77, 85, 271-2
Jokumara rain-making ceremony, 306, 307
Journey, omens, 23-5
Jupiter, planet, 276

KĀDIR, 83, 232
Kaikōlan, 144
Kakkalan, 129
Kāli or Durga, festival, 282
Kalla Alagar, 42
Kallan, 42, 133, 169, 244, 286
Kamma, 50, 256
Kammālan, 42, 174
Kaniyan, 213, 273-7, 290
Kāppiliyan, 57, 139
Kāpu, 53, 87-8, 118, 266, 306, 307
Karamadai festival, 147-8
Kāvadi, fish, 138; milk, 137-40
Kēvuto, 82
Khatri, 118
Kodumpāvi, 308, 309
Kōliyan, 117
Konda Dora, 265
Kondh, 21, 56, 66, 76, 83, 86, 87, 111, 199-207, 236, 260, 305
Konga Vellāla, 52
Koraga, 26, 67, 81, 151, 299
Korama, 58
Korava or Yerukala, 14, 21, 30, 34-5, 40, 55, 68, 75, 120, 208, 282, 283
Kota, 234, 279, 301
Koyi, 21, 36, 56, 79, 87, 88, 90, 175, 207, 243, 262, 264, 265, 302, 303
Kudubi, 177
Kudumi (caste), 26, 94
—— (hair knot), 31, 162
Kumbāra, 26
Kunkumam (red powder), 40, 144, 166, 176, 192, 269
Kuruba, 26, 52, 194, 307, 308
Kurumba, 14, 232-4, 277, 299, 300
Kuruvikkāran, 39, 52, 282
Kusavan potter, 166-7
Kuttichāttan, 237-8

LAKSHMI or Lutchmi, 61, 195
Lambādi or Brinjāri, 101, 136, 154, 155, 181, 209, 210
Lamp and wick, 18, 32, 39, 50, 97, 106, 116, 117, 118, 121, 130, 136, 143, 149, 178, 184, 209, 212, 229, 243, 244, 251, 261, 268, 270, 278, 290, 294
Leaf garments, 149-52
Leaf-cup, 33, 46, 290
Leather, beating with, 146-7; burnt in lying-in chamber, 53; refusal to touch, 81
Leaves, devil ceremony, 246; omen, 40
Leopard, 76, 78, 280
Leprosy, 97, 98, 108, 310
Lime fruit, 22, 39, 50, 160, 244, 245, 249, 269
Lingadar bottles evil spirits, 250
Lingam, 91, 144-5, 183, 304, 305, 308

Lingâyat, 135, 144, 239, 256
Lizard, 48-9, 70-1, 98-9, 105, 162, 253
Looking-glass (mirror), 17, 18, 20, 293
Loris, eye used as love charm, 240
Love philtre, 239, 240, 241

MĀDIGA, 27, 77, 119, 151
Magicians pretend to cure disease, 264-5, 267-8; to discover treasure, 268; to drive out devils, 268-70; to make stone bull eat, 272
Magnesite, legend, 88
Mahseer, 101
Māla, 194, 216, 259
Malaiāli, 48, 146
Malai Vellāla, 83
Malayan, 211, 212, 237, 245
Mammals, superstitions, 73-85
Mandula, 94, 193
Mango, 60, 187, 285, 293
Mannarsala, snake worship, 125-6
Mantram, 37, 92, 93, 133, 135, 163, 166, 180, 181, 182, 186, 187, 213, 225, 227, 242, 244, 247, 248, 250, 258, 261, 267, 269, 270, 276, 277
Mantrasara, 180-1
Māppilla, 87, 111, 128, 129, 187, 188, 193
Maravan, 53, 117
Markandēya, 25
Marks, unlucky, in girls, 52, 180
Marriage of bachelor after death, 51; of boys and girls to dolls, 159; of idol to Paraiyan, 297; omens, 14, 43-4, 47-50, 52, 55, 58, 63, 64; wave offerings, 117-8
Marriage pots, sacrifice to, 119
Mātangi, 27
Meals, omens, 20, 26
Mēlkote temple, 297
Menstruation, 21, 26, 46, 132, 185-6. *See* Puberty
Mercury cups, 196
Meriah sacrifice, 199-207
Metal bowls, blessed at Mecca, 188
Metal votive, and other offerings, 160-4
Milk, 21, 35, 79, 82, 111, 118, 121, 124, 131, 133, 134, 135, 136, 138, 139, 140, 285, 287, 300, 301, 304
——, human, for scorpion sting, 105
Milk-hedge (*Euphorbia Tirucalli*), 105, 259
——-post, 49, 50, 256
Mimusops hexandra, milk-post, 49
Minige (*Argyreia*) in Badaga ceremony, 301
Mohwa or ippa (*Bassia*), 56, 302
Mondi mendicant, 145
Monkey, 17, 73, 205, 207, 240
Monster, birth, 53; regarded as a devil, 230
Months, lucky and unlucky, 45, 46
Moon, 17, 22, 43, 55, 104, 105, 190, 191, 220, 229, 239, 299, 302, 306
Moon-shaped amulets, 195
Morning, omen on waking, 19
Mosquito, 82, 105
Mouse, 240
Mouth-lock, 139
Muduvar, 73, 76
Muhammadan, 29, 30, 31, 98, 119, 120, 163, 164, 170, 171, 187, 188, 195, 230, 249, 266, 269, 297
Mungoose, 98
Muni or Munisvara, 177, 209, 258, 295
Munro, Sir Thomas, 34
Murrel (*Ophiocephalus*), 102
Museum, visit unlucky, 54
Musk in agricultural ceremony, 293
Mustard in evil eye ceremony, 119

NĀGARAPANCHAMI, 123, 124, 135
Nail-cuttings burnt against evil eye, 115; in lying-in chamber, 53
Nalke devil-dancer, 237
Nambiathy priest at snake shrine, 125-6
Names, lucky and unlucky, 20, 34, 55, 56, 133-4, 143
—— of holy persons drunk as charm, 187
Nandi (sacred bull), 154, 304, 308
Nāttukōttai Chetti, 117
Nayādi, curse, 119
Nāyar, 16, 17, 18, 111, 118, 128-9, 138, 161, 193, 256
Nētra mangalya, 167
Nīm or margosa (*Melia Azadirachta*), 36, 53, 55, 94, 105, 115, 133, 144, 149, 150, 151, 156, 214, 254, 285, 304, 306
Nobili, Dr, and magician, 271-2
Nudity, 37, 104, 151, 224-5, 227, 309
Numbers, lucky and unlucky, 23, 26, 30, 31, 33, 34, 49, 52, 56, 68, 75, 117, 133, 135, 136, 184, 186, 194, 228, 229, 248, 249, 251-2, 253, 299, 309

ODDĒ, 68, 70, 93, 109, 256
Odi cult, 226-30
Odina Wodier, abode of devils, 286; milk-post, 49
Odiyan, 226
Offspring, desire for, 218; cocoanut broken on head, 146; diet of monkey flesh, 73; ear-boring ceremony on doll, 159; eating cakes, 54; offerings and vows, 40, 72, 124, 132, 133, 141, 142, 143, 147-8, 150, 151, 155, 158-9, 164, 166, 185; snake songs, 128

Oil, ceremonial use, 18, 29, 40, 45, 50, 119, 178, 201, 243, 282, 292; magic oil, 96, 97, 226-9; marks on door, 119; omen, 40; reflection of image, 45, 55
Oleander (*Nerium*), used in anointing body, 45
Omens, good and bad, 15-7
Ordeal, charcoal, 286; fire, 146; iron, 52, 154; oil, 146, 197, 264, 282; rice, 285, 288; sieve, 288; snake-bite, 123
Ordure, omen, 59; pelting with, 303; thrown into houses, 145
Owl, 65-7

PALIYAN, 69, 78, 81, 94
Pallan, 117, 133
Palli, 49-50, 52, 117, 133, 152, 153, 216
Palm - leaf book (grāndha), 18, 225, 253, 275, 293; charm, 43, 189, 246, 253; scroll, 172
Palmyra palm, climbing, 84; fruits to ward off evil eye, 113; leaf charm, 187; many-branched tree worshipped, 177-8
Palni shrine, 137-8, 143, 157
Pāmpanmekkat (snake guardian), Nambutiri, 126-8
Pānan, 211, 228, 237
Pānchagavyam, 79
Panchamritham, 78
Pandanus fascicularis, believed to harbour snake, 96
Pāndavas, 79, 85, 152, 265, 305, 309
Pāndu kuli supposed to contain treasure, 215-6
Paniyan, 68, 83, 231, 260
Pāno, 221
Paraiyan (Pariah) Malayālam, 83, 225, 227-8, 232, 246, 255
Paraiyan, Tamil, 17, 27, 51, 57, 84, 117, 118, 133, 148, 158, 194, 197, 240, 244, 297, 309
Parasurāma, 122, 150
Parava devil-dancer, 237
Parivaram, 254
Partridge, 88
Pavai (sorcery effigy), 247
Peacock, 36, 41, 88, 200, 201
Pepper in magic ceremony, 253
Periyapālayam, leaf festival, 148-51
Phaseolus Mungo, thrown into ant-hill, 136
Pig, 83; sacrifice, 56, 65, 165, 189, 201, 211, 284, 305
Pigeon, 70, 176, 228
Pīpal (*Ficus religiosa*), 118, 133, 138, 288
Placenta, burial, 55; tied to tree, 81
Plague, 171, 266-7
Plantain, 65, 78, 117, 121, 131, 147, 160, 185, 202, 212, 251, 252, 293, 294
Plumbago zeylanica, in magic, 228
Pollution and purification, 26-7, 28, 29, 34, 40, 43, 59, 67, 79, 81, 83, 110, 121, 123, 131-2, 159, 179, 200, 297, 298, 301
Pompada devil-dancer, 237
Pongal festival, 35, 133, 202
Porcupine, 85
Portuguese, spirits propitiated, 179
Possession of men by gods, 56, 142, 144, 147, 172, 213, 255, 267, 278, 279, 282, 284, 287, 301, 308
Pot broken at boundary, 37; to cure disease, 243; to scare away owls, 66; offered to cholera god, 176; to ward off evil eye, 112, 113, 114; worn as charm, 194
Prayogasara, 181
Pregnancy 44, 53-4, 70, 85, 100, 246
Pregnant corpses exposed in jungle, 74-5
Prehistoric stone celts offered at shrines, 178
Priapi to ward off evil eye, 112, 113, 114
Prophecy, 272-7, 307-8
Puberty, 46, 57-8, 117, 255-6, 284
Pulaya, 17, 27, 255
Pulluvan, 42, 129-32
Pumpkin, 295, 302
Puri, car festival, 142

QUAIL, 88
Quivering of animals, 14-5, 295; of human body, 13

RĀGI (*Eleusine Coracana*), 301
Rags tied to bushes and trees, 155-6; to scare away owls, 66; torches, 147
Rāhu, 43
Rain caused by monsters in the air, 310-1
Rāma, legends, 17, 24, 83-4, 87
Rāmānuja, 297
Rāma tanka, 235
Rat-snake (*Zamenis*), 25, 71, 98
Red sanders (*Pterocarpus santalinus*), wooden figures carved at Tirupati, 159
Reptiles, omens, 70-1; superstitions, 89-100
Rice at agricultural ceremonies, 290, 291, 293, 294, 295, 300, 302, 304; at Badaga festival, 116; at Koyi festival, 303; at meriah sacrifice, 201, 202; at rain-making ceremony, 309; at Vishu festival, 18, 289; effigies, 130, 185, 244, 245; in fortune-telling, 283; in learning

Rice—*continued.*
alphabet, 30; in parturition, 54; offerings, 15, 68, 73, 125, 133, 134, 135, 147, 150, 156, 175, 221, 243, 287, 299; omens, 20, 33, 34-5, 36, 37, 65; ordeal, 146, 285, 288; pot smeared with, 170; poured over bullock, 166; Russell's viper stuffed with, 98; thrown on corpse, 264; tied to marriage cloth, 49
—— balls, 22, 26, 67, 86, 115, 117, 253, 262
——, boiled, 34, 37-8, 39, 284
——, charred, charm, 187
—— ears, food for sparrows, 87
—— flour, 32, 157-8, 212
—— unhusked (paddy), 27, 136, 169
Right and left hand factions, 222
Rings worn as amulets, 95, 191, 192, 193; as vow, 161
Roller or blue jay, 88, 279-80
Russell's viper, 98

SAHAVĀSI, 102
Sakti, 220
Sakuna Pakshi, 104, 279
Sālagrāma stone, 288
Saliva, 27, 98, 248
Salt, 28, 115, 116, 118, 146
Sandal (*Santalum*), 20, 41, 120, 123, 222, 251, 293
Sandals offered to deity, 157-8, 160
Sand-snake (*Eryx*), 97-8
Sanyāsi, 159, 219, 269
Sarasvati, 174, 276
Savara, 33, 73, 75, 155, 164, 165, 189, 262
Scorpion, 20, 82, 102-5, 192
Sēdan, 144
Sembadavan, 118
Servile classes, privileges, 27, 296-8
Setaria italica (tenai), 300
Seven, number, 26, 30, 31, 33, 34, 49, 52, 56, 68, 186, 228, 229, 253, 291, 299, 309
Shadow of European thrown on a feast, 109
Shānān, 84, 174, 178, 246
Shark-charmer, 198
Sheep, 14, 22, 52, 191; sacrifice, 37, 38, 41, 119, 137, 148, 149, 150, 176, 183, 214, 249, 287, 302
Shoe-leather, omen, 57
Shoes in lying-in chamber, 53; unlucky, 29
Sickle, unlucky for cutting crop, 59
Silence, 38, 287; vow, 139
Sin, killing insects, 295; omens, 40, 86
Siva, 24, 65, 71, 86, 101, 115, 162, 163, 184, 279, 297, 305, 307, 308
Skewer through cheeks and tongue, 138, 143, 144, 145
Skull, human, used in sorcery, 228, 241
—— of bull to ward off evil eye, 113
Sleep, omens, 19
Slippers, beating with, 28
Smallpox, 29, 36, 39, 59, 115, 166 175, 212, 235
Smasanākollai festival, 136
Snake, 20, 25, 43, 71, 89-91, 96, 98, 186, 260
——, cremation, 123
—— gods, propitiation by Pulluvans, 129-32
—— grove, 122-3, 126-7, 129, 131
—— mosque at Manarghāt, 129
—— shrine (nāga kovil), 92
—— songs, 128
—— stones, 120, 123-6, 131-3
Snake-bite, 92-6, 193
——-charmers, 92-6, 129
——-wood tree, 91
Snakes, images, 43, 124, 127, 160
—— inhabit white-ant hills, 129, 133-6
Sneezing, omen, 25, 26
Sonaga, 196
Sparrow, 70, 87-8
Spider, 105, 240
Spitting, 26, 27
Square, magic, 32, 36-7, 74, 78, 183, 184, 194, 215, 274, 276
Squirrel, 83-4
Srādh (anniversary ceremony for dead), 67-8, 83
Srāvana Belgola, colossal Jain figure, 135
Srinivāsa fish, 102
Sterility, umbilical cord a cure, 55
Stone, magic (yantram rāyi), 180, 183-5
Stones piled up as vow, 158; in honour of deity, 155-7; throwing into house, 239; water-worn in shrine, 14
Strangers, unlucky omen, 111
Strychnos Nux-vomica, 248, 251, 290
Sugar, 78, 86, 140, 147, 170, 171, 213. *See* Jaggery
Sukra, 308, 309
Sun, 43, 51, 64, 204, 206, 276
—— god, 35
Suttee, 75
Sword balanced on pot, 39; boundary ceremony, 36; cutting body, 144, 145, 278; in worship, 153, 177
Syphilis, 76, 243

TĀLI, 46, 47, 48, 51, 143, 153, 158, 166, 195, 297

Tamarind, 119, 154
Teeth, extraction, 257-60
Telli, 81
Temple car, 53, 114, 144, 222-3, 297; festival, 142
Terminalia tomentosa, 36, 304
Tēyyambādi, 128
Thanda Pulayan, 246
Thelyphonus (whip-scorpion), 105
Thorns fixed to door, 296; lying and sitting on, 145; stuck into effigies, 120, 251, 252, 254; to catch earth spirit, 243
Thread, sacred, 194
—— (string), charm, 193; for tying yantram, 220; movement as omen, 15, 41; wound round ant-hill, 135-6
Thulabhāram ceremony, 171-2
Thunder, 19
Tiger, 14, 57, 74-6, 189, 260, 261, 262, 280
Tīpu Sultan, 44-5, 101, 188
Tirupati (Tirumala), 55, 137, 141, 143, 148, 156-9, 161, 168-9
Tiyan, 46, 82, 128, 162-3, 246
Toad, 100
Tobacco, 20, 27, 178, 208, 250, 259
Toda, 141, 210, 233, 234, 279
Toddy, 186, 187, 200, 251, 252, 253, 262, 263, 287, 295, 299, 302
Torch, against evil eye, 115; beating body, 146; in death ceremony, 244; rain ceremony, 309; snake ceremony, 131; rag torch tied to tree, 156
Tortoise, 71, 192
Tottiyan, 14, 28, 94, 260
Treading on charm, 185, 243, 247, 252, 307; on name cut on road, 159; water poured on footsteps, 51. *See* Earth
Treasure, beliefs, 85, 90-1, 102, 221; human sacrifice, 215-21
Tree of testimony as charm, 188
Tree-snake, *Dendrophis*, 96; *Dryophis*, 96, 97
Trisula (Siva's trident), 183-4
Tūd (*Meliosma pungens*) in Badaga ceremony, 300
Tulsi (*Ocimum sanctum*), 53, 291
Turban, omen, 41
Turmeric, 36, 40, 77, 114, 117, 125, 130, 166, 170, 171, 175, 176, 177, 185, 190, 194, 199, 202, 206, 212, 227, 243, 246, 269, 278, 283, 284, 292, 293, 295
Twins, 54

UMBILICAL cord, 25, 54-5, 105
Umbrella, unlucky, 29, 63; silver, offering, 160
Uncle, 55; maternal, 54, 55, 70; paternal, 55
Urāli, 48, 68
Urine of animals as omen, 15, 21, 58; of enemy in magic, 187, 248; of cattle, 58, 59, 79, 97; of monkey, 73; of monsters, 310-1; of wild dogs, 79

VADA, 40-1
Valaiyan, 56, 133, 244, 286
Valluvan magician, 268
Valmīki, 135
Varuna, 122, 305
Varuna japam, prayer to the rain god, 308-10
Velama, 216
Velichchapād, 277-8
Vellālan, 133
Venus, planet, 44
Vettiyan grave-digger, 309
Vettuvan, 151
Vigna Catiang seeds as omens, 39
Vīramushti, 94, 144
Virgin and Child, picture works miracles, 161
——, catamenial blood in magic, 240; corpse in sorcery, 242; vows, 158
Vishnupād (feet of Vishnu), 193
Vishu festival, 17-9, 289
Vontigadu ceremony, 50-1
Vulture, sarced, 86

WASHING of feet, ceremonial, 22, 31
Water, charm, 189; drunk as charm, 187; holy, 14, 123, 220; poured over idol as vow, 147; *cf.* 142
Water-snake, 96, 98
Wave offering, 114, 115, 117-9, 135, 171, 245
White-ant. *See* Ant
Whooping-cough caused by Bhairava, the dog-god, 196
Widow, 21, 30, 46, 51, 52
Winnowing basket, 292, 293; fan, 26, 283, 306; sieve, 20, 80, 117, 287; tray, 68, 283
Wolf, 77
Woodpecker, 85
Wool of black sheep, charm, 191
Words, lucky and unlucky, 29, 30, 31

YĀNĀDI, 82, 95, 285
Yantram, 182, 185-7, 196-7, 219, 227
Yantrasara, 181
Yerukala. *See* Korava
Yetah fish (*Bagarius*), used in magic, 253
Yōgi, 104